The Early Modern Englishwoman:
A Facsimile Library of Essential Works

Part 1: Printed Writings, 1500–1640

Volume 2
Works by and attributed to
Elizabeth Cary

The Early Modern Englishwoman:
A Facsimile Library of Essential Works

Part 1: Printed Writings, 1500–1640

Volume 2
Works by and attributed to
Elizabeth Cary

Introduced by
Margaret W. Ferguson

General Editors
Betty S. Travitsky and Patrick Cullen

Routledge
Taylor & Francis Group

LONDON AND NEW YORK

First published 1996 by Ashgate Publishing

2 Park Square, Milton Park, Abingdon, Oxfordshire OX14 4RN
52 Vanderbilt Avenue, New York, NY 10017

Routledge is an imprint of the Taylor & Francis Group, an informa business

First issued in paperback 2018

British Library Cataloguing-in-Publication data.

Early Modern Englishwoman: Facsimile Library of Essential Works. – Part 1: Printed
Writings, 1500–1640. – Vol. 2: "Tragedie of Mariam", "History of the Life, Reign and
Death of Edward II", "History of the Most Unfortunate Prince" by E. Cary. – facsim. of
1613 & 1680 ed
   822.3

Library of Congress Cataloging-in-Publication data.

The early modern Englishwoman: a facsimile library of essential works. Part 1. Printed
writings, 1500–1640 / general editors, Betty S. Travitsky and Patrick Cullen.

See page vi for complete CIP Block 95-20837

The woodcut reproduced on the title page and on the case is from the title page of Margaret
Roper's translation of Erasmus's *A Devout Treatise upon the Pater Noster* (circa 1524).

ISBN 978-1-85928-093-5 (hbk)
ISBN 978-1-138-38017-2 (pbk)

Transferred to Digital Printing in 2010

CONTENTS

Library of Congress Cataloging-in-Publication Data

The early modern Englishwoman : a facsimile library of essential works. Part 1. Printed
   writings, 1500–1640 / general editors, Betty S. Travitsky & Patrick Cullen.
      Contents: v. 1. Anne Askew / intro. J.N. King – v. 2. Works by and attributed
   to Elizabeth Cary / intro. M.W. Ferguson – v. 3. Katherine Parr / intro. J. Mueller
   – v. 4. Defences of Women, Jane Anger, Rachel Sowernam, and Constantia
   Munda / intro. S.G. O'Malley – v. 5. Admirable events / S. DuVerger / intro.
   J. Collins – v. 6. M. Sidney Herbert, A discourse of life and death / intro. G.
   Waller – v. 7. Alice Sutcliffe / intro. P. Cullen – v. 8. Margaret Tyler / intro.
   K. Coad – v. 9. Anne Wheathill / intro. P. Cullen – v. 10. Mary Wroth /
   intro. J.A. Roberts.
   ISBN 1-85928-226-1 (set) – ISBN 1-85928-092-7 (v. 1) – ISBN 1-85928-093-5
   (v. 2) – ISBN 1-85928-094-3 (v. 3) – ISBN 1-85928-095-1 (v. 4) –
   ISBN 1-85928-096-X (v. 5) – ISBN 1-85928-097-8 (v. 6) – ISBN 1-85928-098-6
   (v. 7) – ISBN 1-85928-099-4 (v. 8) – ISBN 1-85928-100-1 (v. 9) –
   ISBN 1-85928-101-X (v. 10)
      1. English literature—Early modern, 1500–1700.   2. Women—England—
   History—Renaissance, 1450–1600—Sources.   3. Women—England—History
   —17th century—Sources.   4. English literature—Women authors.   5. Women—
   Literary collections.   6. Women—
   England—Biography.
   I. Travitsky, Betty S.   II. Cullen, Patrick.
   PR1121.E19   1995
   820.8′ 09287′ 09031—dc20   95-20837
                                                                        CIP

PREFACE
BY THE GENERAL EDITORS

Until very recently, scholars of the early modern period have assumed that there were no Judith Shakespeares in early modern England. Much of the energy of the current generation of scholars has been devoted to constructing a history of early modern England that takes into account what women actually wrote, what women actually read, and what women actually did. In so doing the masculinist representation of early modern women, both in their own time and ours, is deconstructed. The study of early modern women has thus become one of the most important – indeed perhaps the most important – means for the rewriting of early modern history.

The Early Modern Englishwoman: A Facsimile Library of Essential Works is one of the developments of this energetic reappraisal of the period. As the names on our advisory board and our list of editors testify, it has been the beneficiary of scholarship in the field and we hope it will also be an essential part of that scholarship's continuing momentum.

The Early Modern Englishwoman is designed to make available a comprehensive and focused collection of writings in English from 1500 to 1700, both by women and for and about them. The first series in the facsimile library provides a comprehensive if not entirely complete collection of the separately published writings by women. In reprinting these writings we intend to remedy one of the major obstacles to the advancement of feminist criticism of the early modern period, namely the unavailability of the very texts upon which the field is based. The volumes in the facsimile library reproduce carefully chosen copies of these texts, incorporating significant variants (usually in appendices). Each text is preceded by a short introduction providing an overview of the life and work of the writer along with a survey of important scholarship. These works, we strongly believe, deserve a large readership – of historians, literary critics, feminist critics, and non-specialist readers.

The Early Modern Englishwoman: A Facsimile Library of Essential Works is published in two parts: *Printed Writings, 1500–1640* and *Printed Writings, 1641–1700*. We project that it will be complemented by separate facsimile series of *Essential Works for the Study of Early Modern Women* and of *Manuscript Writings*, and by a series of original monographs on early modern gender studies, also under our general editorship.

New York City
1996

INTRODUCTORY NOTE

Elizabeth Cary was born around 1585 and died in 1639. The only child (and heir) of Sir Lawrence Tanfield, a wealthy lawyer, and his wife Elizabeth Symondes, Cary was a precocious scholar of languages and theology before she was married (1602) to Sir Henry Cary, later Viscount Falkland, who went to Ireland as Lord Deputy in 1622. Three years later, she returned to England and earned Falkland's ire, and that of her father as well, by publicly converting to Catholicism. A biography of Cary written after her death by one of her daughters tells us that she had eleven children 'born alive' during her troubled marriage; four of her daughters, among them the author of the biography, became nuns in a Benedictine convent in France. The *Life* tells us that Cary wrote several things 'for her private recreation' and mentions various works now lost, among them lives of the saints, poems to the Virgin Mary, and a life of Tamburlaine. She also wrote a translation of a Catholic treatise by the Cardinal of Perron (reproduced in this series). The biography does not mention the works for which Cary is best known today: the play entitled *The Tragedie of Mariam*; and two versions of a historical narrative about Edward II which many scholars believe she wrote after separating from her husband.

The Tragedie of Mariam, Faire Queene of Jewry

On the title page of *Mariam*, printed in quarto in 1613, the author is identified only as 'that learned, vertuous, and truly noble Ladie, E.C.' Two extant copies of the play, one at Harvard's Houghton Library, the other, reproduced here, at the Huntington Library, contain a sonnet dedicating the play to a 'worthy Sister, Mistress Elizabeth Carye.' Whether the sonnet was addressed to a sister or a sister-in-law of Sir Henry Cary, it does much to support the modern scholarly consensus that *Mariam* was written by his wife. The fact that the dedicatory sonnet unveiling the author's identity was removed from all but two copies of the play suggests, however, that someone – perhaps the playwright, perhaps her husband – regretted the female author's exposure as a public rather than a private being. Whatever the circumstances of its publication, Cary's play about a heroine who defies the law of wifely silence – and thereby provokes her husband to order her beheaded – was printed by Thomas Creede for Richard Hawkins, who entered it in the Register of the Stationers' Company on 17 December 1612. The play had probably circulated for some years in manuscript, having been written, scholars surmise, sometime between the year of Elizabeth's marriage and 1609, the year when her first child was born.

The play is the first original drama by a woman to be printed in England. Sir John Davies offers a further clue to the author's identity when, in his *Muses Sacrifice* (1612), he praises Elizabeth Cary for writing a play set in Palestine and urges her, and two other noble ladies, to 'press the Presse' with their works. Based on a story told by Josephus, whose *Antiquities of the Jews*, ca. 93 C.E., had been translated into English by Thomas Lodge in 1602, *Mariam* explores the turbulent marriage of King Herod and his second wife, the Maccabean princess Mariam. The story had been dramatized by other Renaissance authors, among them Lodovico Dolce and Hans Sachs; but Cary depicts Mariam's relation to her husband and to other female characters, especially Herod's villainous sister Salome and his first wife Doris, in ways that seem highly reflective of Cary's status as an English noblewoman with ambivalent feelings toward her mother and with leanings toward Roman Catholicism – leanings not shared by her husband. Recent critics have argued for political as well as autobiographical allegories in Cary's play; its concerns with husbandly tyranny and with questions about when and for whom divorce might be legitimate, for instance, suggest parallels between Herod and King Henry VIII of England. Critics have also noticed significant parallels between the plot of *Mariam* and that of Shakespeare's *Othello*. In both tragedies a jealous husband comes too late to value his 'jewel', the chaste wife whom he mistakenly kills.

Unlike Shakespeare's play, however, Cary's was never performed on stage and existed in only one edition until 1914, when Dunstan and Greg did a facsimile edition for the Malone Society based on three copies of the play in the British Museum and one in the Bodleian Library. Unable to examine copies in the United States, Dunstan and Greg erroneously surmised that the leaf of forematter marked A (containing the dedicatory sonnet and a list of 'the Speakers') which exists in the Huth and White copies, now in the Houghton and Huntington libraries respectively, was an addition to the text. Greg later corrected this view, and a discussion of that prefatory leaf as suppressed or 'cancelled' may now be found in 'A Supplement to the Introduction,' by Straznicky and Rowland, in the 1992 reprint of the Malone Society edition. A detailed discussion of the suppressed leaf, and of seventeen copies of the play in North America, England, and Scotland, appears in the modern critical edition of *Mariam* prepared by Weller and Ferguson. This edition also includes the text of *The Lady Falkland: Her Life*, written ca. 1643–1649 and first printed in 1861. The Huntington Library copy of *Mariam* was chosen because it is in excellent condition and contains the important leaf of 'forematter'. It also has the name 'Eliz. Carew', in a seventeenth-century hand, strikingly inscribed on the blank page facing the title page. 'Eliz. Carew' could refer to the play's author, Carew being a common alternative spelling of Carey; or it could refer to the sister-in-law addressed in the dedicatory sonnet. The name is not in the usual 'ownership position', the upper right-hand corner of the recto. This copy (12.4 × 18 cm; sig. C 8.3 × 16.8) was acquired by Mr. W.A. White of New York in 1890 from a London bookseller.

Also reproduced here, and again by permission of the Huntington Library, are two texts about Edward II which were first published in 1680. Elizabeth Cary may have written one or both of these texts, which offer a more psychologically complex (and some critics think a more sympathetic) portrait of Edward's Queen Isabel than do earlier versions of Edward's story either in chronicles by Fabyan (1533), Holinshed (1577), and Stowe (1615) or in the well known play by Marlowe which was first printed in 1594. There is less scholarly consensus about Cary's authorship of the shorter, octavo text than there is about her authorship of the folio; and there is considerably less consensus about her authorship of either of these texts than there is about her authorship of *Mariam*. Nonetheless, a number of recent critics strongly believe that Cary did write one or both of these texts, and we reproduce them so that the reader can join the debate.

The History of the Life, Reign, and Death of Edward II. King of England and Lord of Ireland. With the Rise and Fall of his Great Favourites, Gaveston and the Spencers. Written by E.F. in the year 1627. And printed Verbatim from the Original.

This is the full title of the folio text (18.4 × 28.2 cm; sig. C 14 × 23 [though reduced in this reproduction]), and its use of the initials 'E.F.' is a major piece of evidence for those who argue the case for Cary's authorship. She regularly signed herself 'Elizabeth Falkland' in letters written after 1620. The date has also been used to support the case for Cary's authorship; in 1627, she was living impoverished in London, separated from her husband; she could thus have penned the narrative of Edward II's life for the reason mentioned in the 'Author's Preface to the Reader': 'to out-run those weary hours of a deep and sad Passion.' It was, however, conventional to say one was writing to distract oneself from grief, and we cannot assume that the 'Author's Preface' is a transparent autobiographical statement. A number of critics have nonetheless emphasized the auto-biographical dimensions of the *History*, noting, for instance, a parallel between Cary's situation at the alleged time of writing and the text's portrait of a queen abandoned by a proud and cruel husband.

The publisher's prefatory letter to the reader refers to the author as a 'Gentleman' and praises him for using 'so Masculine a Stile'. Many readers have assumed that the author of the folio was Henry Falkland, though his name is mentioned only in the octavo version of the text. Some previous owner of The Huntington Library folio has indeed graphically insisted on Henry Cary's authorship of the folio: crossing out the initial 'E.' both on the title page and at the end of the 'Author's Preface', the anonymous emendator substituted 'H' for 'E' and spelled out Henry Cary's name to remove all doubt on the question of authorship. Doubt nonetheless remains, partly because the relation between the folio and the octavo texts is construed so differ-ently by critics who believe Cary wrote the folio but not the octavo (for example, Lewalski and Foster), by those who believe she wrote both texts (for example, Stauffer, Krontiris, and Travitsky) and by one who insists that no Falkland wrote either text (Woolf).

The *History* unfolds in a complex mixture of prose and blank verse and with much more attention to motive and characterization than the chronicle versions display. The additions to the chronicles show the influence, as Lewalski has observed, of classical historians 'recently made available in good translations', historians such as Thucydides, Livy, Sallust, and especially Tacitus (Lewalski 203). The folio was printed in 1680 by 'J.C.' for three booksellers; it was reprinted in 1689, without the 'Author's Preface to the Reader', as *The Parallel: Or the History of the Life, Reign, Deposition, and Death, of King Edward the Second* (London: R. Baldwin). There is no modern edition.

The History of the Most Unfortunate Prince King Edward II. With Choice Political Observations on Him and his Unhappy Favourites, Gaveston & Spencer. Containing some rare passages of those Times, not found in other historians. Found among the papers of, and (supposed to be) Writ by the Right Honourable Henry Viscount Faulkland, Sometime Lord Deputy of Ireland.

The publisher's preface to this octavo text (10.5 × 17 cm.; sig. C 7.8 × 15) about Edward repeats the title page's claim that the text was found among Henry Cary's papers and is 'supposed to be written' by him. Publishers, however, often sought to bolster sales by giving a 'noble' genealogy to a work, and Woolf cites this practice in support of his argument that both the folio and the octavo narratives about Edward II and his disastrous reliance on his 'favourite', Gaveston, pertain to the tense political situation in 1680 and hence could not have been written by Henry Cary. Woolf, however, does not even consider the case for Elizabeth Cary's authorship; and his own case for a late composition date is considerably weakened by his failure to address the relevance of the Edward II story to the English monarchy in the 1620's, when King James I was widely criticized for granting excessive powers to his favourite, Buckingham. Although Buckingham's wife was a friend of Elizabeth Cary, and Buckingham himself was a patron of Henry Cary, such alliances would not necessarily prevent Elizabeth from writing a manuscript – or two manuscripts – critical of kingly favouritism; such alliances might well, however, have contributed to her desire to keep such thoughts unpublished. Critics have found topical allusions both to the 1620's and to the period of the so-called 'Exclusion Crisis' of 1679–81 in the octavo *Edward*, so the issue of its dating remains open.

Even among those critics who date the octavo and the folio to Cary's lifetime and maintain she wrote some portion of both texts, there is substantial disagreement. Some critics consider the octavo a later, streamlined and aesthetically superior version of the folio; others think it is an early draft, in prose, of a work Cary later elaborated in the folio's mixture of prose and verse. Whenever it was initially written, the octavo was included in *The Harleian Miscellany or a Collection of Scarce, Curious, and Entertaining Pamphlets and Tracts*, in 1744 (London: Printed for T. Osborne, Vol. 1, 66–91) and reprinted again in 1965 (New York: AMS Press).

References

STC 4613; Wing 313, 314

Dunstan, A.C. and W.W. Greg (eds.), (1914), *The Tragedie of Mariam* [Facsimile reprint with introduction and list of textual variants], London: Printed for the Malone Society by Horace Hart for Oxford University Press; rpt. 1992 with a new introduction by Marta Straznicky and Richard Rowland

Foster, Donald (1994), 'Resurrecting the Author: Elizabeth Cary Tanfield', in Brink, Jean (ed.), *Privileging Gender in Early Modern England*, Kirksville, MO: Sixteenth Century Journal Publishers

Guttierrez, Nancy (1991), 'Valuing *Mariam*: Genre Study and Feminist Analysis', *Tulsa Studies in Women's Literature* 10: 233–51

Krontiris, Tina (1990), 'Style and Gender in Elizabeth Cary's *Edward II*' in Haselkorn, Anne M. and Betty S. Travitsky (eds.), *The Renaissance Englishwoman in Print: Counterbalancing the Canon*, Amherst, MA: University of Massachusetts Press

Lewalski, Barbara Kiefer (1993), *Writing Women in Jacobean England*, Cambridge, MA: Harvard University Press

Pearse, Nancy Cotton (1977), 'Elizabeth Cary, Renaissance Playwright', *Texas Studies in Language and Literature* 18: 601–8

Stauffer, Donald A. (1935), 'A Deep and Sad Passion' in Craig, Hardin (ed.), *The Parrott Presentation Volume: Essays in Dramatic Literature*, Princeton, NJ: Princeton University Press

Travitsky, Betty (1987), 'The Feme Covert in Elizabeth Cary's *Mariam*' in Levin, Carole and Jeanie Watson (eds.), *Ambiguous Realities: Women in the Middle Ages and Renaissance*, Detroit: Wayne State University Press

Weller, Barry, and Margaret W. Ferguson (eds.), (1994), *"The Tragedy of Mariam, The Fair Queen of Jewry," with "The Lady Falkland: Her Life," by One of Her Daughters*, Berkeley: University of California Press [with extensive bibliography]

Woolf, D. R. (1988), 'The True Date and Authorship of Henry, Viscount Falkland's *History of the Life, Reign and Death of King Edward II*', *Bodleian Library Record* 12, no. 6: 440–53

MARGARET W. FERGUSON

The Tragedie of Mariam (STC 4613) is reproduced, by permission, from the copy at The Huntington Library. The text block of the copy measures 8.3 × 16.8 cm.

Lines 17 and 18 on signature A3ᵛ are blurred, but should read as follows:

Which still he thought on earth too long immur'd.
How happie was it that *Sohemus* minde

Eliz: Carew

THE
TRAGEDIE
OF MARIAM,
THE FAIRE
Queene of Iewry.

Written by that learned,
vertuous, and truly noble Ladie,
E. C.

LONDON.
Printed by Thomas Creede, for Richard
Hawkins, and are to be folde at his fhoppe
in Chancery Lane, neere vnto
Sargeants Inne.
1613.

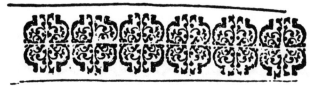

TO DIANAES
EARTHLIE DEPVTESSE,
and my worthy Sister, Miſtris Elizabeth Carye.

WHen cheerfull *Phœbus* his full courſe hath run,
His ſiſters fainter beams our harts doth cheere:
So your faire Brother is to mee the Sunne,
And you his Siſter as my Moone appeere.

You are my next belou'd, my ſecond Friend,
For when my *Phœbus* abſence makes it Night,
Whilſt to th'*Antipodes* his beames do bend,
From you my *Phœbe*, ſhines my ſecond Light.

Hee like to *SOL*, cleare-ſighted, conſtant, free,
You *LVNA*-like, vnſpotted, chaſt, diuine:
Hee ſhone on *Sicily*, you deſtin'd bee,
T'illumine the now obſcurde *Paleſtine*.
My firſt was conſecrated to *Apollo*,
My ſecond to *DIANA* now ſhall follow.

E. C.

A   The

The names of the Speakers.

Herod, King of Iudea..
Doris, his first Wife.
Mariam, his second Wife.
Salome, Herods Sister.
Antipater his sonne by Salome.
Alexandra, Mariams mother.
Sillius, Prince of Arabia.
Constabarus, husband to Salome.
Pheroras, Herods Brother.
Graphina, his Loue.
Babus first Sonne.
Babus second Sonne.
Annanell, the high Priest.
Sohemus, a Counseller to Herod.
Nuntio.
Bu. another Messenger.
  Chorus, a Companie of Iewes..

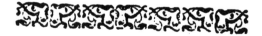

The

The Argument.

HErod the fonne of *Antipater* (an *Idumean*,) hauing crept by the fauor of the *Remanes*, into the Iewifh Monarchie, married *Mariam* the daughter of *Hircanus*, the rightfull *King and Prieft*, and for her (befides her high blood, being of fingular beautie) hee reputiated *Doris*, his former Wife, by whome hee had Children.

This *Mariam* had a Brother called *Ariftobulus*, and next him and *Hircanus* his Graund-father, *Herod* in his Wiues right had the beft title. Therefore to remooue them, he charged the firft with treafon : and put him to death ; and drowned the fecond vnder colour of fport. *Alexandra*, Daughter to the one, and Mother to the other, accufed him for their deaths before *Anthony*.

So when hee was forc'te to goe anfwere this Accufation at *Rome*, he left the cuftodie of his wife to *Iofephus* his Vncle, that had married his Sifter *Salome*, and out of a violent affection (vnwilling any fhould enioy her after him) hee gaue ftrict and priuate commaundement, that if hee were flaine, fhee fhould be put to death. But he returned with much honour, yet found his Wife extreamely difcontented, to whom *Iofophus* had (meaning it for the beft, to proue *Herod* loued her) reuealed his charge.

So by *Salomes* accufation hee put *Iofephus* to death, but was reconciled to *Mariam*, who ftill bare the death of her Friends exceeding hardly.

In this meane time *Herod* was againe neceffarily to reuifite *Rome*, for *Cæfar* hauing ouerthrowne *Anthony* his

great

great friend, was likely to make an alteration of his Fortune.

In his abfence, newes came to *Ierufalem* that *Cæfar* had put him to death, their willingnes it fhould be fo, together with the likelyhood, gaue this Rumor fo good credit, as *Sohemus* that had fucceeded *Iofephus* charge, fucceeded him likewife in reuealing it. So at *Herods* returne which was fpeedy and vnexpected, he found *Mariam* fo farre from ioye, that fhe fhewed apparant fignes of forrow. Hee ftill defiring to winne her to a better humour, fhe being very vnable to conceale her paffion, fell to vpbraiding him with her Brothers death. As they were thus debating, came in a fellow with a Cuppe of Wine, who hired by *Salome*, faide firft, it was a Loue potion, which *Mariam* defired to deliuer to the King: but afterwards he affirmed that it was a poyfon, and that *Sohemus* had tolde her fomewhat, which procured the vehement hate in her.

The King hearing this, more moued with Iealoufie of *Sohemus*, then with this intent of poyfon, fent her away, and prefently after by the inftigation of *Salome*, fhe was beheaded. Which rafhnes was afterward punifhed in him, with an intollerable and almoft Frantike paffion for her death.

Actus primus. Scœna prima.

Marium sola.

HOw oft haue I with publike voyce runne on?
To cenſure *Romes* laſt *Hero* for deceit:
    Becauſe he wept when *Pompeu* life was gone,
Yet when he liu'd, hee thought his Name too great.
But now I doe recant, and *Roman* Lord
Excuſe too raſh a judgement in a woman:
My Sexe pleads pardon, pardon then afford,
Miſtaking is with vs, but too too common.
Now doe I finde by ſelfe Experience taught,
One Object yeelds both griefe and ioy: *onely*
You wept indeed, when on his worth you thought,
But ioyd that ſlaughter did your Foe deſtroy.
So at his death your Eyes true droppes did raine,
Whom dead, you did not wiſh aliue againe.
When *Herod* liu d, that now is done to death,
Oft haue I wiſht that I from him were free:
Oft haue I wiſht that he might loſe his breath,
Oft haue I wiſht his Carkas dead to ſee.
Then Rage and Scorne had put my loue to flight,
That Loue which once on him was firmely ſet:
Hate hid his true affection from my ſight,
And kept my heart from paying him his debt.
And blame me not, for *Herods* Iealouſie
Had power euen conſtancie it ſelfe to change:
For hee by barring me from libertie,
To ſhunne my ranging, taught me firſt to range.
But yet too chaſt a Scholler was my hart,
To learne to loue another then my Lord:
To leaue his Loue, my leſſons former part,

I quickly learn'd, the other I abhord.
But now his death to memorie doth call,
The tender loue, that he to *Mariam* bare:
And mine to him, this makes those riuers fall,
Which by an other thought vnmoiftned are.
For *Ariftobolus* the lowlyeft youth
That euer did in Angels fhape appeare:
The cruell *Herod* was not mou'd to ruth,
Then why grieues *Mariam Herods* death to heare?
Why ioy I not the tongue no more fhall fpeake,
That yeelded forth my brothers lateft dome:
Both youth and beautie might thy furie breake,
And both in him did ill befit a Tombe.
And worthy Grandfire ill did he requite,
His high Affent alone by thee procur'd,
Except he murdred thee to free the fpright
Which in he thought on earth too long jmmur'd.
How happie was it that *Sohemus* maide
Was mou'd to pittie my diftreft eftate?
Might *Herods* life a truftie feruant finde,
My death to his had bene vnfeparate.   (heare,
Thefe thoughts haue power, his death to make me
Nay more, to wifh the newes may firmely hold:
Yet cannot this repulfe fome falling teare,
That will againft my will fome griefe vnfold.
And more I owe him for his loue to me,
The deepeft loue that euer yet was feene:
Yet had I rather much a milke-maide bee,
Then be the Monarke of *Iudeas* Queene.
It was for nought but loue, he wifht his end
Might to my death, but the vaunt-currier prouе:
But I had rather ftill be foe then friend,
To him that faues for hate, and kills for loue.
Hard-hearted *Mariam*, at thy difcontent,
What flouds of teares haue drencht his manly face?
How canft thou then fo faintly now lament,
Thy trueft louers death, a deaths difgrace:
I now mine eyes you do begin to right

                                              Th

The wrongs of your admirers And my Lord,
Long since you should haue put your smiles to flight,
Ill doth a widowed eye with ioy accord.
Why now me thinkes the loue I bare him then,
When virgin freedome left me vnreftraind :
Doth to my heart begin to creepe agen,
My paffion now is far from being faind.
But teares flie backe, and hide you in your bankes,
You muft not be to *Alexandra* feene:
For if my mone be fpide, but little thankes
Shall *Mariam* haue, from that incenfed Queene.

Actus primus : Scœna Secunda.

Mariam. Alexandra.

Alex :   (miftake,
WHat meanes thefe teares? my *Mariam* doth
         The newes we heard did tell the *Tyrants* end:
What weepft thou for thy brothers murthers fake,
Will euer wight a teare for *Herod* fpend?
My curfe purfue his breathles trunke and fpirit,
Bafe *Edomite* the damned *Efaus* heire:
Muft he ere *Iacobs* child the crowne inherit?
Muft he vile wretch be fet in *Dauids* chaire?
No *Dauids* foule within the bofome plac'te,
Of our forefather *Abram* was afham'd:
To fee his feat with fuch a toade difgrac'te,
That feat that hath by *Iudas* race bene faind.
Thou fatall enemie to royall blood,
Did not the murther of my boy fuffice,
To ftop thy cruell mouth that gaping ftood?
But muft thou dim the milde *Hercanus* eyes?
My gratious father, whofe too readie hand
Did lift this *Idumean* from the duft :
And he vngratefull catiffe did withftand,
The man that did in him moft friendly truft.
What kingdomes right could cruell *Herod* claime,
Was he not *Efaus* Iffue, heyre of hell?
Then what fucceffion can he haue but fhame?
Did not his Anceftor his birth-right fell?   O

O yes,he doth from *Edom* name deriue,
His cruell nature which with blood is fed :
That made him me of Sire and fonne depriue,
He euer thirfts for blood,and blood is red.
Wee pft thou becaufe his loue to thee was bent?
And readft thou loue in crimfon caraƈters?
Slew he thy friends to worke thy hearts content?
No : hate may Iuftly call that aƈtion hers.
He gaue the facred Prieſthood for thy fake,
To *Ariſtobolus.* Yet doomde him dead:
Before his backe the *Ephod* warme could make,
And ere the *Myter* fetled on his head.
Qh had he giuen my boy no leſſe then right,
The double oyle fhould to his forehead bring :
A double honour, fhining doubly bright,
His birth annoynted him both Prieſt and King.
And fay my father,and my fonne he flewe,
To royalize by right your Prince borne breath:
Was loue the caufe, can *Mariam* deeme it true,
That *Mariam* gaue commandment for her death?
I know by fits,he fhewd fome fignes of loue,
And yet not loue,but raging lunacie:
And this his hate to thee may iuftly proue,
That fure he hates *Hercanus* familie.
Who knowes if he vnconftant wauering Lord,
His loue to *Doris* had renew'd againe?
And that he might his bed to her afford,
Perchance he wifht that *Mariam* might be flaine.

    Nun: Doris, Alas her time of loue was paft,
Thofe coales were rakte in embers long agoe :
If *Mariams* loue and fhe was now difgraft,
Nor did I glorie in her ouerthrowe.
He not a whit his firft borne fonne efteem'd,
Becaufe as well as his he was not mine:
My children onely for his owne he deem'd,
Thefe boyes that did defcend from royall line.
Thefe did he ftile his heyres to *Dauids* throne,
My *Alexander* if he liue, fhall fit

                            In

In the Maiesticke seat of *Salomon*,
To will it so, did *Herod* thinke it fit.

  Alex. Why? who can claime from *Alexanders* brood
That Gold adorned Lyon-guarded Chaire?
Was *Alexander* not of *Dauids* blood?
And was not *Mariam Alexanders* heire?
What more then right could *Herod* then bestow,
And who will thinke except for more then right,
He did not raise them, for they were not low,
But borne to weare the Crowne in his despight:
Then send those teares away that are not sent
To thee by reason, but by passions power:
Thine eyes to cheere, thy cheekes to smiles be bent,
And entertaine with ioy this happy houre.
Felicitie, if when shee comes, she findes
A mourning habite, and a cheerlesse looke,
Will thinke she is not welcome to thy minde,
And so perchance her lodging will not brooke.
Oh keepe her whilest thou hast her, if she goe
She will not easily returne againe:
Full many a yeere haue I indur'd in woe,
Yet still haue sude her presence to obtaine:
And did not I to her as presents send
A Table, that best Art did beautifie
Of two, to whom Heauen did best feature lend,
To woe her loue by winning *Anthony* :
For when a Princes fauour we doe craue,
We first their Mynions loues do seeke to winne:
So I, that sought Felicitie to haue,
Did with her Mynion *Anthony* beginne,
With double slight I sought to captiuate
The warlike louer, but I did not right:
For if my gift had borne but halfe the rate,
The *Roman* had beene ouer-taken quite.
But now he fared like a hungry guest,
That to some plenteous festiuall is gone,
Now this, now that, hee deems to eate were best,
Such choice doth make him let them all alone.

        B   The

The boyes large forehead firſt did fayreſt ſeeme.
Then glauntſt his eye vpon my *Mariams* cheeke:
And that without compariſon did deeme,
VVhat was in eyther but he meſt did leeke.
And thus diſtracted, eythers beauties might
VVithin the others excellence was drown'd:
Too much delight did bare him from delight,
For eithers loue, the others did confound.
VVhere if thy portraiture had onely gone,
His life from *Herod*, *Anthony* had taken:
He would haue loued thee, and thee alone,
And left the browne *Egyptian* cleane forſaken.
And *Cleopatra* then to ſeeke had bene,
So firme a louer of her wayned face :
Then great *Anthonius* fall we had not ſeene,
By her that fled to haue him holde the chaſe.
Then *Mariam* in a *Romans* Chariot ſet,
In place of *Cleopatra* might haue ſhowne:
A mart of Beauties in her viſage met,
And part in this, that they were all her owne.

Ma. Not to be Empriſe of aſpiring *Rome*,
Would *Mariam* like to *Cleopatra* liue:
With pureſt body will I preſſe my Toome,
And wiſh no fauours *Anthony* could giue.

Alex. Let vs retire vs, that we may reſolue
How now to deale in this reuerſed ſtate :
Great are th'affaires that we muſt now reuolue,
And great affaires muſt not be taken late.

.Actus primus. Scœna tertia.

Mariam. Alexandra. Salome.

Salome.

MOre plotting yet? Why? now you haue the thing
For which ſo oft you ſpent your ſupliant breath:
And *Mariam* hopes to haue another King,
Her eyes doe ſparkle ioy for *Herods* death.

Alex.

Alex. If she desir'd another King to haue,
She might before she came in *Herods* bed
Haue had her wish. More Kings then one did craue,
For leaue to set a Crowne vpon her head.
I thinke with more then reason she laments,
That she is freed from such a sad annoy :
Who ist will weepe to part from discontent,
And if she ioy, she did not causelesse ioy.

Sal. You durst not thus haue giuen your tongue the
If noble *Herod* still remaind in life :   (raine,
Your daughters betters farre I dare maintaine,
Might haue reioyc'd to be my brothers wife.

Mar. My betters farre, base woman t'is vntrue,
You scarce haue euer my superiors seene :
For *Mariams* seruants were as good as you,
Before she came to be *Iudeas* Queene.

Sal. Now stirs the tongue that is so quickly mou'd,
But more then once your collor haue I borne :
Your furnish words are sooner sayd then prou'd,
And *Salomes* reply is onely scorne.

Mar. Scorne those that are for thy companions
Though I thy brothers face had neuer seene,   (held,
My birth, thy baser birth so farre exceld,
I had to both of you the Princesse bene.
Thou party Iew, and party Edomite,
Thou Mongrell : issu'd from reiected race,
Thy Ancestors against the Heauens did fight,
And thou like them wilt heauenly birth disgrace.

Sal. Still twit you me with nothing but my birth,
What ods betwixt your ancestors and mine ?
Both borne of *Adam,* both were made of Earth,
And both did come from holy *Abrahams* line.

Mar. I fauour thee when nothing else *I* say,
VVith thy blacke acts ile not pollute my breath : :
Else to thy charge *I* might full iustly lay
A shamefull life, besides a husbands death.

Sal. Tis true indeed, *I* did the plots reueale,
That past betwixt your fauorites and you :
I ment not *I,* a traytor to conceale.

Thus *Salome* your Mynion *Ioseph* flue.

Mar. Heauen, dost thou meane this Infamy to smo-
Let slandred *Mariam* ope thy clofed eare :   (ther?
Selfe-guilt hath euer bene fufpitious mother,
And therefore I this fpeech with patience beare.
No, had not *Salomes* vnstedfast heart,
In *Iofephus* stead her *Conftabarus* plast,
To free her felfe, she had not vfde the art,
To slander haplesse *Mariam* for vnchast.

Alex. Come *Mariam*, let vs goe: it is no boote
To let the head contend against the foote.

Actus primus. Scœna quarta.

Salome, Sola.

Lues *Salome*, to get fo bafe a stile
As foote, to the proud *Mariam Herods* fpirit:
In happy time for her endured exile,
For did he liue she should not miffe her merit:
But he is dead : and though he were my Brother,
His death fuch store of Cinders cannot cast
My Coales of loue to quench : for though they fmo-
The flames a while, yet will they out at last.   (ther
Oh blest *Arabia*, in best climate plast,
I by the Fruit will cenfure of the Tree:
Tis not in vaine, thy happy name thou hast,
If all *Arabians* like *Silleus* bee:
Had not my Fate bene too too contrary,
When I on *Conftabarus* first did gaze,
Silleus had beene obiect to mine eye:
Whofe lookes and perfonage must allyes amaze.
But now ill Fated *Salome*, thy tongue
To *Conftabarus* by it felfe is tide:
And now except I doe the Ebrew wrong
I cannot be the faire *Arabian* Bride:
What childish lets are thefe? Why stand I now
On honourable points? Tis long agoe

Since

Since shame was written on my tainted brows
And certaine tis, that shame is honours foe.
Had I vpon my reputation stood,
Had I affected an vnspotted life,
Iosephus vaines had still bene stuft with blood,
And I to him had liu'd a sober wife.
Then had I neuer cast an eye of loue,
On *Constabarus* now detested face,
Then had I kept my thoughts without remoue:
And blusht at motion of the least disgrace:
But shame is gone, and honour wipt away,
And Impudencie on my forehead sits:
She bids me worke my will without delay,
And for my will I will imploy my wits.
He loues, I loue; what then can be the cause,
Keepes me for being the *Arabians* wife?
It is the principles of *Moses* lawes,
For *Contabarus* still remaines in life,
If he to me did beare as Earnest hate,
As I to him, for him there were an ease,
A separating bill might free his fate:
From such a yoke that did so much displease.
Why should such priuiledge to man be giuen?
Or giuen to them, why bard from women then?
Are men then we in greater grace with Heauen?
Or cannot women hate as well as men?
Ile be the custome-breaker: and beginne
To shew my Sexe the way to freedomes doore,
And with an offring will I purge my sinne,
The lawe was made for none but who are poore.
If *Herod* had liu'd, I might to him accuse
My present Lord. But for the futures sake
Then would I tell the King he did refuse
The sonnes of *Baba* in his power to take.
But now I must diuorse him from my bed,
That my *Silleus* may possesse his roome:
Had I not begd his life he had bene dead,
I curse my tongue the hindrer of his doome,

But

But then my wandring heart to him was fast,
Nor did *I* dreame of chaunge: *Silleus* said,
He would be here, and see he comes at last,
Had *I* not nam'd him longer had he staid.

Actus primus. Scœna quinta.

Salome, Silleus.

Silleus. WEll found faire *Salome Iudeas* pride,
Hath thy innated wisedome found
To make *Silleus* deeme him deified,   (the way
By gaining thee a more then precious pray?
   Salo. I haue deuisde the best I can deuise,
A more imperfect meanes was neuer found:
But what cares *Salome*, it doth suffice
If our indeuours with their end be crown'd.
In this our land we haue an ancient vse,
Permitted first by our law-giuers head:
Who hates his wife, though for no iust abuse,
May with a bill diuorce her from his bed.
But in this custome women are not free,
Yet I for once will wrest it, blame not thou
The ill I doe, since what I do'es for thee,
Though others blame, *Silleus* should allow.
   Silleus. Thinkes *Salome*, *Silleus* hath a tongue
To censure her faire actions: let my blood
Bedash my proper brow, for such a wrong,
The being yours, can make euen vices good:
Arabia ioy, prepare thy earth with greene,
Thou neuer happie wert indeed till now:
Now shall thy ground be trod by beauties Queene,
Her foote is destin'd to depresse thy brow.
Thou shalt faire *Salome* commaund as much
As if the royall ornament were thine:
The weaknes of *Arabias* King is such,
The kingdome is not his so much as mine:
My mouth is our *Obodas* oracle,
Who thinkes not ought but what *Silleus* will?

                    And

And thou rare creature. *As us* miracle,
Shalt be to me as *It: Obocus* ftill.

   Salome. Tis not for glory *I* thy loue accept,
Iudea yeelds me honours worthy ftore:
Had not affection in my bosome crept,
My natiue country should my life deplore.
Were not *Sillius* he with home I goe,
I would not change my *Palaftine* for *Rome:*
Much lesse would I a glorious ftate to shew,
Goe far to purchase an *Arabian* toome.

   Silleus. Far be it from *Silleus* fo to thinke,
I know it is thy gratitude requites
The loue that is in me, and shall not shrinke
Till death doe feuer me from earths delights.   (talke,

   Salom. But whift; me thinkes the wolfe is in our
Be gone *Silleus*, who doth here arriue?
Tis *Conftabarus* that doth hither walke,
Ile find a quarrell, him from me to driue.

   Sille. Farewell, but were it not for thy commaund,
In his defpight *Silleus* here would ftand.

Actus primus : Sœna Sexta.

Salome : Conftabarus.

Conft: OH *Salome*, how much you wróg your name,
   Your race, your country, and your husband
A ftraungers priuate conference is shame,   (moft?
I blush for you, that haue your blushing loft.
Oft haue I found, and found you to my griefe,
Conforted with this bafe *Arabian* heere:
Heauen knowes that you haue bin my comfort chiefe,
Then doe not now my greater plague appeare.
Now by the ftately Garued edifice
That on Mount *Sion* makes fo faire a show,
And by the Altar fit for facrifice,
I loue thee more then thou thy felfe doeft know.
Oft with a filent forrow haue I heard
How ill *Iudeas* mouth doth cenfure thee:

                          And

And did I not thine honour much regard,
Thou shouldst not be exhorted thus for mee.
Didst thou but know the worth of honest fame,
How much a vertuous woman is esteem'd,
Thou wouldest like hell eschew deserued shame,
And seeke to be both chast and chastly deem'd.
Our wisest Prince did say, and true he said,
A vertuous woman crownes her husbands head.

    Salome. Did I for this, vpreare thy lowe estate?
Did I for this requitall begge thy life,
That thou hadst forseited haples fate?
To be to such a thankles wretch the wife.
This hand of mine hath lifted vp thy head,
Which many a day agoe had falne full lowe,
Because the sonnes of *Baba* are not dead,
To me thou doest both life and fortune owe.

    Const. You haue my patience often exercisde,
Vse make my choller keepe within the bankes:
Yet boast no more, but be by me aduisde.
A benefit vpbraided, forseits thankes :
I prethy *Salome* dismisse this mood,
Thou doest not know how ill it fits thy place:
My words were all intended for thy good,
To raise thine honour and to stop disgrace.

    Sa. To stop disgrace? take thou no care for mee,
Nay do thy worst, thy worst I set not by:
No shame of mine is like to light on thee,
Thy loue and admonitions I defie.
Thou shalt no hower longer call me wife,
Thy Iealousie procures my hate so deepe :
That I from thee doe meane to free my life,
By a diuorcing bill before I sleepe.

    Const. Are Hebrew women now trasform'd to men?
Why do you not as well our battels fight,
And weare our armour? suffer this, and then
Let all the world be topsie turued quite.
Let fishes graze, beastes, swine, and birds descend,
Let fire burne downewards whilst the earth aspires:

                      Let

Let Winters heat and Summers cold offend,
Let Thistels growe on Vines, and Grapes on Briers,
Set vs to Spinne or Sowe, or at the best
Make vs Wood-hewers, Waters-bearing wights:
For sacred seruice let vs take no rest,
Vse vs as *Ioshua* did the *Gibonites*.

   Salom. Hold on your talke, till it be time to end,
For me I am resolu'd it shall be so :
Though I be first that to this cou.se do bend,
I shall not be the last full well I know.

   Const. Why then be witnesse Heau'n, the Iudge of
Be witnesse Spirits that eschew the darke: (sinnes,
Be witnesse Angels, witnesse Cherubins,
Whose semblance sits vpon the holy Arke:
Be witnesse earth, be witnesse *Palestine*,
Be witnesse *Dauids* Citie, if my heart
Did euer merit such an act of thine:
Or if the fault be mine that makes vs part,
Since mildest *Moses* friend vnto the Lord,
Did worke his wonders in the land of *Ham*,
And slew the first-borne Babes without a sword,
In signe whereof we eate the holy Lambe:
Till now that foureteene hundred yeeres are past,
Since first the Law with vs hath beene in force:
You are the first, and will I hope, be last,
That euer sought her husband to diuorce.

   Salom. I meane not to be led by president,
My will shall be to me in stead of Law.

   Const. I feare me much you will too late repent,
That you haue euer liu'd so void of awe:
This is *Sileus* loue that makes you thus
Reuerse all order: you must next be his.
But if my thoughts aright the cause discusse,
In winning you, he gaines no lasting blisse,
I was *Sileus*, and not long agoe
Iosephus then was *Constabarus* now :
When you became my friend you prou'd his foe,
As now for him you breake to me your vowd.

          C   *Salom.*

Sal. If once I lou'd you, greater is your debt:
For certaine tis that you deſerued it not.
And vndeſerued loue we ſoone forget,
And therefore that to me can be no blot.
But now fare ill my once beloued Lord,
Yet neuer more belou'd then now abhord.

   Conſt. Yet *Conſtabarus* biddeth thee farewell.
Farewell light creature. Heauen forgiue thy ſinne:
My prophecying ſpirit doth foretell
Thy wauering thoughts doe yet but new beginne.
Yet I haue better ſcap'd then *Ioſeph* did,
But if our *Herods* death had bene delayd,
The valiant youths that I ſo long haue hid,
Had bene by her, and I for them betrayd.
Therefore in happy houre did *Cæſar* giue
The fatall blow to wanton *Anthony*:
For had he liued, our *Herod* then ſhould liue,
But great *Anthonius* death made *Herod* dye.
Had he enioyed his breath, not I alone
Had beene in danger of a deadly fall:
But *Mariam* had the way of perill gone,
Though by the Tyrant moſt belou'd of all.
The ſweet fac'd *Mariam* as free from guilt
As Heauen from ſpots, yet had her Lord come backe
Her pureſt blood had bene vniuſtly ſpilt.
And *Salome* it was would worke her wracke.
Though all *Iudea* yeeld her innocent,
She often hath bene neere to puniſhment.

Chorus.

THoſe mindes that wholy dote vpon delight,
  Except they onely ioy in inward good:
Still hope at laſt to hop vpon the right,
  And ſo from Sand they leape in loathſome mud.
Fond wretches, ſeeking what they cannot finde,
For no content attends a wauering minde.
If wealth they doe deſire, and wealth attaine,

Then

Then wondrous faine would they to honor lep:
Of meane degree they doe in honor gaine,
They would but wish a little higher step.
   Thus step to step, and wealth to wealth they ad,
   Yet cannot all their plenty make them glad.

Yet oft we see that some in humble state,
Are chreefull, pleasant, happy, and content:
When those indeed that are of higher state,
With vaine additions do their thoughts torment.
   Th'one would to his minde his fortune binde,
   T'hother to his fortune frames his minde.

To wish varietie is signe of griefe,
For if you like your state as now it is,
Why should an alteration bring reliefe?
Nay change would then be fear'd as losse of blis.
   That man is onely happy in his Fate,
   That is delighted in a setled state.

Still *Mariam* wisht she from her Lord were free,
For expectation of varietie:
Yet now she sees her wishes prosperous bee,
She grieues, because her Lord so soone did die.
   Who can those vast imaginations feede,
   Where in a propertie, contempt doth breede?

Were *Herod* now perchance to liue againe,
She would againe as much be grieued at that:
All that she may, she euer doth disdaine,
Her wishes guide her to she knowes not what.
   And sad must be their lookes, their honor sower,
   That care for nothing being in their power.

Actus secundus. Scœna prima.

Pheroras and Graphina.

Pher. 'Tis true *Graphina*, now the time drawes nye
   Wherin the holy Priest with hallowed right,

The happy long defired knot fhall tie,
Pheroras and *Graphina* to vnite:
How oft haue I with lifted hands impler'd
This bleffed houre, till now implord in vaine,
Which hath my wifhed libertie reftor'd,
And made my fubiect felfe my owne againe.
Thy loue faire Mayd vpon mine eye doth fit,
Whofe nature hot doth dry the moyfture all,
Which were in nature, and in reafon fit
For my monachall Brothers death to fall:
Had *Herod* liu'd, he would haue pluckt my hand
From faire *Graphinas* Palme perforce: and tide
The fame in hatefull and defpifed band,
For I had had a Baby to my Bride:
Scarce can her Infant tongue with eafie voice
Her name diftinguifh to anothers care:
Yet had he liu'd, his power, and not my choife
Had made me folemnly the contract fweare.
Haue I not caufe in fuch a change to ioy?
What? though fhe be my Neece, a Princeffe borne:
Neere bloods without refpect: high birth a toy.
Since Loue can teach blood and kindreds fcorne.
VVhat booted it that he did raife my head,
To be his Realmes Copartner, Kingdomes mate,
Withall, he kept *Graphina* from my bed,
More wifht by me then thrice *Indeas* ftate.
Oh, could not he be skilfull Iudge in loue,
That doted fo vpon his *Mariams* face?
He, for his paffion, *Doris* did remoue.
I needed not a lawfull Wife difplace,
It could not be but he had power to iudge,
But he that neuer grudg'd a Kingdomes fhare,
T. is well knowne happineffe to me did grudge:
And ment to be therein without compare.
Elfe had I bene his equall in loues hoaft,
For though the Diadem on *Mariams* head
Corrupt the vulgar iudgements, I will boaft
Graphinas brow's as white, her cheekes as red.

Why

Why fpeaks thou not faire creature?moue thy tongue,
For Silence is a figne of difcontent :
It were to both our loues too great a wrong
If now this hower do find thee fadly bent.

   Graph. Miftake me not my Lord,too oft haue I
Defir'd this time to come with winged feete,
To be inwrapt with griefe when tis too nie,
You know my wifhes euer yours did meete :
If I be filent, tis no more but feare
That I fhould fay too little when I fpeake:
But fince you will my imperfections beare,
In fpight of doubt I will my filence breake :
Yet might amazement tie my mouing tongue,
But that I know before *Pheroras* minde,
I haue admired your affection long :
And cannot yet therein a reafon finde.
Your hand hath lifted me from loweft ftate,
To higheft eminencie wondrous grace,
And me your hand-maid haue you made your mate,
Though all but you alone doe count me bafe.
You haue preferued me pure at my requeft,
Though you fo weake a vaffaile might confftraine
To yeeld to your high will, then laft not beft
In my refpect a Princeffe you difdaine,
Then need not all thefe fauours ftudie craue,
To be requited by a fimple maide:
And ftudie ftill you know mult filence haue,
Then be my caufe for filence iuftly waide,
But ftudie cannot boote nor I requite,
Except your lowly hand-maides fteadfaft loue
And faft obedience may your mind delight,
I will not promife more then I can proue.

   Phero. That ftudie needs not let *Graphina* fmile,
And I defire no greater recompence :
I cannot vaunt me in a glorious ftile,
Nor fhew my loue in far-fetcht eloquence:
But this beleeue me, neuer *Herods* heart
Hath held his Prince-borne beautie famed wife

C 3

In

In neerer place then thou faire virgin art,
To him that holds the glory of his life.
Should *Herods* body leaue the Sepulcher,
An d entertaine the feuer'd ghoft againe:
He fhould not be my nuptiall hinderer,
Except he hindred it with dying paine.
Come faire *Graphina*, let vs goe in ftate,
This wifh-indeered time to celebrate.

Actus 2. Scena. 2.

Conftabarus and *Babus Sonnes.*

Babus. 1. Sonne.

NOw valiant friend you haue our liues redeem'd,
Which liues as fau'd by you, to you are due:
Command and you fhall fee your felfe efteem'd,
Our liues and liberties belong to you.
This twice fixe yeares with hazard of your life,
You haue conceal'd vs from the tyrants fword:
Though cruell *Herods* fifter were your wife,
You durft in fcorne of feare this grace afford.
In recompence we know not what to fay,
A poore reward were thankes for fuch a merit,
Our trueft friendfhip at your feete we lay,
The beft requitall to a noble fpirit.   (youth,
    Conft. Oh how you wrong our friendfhip valiant
With friends there is not fuch a word as det:
Where amitie is tide with bond of truth,
All benefits are there in common fet.
Then is the golden age with them renew'd,
All names of properties are banifht quite:
Diuifion, and diftinction, are efchew'd :
Each hath to what belongs to others right.
And tis not fure fo full a benefit,
Freely to giue, as freely to require:
A bountious act hath glory following it,
They caufe the glory that the act defire.

All friendship should the patterne imitate,
Of *Iesses* Sonne and valiant *Ionathane*
For neither Soueraignes nor fathers hate,
A friendship fixt on vertue seuer can.
Too much of this,'tis written in the heart,
And need no amplifying with the tongue:
Now may you from your liuing tombe depart,
Where *Herods* life hath kept you ouer long.
Too great an iniury to a noble minde,
To be quicke buried,you had purchast fame,
Some yeares a goe,but that you were confinde.
While thousand meaner did aduance their name.
Your best of life the prime of all your yeares,
Your time of action is from you bereft.
Twelue winters haue you operpast in feares:
Yet if you vse it well,enough is left.
And who can doubt but you will vse it well?
The sonnes of *Babus* haue it by descent:
In all their thoughts each action to excell,
Boldly to act,and wisely to inuent.

Babus 2. *Sonne.*

Had it not like the hatefull cuckoe beene,
Whose riper age his infant nurse doth kill:
So long we had not kept our selues vnseene,
But *Constabarus* safely crost our will :
For had the Tyrant fixt his cruell eye,
On our concealed faces wrath had swaide
His Iustice so, that he had forst vs die.
And dearer price then life we should haue paid,
For you our truest friend had falne with vs :
And we much like a house on pillers set,
Had cleane deprest our prop, and therefore thus
Our readie will with our concealement met.
But now that you faire Lord are daungerlesse,
The Sonnes of *Baba* shall their rigor show:
And proue it was not basenes did oppresse
Our hearts so long,but honour kept them low.

Ba. 1.*Sonne.* Yet do I feare this tale of *Herods* death,
At last will proue a very tale indeed:

It

It giues me strongly in my minde, his breath
Wili be preferu'd to make a number bleed :
I wish not therefore to be set at large ,
Yet perill to my selfe I do not feare :
Let vs for some daies longer be your charge,
Till we of *Herods* state the truth do heare.

   Const. What art thou turn'd a coward noble youth,
That thou beginst to doubt, vndoubted truth?

   Babus. 1. Son. Were it my brothers tongue that cast
I fró his hart would haue the question out:(this doubt,
With this keene fauchion, but tis you my Lord
Against whose head I must not lift a sword :
I am so tide in gratitude *Const.* belieue
You haue no cause to take it ill,
If any word of mine your heart did grieue
The word discented from the speakers will,
I know it was not feare the douht begun,
But rather valour and your care of me,
A coward could not be your fathers sonne,
Yet know I doubts vnnecessarie be:
For who can thinke that in *Anthonius* fall,
Herod his bosome friend should scape vnbrusde :
Then *Cæsar* we might thee an idiot call,
If thou by him should'st be so farre abusde.

   Babus. 2. Sonne. Lord *Constab:* let me tell you this,
Vpon submission *Cæsar* will forgiue :
And therefore though the tyrant did amisse,
It may fall out that he will let him liue.
Not many yeares agone it is since I
Directed thither by my fathers care,
In famous *Rome* for twice twelue monthes did liue,
My life from *Hebrewes* crueltie to spare,
There though I were but yet of boyish age,
I bent mine eye to marke, mine eares to heare.
Where I did see *Octauious* then a page,
When first he did to *Iulions* fight appeare:
Me thought *I* faw such mildnes in his face,
And such a sweetnes in his lookes did grow,

Withall

Withall, commixt with so maieflicke grace,
His Phinomy his Fortune did fore-show:
For this I am indebted to mine eye,
But then mine eare receiu'd more euidence,
By that I knew his loue to clemency,
How he with hottest choller could dispence.

   Conſt. But we haue more then barely heard the news,
It hath bin twice confirm'd. And though some tongue
Might be so falle, with falle report t'abuse,
A falle report hath neuer lafted long.
But be it so that *Herod* haue his life,
Concealement would not then a whit auaile:
For certaine t'is, that fhe that was my wife,
Would not to fet her acculation faile.
And therefore now as good the venture giue,
And free our felues from blot of cowardile:
As fhow a pittifull defire to liue,
For, who can pittie but they muft defpife?

             Babus firſt ſonne.
I yeeld, but to neceſſitie I yeeld,
I dare vpon this doubt ingage mine arme:
That *Herod* fhall againe this kingdome weeld,
And proue his death to be a falle alarme.

            Babus ſecond ſonne.
I doubt it too: God grant it be an error,
Tis beft without a caufe to be in terror:
And rather had I, though my foule be mine,
My foule fhould lie, then proue a true diuine.

   Conſt. Come, come, let feare goe feeke a daftards
Vndanted courage lies in a noble breft.   (neft,

Actus 2.   Scœna 3.

Doris and Antipater.

Dor. YOur royall buildings bow your loftie fide,
     And fcope to her that is by right your Queen:
          D   Let

Let your humilitie vpbraid the pride
Of thofe in whom no due refpect is feene:
Nine times haue we with Trumpets haughtie found,
And banifhing fow'r Leauen from our tafte:
Obferu'd the feaft that takes the fruit from ground.
Since I faire Citie did behold thee laft,
So long it is fince *Mariams* purer cheeke
Did rob from mine the glory. And fo long
Since I returnd my natiue Towne to feeke:
And with me nothing but the fence of wrong.
And thee my Boy, whofe birth though great it were,
Yet haue thy after fortunes prou'd but poore:
When thou wert borne how little did I feare
Thou fhouldft be thruft from forth thy Fathers doore.
Art thou not *Herods* right begotten Sonne?
VVas not the haples *Doris, Herods* wife?
Yes: ere he had the Hebrew kingdome wonne,
I was companion to his priuate life.
VVas *I* not faire enough to be a Queene?
Why ere thou wert to me falfe Monarch tide,
My lake of beauty might as well be feene,
As after *I* had liu'd fiue yeeres thy Bride.
Yet then thine oath came powring like the raine,
Which all affirm'd my face without compare:
And that if thou might'ft *Doris* loue obtaine,
For all the world befides thou didft not care.
Then was *I* yong, and rich, and nobly borne,
And therefore worthy to be *Herods* mate:
Yet thou vngratefull caft me off with fcorne,
When Heauens purpofe raifd your meaner fate.
Oft haue I begd for vengeance for this fact,
And with deiected knees, afpiring hands
Haue prayd the higheft power to inact
The fall of her that on my Trophee ftands.
Reuenge I haue according to my will,
Yet where I wifht this vengeance did not light:
I wifht it fhould high-hearted *Mariam* kill.
But it againft my whilome Lord did fight

                                              With

With thee sweet Boy I came, and came to try
If thou before his bastards might be plac'd
In *Herods* royall seat and dignitie.
But *Mariams* infants here are onely grac'd,
And now for vs there doth no hope remaine:
Yet we will not returne till *Herods* end
Be more confirmd, perchance he is not slaine.
So glorious Fortunes may my Boy attend,
For if he liue, hee'll thinke it doth suffice,
That he to *Doris* shows such crueltie:
For as he did my wretched life dispise,
So doe *I* know I shall despised die.
Let him but proue as naturall to thee,
As cruell to thy miserable mother:
His crueltie shall not vpbraided bee
But in thy fortunes. *I* his faults will smother.

    Antipat. Each mouth within the Citie loudly cries
That *Herods* death is certaine: therefore wee
Had best some subtill hidden plot deuise,
That *Mariams* children might subuerted bee,
By poisons drinke, or else by murtherous Knife,
So we may be aduanc'd, it skils not how:
They are but Bastards, you were *Herods* wife,
And foule adultery blotteth *Mariams* brow.

    Doris. They are too strong to be by vs remou'd,
Or else reuenges foulest spotted face:
By our detested wrongs might be approu'd,
But weakenesse must to greater power giue place.
But let vs now retire to grieue alone,
For solitarines best fitteth mone.

Actus secundus. Scœna 4.

Sillens and Constabarus.

Sillens. WEll met *Iudean* Lord, the onely wight
      Sillens wisht to see. I am to call

         Thy

Thy tongue to ſtrict account. *Conſt.* For what deſpight
I ready am to heare, and anſwere all.
But if directly at the cauſe *I* geſſe
That breeds this challenge, you muſt pardon meʒ
And now ſome other ground of fight profeſſe,
For I haue vow'd, vowes muſt vnbroken be.

   Sil. What may be your expectation? let me know.

   Conſt. VVhy? ought concerning *Salom,* my ſword
Shall not be welded for a cauſe ſo low,
A blow for her my arme will ſcorne t'afford.

   Sil. It is for ſlandering her vnſpotted name,
And I will make thee in thy vowes deſpight,
Sucke vp the breath that did my Miſtris blame,
And ſwallow it againe to doe her right.

   Conſi. I prethee giue ſome other quarrell ground
To finde beginning, raile againſt my name :
Or ſtrike me firſt, or let ſome ſcarlet wound
Inflame my courage, giue me words of ſhame,
Doe thou our *Moſes* ſacred Lawes diſgrace,
Depraue our nation, doe me ſome deſpight:
I'm apt enough to fight in any caſe,
But yet for *Salome* I will not fight.

   Sil. Nor I for ought but *Salome* : My ſword
That owes his ſeruice to her ſacred name :
Will not an edge for other cauſe afford,
In other fight I am not ſure of fame.

   Conſt. For her, I pitty thee enough already,
For her, I therefore will not mangle thee :
A woman with a heart ſo moſt vnſteady,
Will of her ſelfe ſufficient torture bee.
I cannot enuy for ſo light a gaine,
Her minde with ſuch vnconſtancie doth runne:
As with a word thou didſt her loue obtaine,
So with a word ſhe will from thee be wonne.
So light as her poſſeſſions for moſt day
Is her affections luſt, to me tis knowne :
As good goe hold the winde as make her ſtay,
Shee neuer loues, but till ſhe call her owne.

                          Sh

She meerly is a painted sepulcher,
That is both faire, and vilely foule at once:
Though on her out-side graces garnish her,
Her mind is fild with worse then rotten bones.
And euer readie lifted is her hand,
To aime destruction at a husbands throat:
For proofes, Iosephus and my selfe do stand,
Though once on both of vs, she seem'd to doat.
Her mouth though serpent-like it neuer hisses,
Yet like a Serpent, poysons where it kisses.   (bite.

Silleus. Well Hebrew well, thou bark'st, but wilt not
Const. I tell thee still for her I will not fight. (heart
Sille: Why then I call thee coward. Const: From my
I giue thee thankes. A cowards hatefull name,
Cannot to valiant mindes a blot impart,
And therefore I with ioy receiue the same.
Thou know'st I am no coward: thou wert by
At the Arabian battaile th'other day:
And saw'st my sword with daring valiancy,
Amongst the faint Arabians cut my way.
The blood of foes no more could let it shine,
And twas inameled with some of thine.
But now haue at thee, not for Salome
I fight: but to discharge a cowards stile:
Here gins the fight that shall not parted be,
Before a soule or two indure exile.   (my blood,

Silleus. Thy sword hath made some windowes for
To shew a horred crimson phisnomie:
To breath for both of vs me thinkes twere good,
The day will giue vs time enough to die.   (time,

Const: With all my hart take breath, thou shalt haue
And if thou list a twelue month, let vs end:
Into thy cheekes there doth a palenes clime,
Thou canst not from my sword thy selfe defend.
What needest thou for Salome to fight,   (her:
Thou hast her, and may'st keepe her, none striues for
I willingly to thee resigne my right,
For in my very soule I do abhorre her.

Thou

Thou feeſt that I am freſh, vnwounded yet,
Then not for feare I do this offer make:
Thou art with loſſe of blood, to fight vnfit,
For here is one, and there another take.

   Silleus. I will not leaue, as long as breath remaines
Within my wounded body : ſpare your words,
My heart in bloods ſtead, courage entertaines,
Salomes loue no place for feare affords.

   Conſt: Oh could thy ſoule but propheſie like mine,
I would not wonder thou ſhould'ſt long to die:
For *Salome* if I aright diuine
Will be then death a greater miſerie.   (will,

   Sillec Then liſt, Ile breath no longer. *Conſt:* Do thy
I hateles fight, and charitably kill. I, I, they fight,
Pittie thy ſelfe *Silleus*, let not death
Intru'd before his time into thy hart :
Alas it is too late to feare, his breath
Is from his body now about to part.
How far'ſt thou braue *Arabian* ? *Silleus* very well,
My legge is hurt, I can no longer fight :
It onely grieues me, that ſo ſoone I fell,
Before faire *Saloms* wrongs I came to right.   (feare,

   Conſt: Thy wounds are leſſe then mortall. Neuer
Thou ſhalt a ſafe and quicke recouerie finde:
Come, I will thee vnto my lodging beare,
I hate thy body, but I loue thy minde.

   Silleus. Thankes noble Iew, I ſee a courtious foe,
Sterne enmitie to friendſhip can no arts:
Had not my heart and tongue engagde me ſo,
I would from thee no foe, but friend depart.
My heart to *Salome* is tide ſo faſt,
To leaue her loue for friendſhip, yet my skill
Shall be imploy'd to make your fauour laſt,
And I will honour *Conſtabarus* ſtill.

   Conſt: I ope my boſome to thee, and will take
Thee in, as friend, and grieue for thy complaint:
But if we doe not expedition make,
Thy loſſe of blood I feare will make thee faint.

                             Chorus.

Chorus.

TO heare a tale with eares preiudicate,
   It spoiles the iudgement, and corrupts the sence:
That humane error giuen to euery state,
Is greater enemie to innocence.
    It makes vs foolish, heddy, rash, vniust,
    It makes vs neuer try before we trust.

It will confound the meaning, change the words,
For it our sence of hearing much deceiues:
Besides no time to Iudgement it affords,
To way the circumstance our eare receiues.
    The ground of accidents it neuer tries,
    But makes vs take for truth ten thousand lies.

Our eares and hearts are apt to hold for good,
That we our selues doe most desire to bee:
And then we drowne obiections in the flood
Of partialitie, tis that we see
    That makes false rumours long with credit past,
    Though they like rumours must conclude at last.

The greatest part of vs preiudicate,
With wishing *Herods* death do hold it true:
The being once deluded doth not bate,
The credit to a better likelihood due.
    Those few that wish it not the multitude,
    Doe carrie headlong, so they doubts conclude.

They not obiect the weake vncertaine ground,
Whereon they built this tale of *Herods* ends:
Whereof the Author scarcely can be found,
And all because their wishes that way bend.
    They thinke not of the perill that ensu'th,
    If this should proue the contrary to truth.

On

On this fame doubt, on this fo light a breath,
They pawne their liues, and fortunes. For they all
Behaue them as the newes of *Herods* death,
They did of moſt vndoubted credit call:
    But if their actions now doe rightly hit,
    Let them commend their fortune, not their wit.

Actus tertius : Scœna prima.

Pheroras : Salome.

Phero. VRge me no more *Graphina* to forſake,
    Not twelue howers ſince I married her
And doe you thinke a ſiſters power cane mak (for loue:
A reſolute decree, ſo ſoone remoue? (affects.
    Salome. Poore minds they are that honour not
    Phero: Who hunts for honour, happines neglects.
    Salom. You might haue bene both of felicitie,
And henour too in equall meaſure ſeaſde.
    Phero: It is not you can tell ſo well as I,
What tis can make me happie, or diſpleaſde.
    Salome. To match for neither beautie nor reſpects
One meane of birth, but yet of meaner minde,
A woman full of naturall defects,
I wonder what your eye in her could finde. (wit,
    Phero: Mine eye found louelines, mine eare found
To pleaſe the one, and to enchant the other:
Grace on her eye, mirrh on her tongue doth ſit,
In lookes a child, in wiſedomes houſe a mother. (elſe,
    Salom: But ſay you thought her faire, as none thinks
Knowes not *Pheroras*, beautie is a blaſt:
Much like this flower which to day excels,
But longer then a day it will not laſt. (ſhow
    Phero: Her wit exceeds her beautie, *Salo:* Wit may
The way to ill, as well as good you know.
    Phero: But wiſedome is the porter of her head,
And bares all wicked words from iſſuing thence.
                             Salome

Sal. But of a porter, better were you sped,
If she against their entrance made defence.

   Phero. But wherefore comes the sacred *Ananell*,
That hitherward his hastie steppes doth bend?
Great sacrificer y'are arriued well,
Ill newes from holy mouth I not attend:

Actus tertius.   Scœna 2.

Phororas. Salome. Ananell.

Ananell.

MY lippes, my sonne, with peacefull tidings blest,
Shall vtter Honey to your listning eare:
A word of death comes not from Priestly brest,
I speake of life: in life there is no feare.
And for the newes I did the Heauens salute,
And fill'd the Temple with my thankfull voice:
For though that mourning may not me pollute,
At pleasing accidents I may reioyce.

   Pheror. Is *Herod* then reuiu'd from certaine death?
   Sall. What? can your news restore my brothers breath?
   Ana. Both so, and so, the King is safe and sound,
And did such grace in royall *Cesar* meet:
That he with larger stile then euer crownd,
Within this houre Ierusalem will greet.
I did but come to tell you, and must backe
To make preparatiues for sacrifice:
I knew his death, your hearts like mine did racke,
Though to conceale it, prou'd you wise.

   Salom. How can my ioy sufficiently appeare?
   Phero. A heauier tale did neuer pierce mine eare.
   Salo. Now *Salome* of happinesse may boast.
   Pheror. But now *Pheroras* is in danger most.
   Salom. I shall enioy the comfort of my life.
   Pherer. And I shall loose it, loosing of my wife.

B

Salom.

Salom. Ioy heart, for *Conſtan:* ſhall be ſlaine.

Phero. Grieue ſoule, *Graphina* ſhall from me be tane.

Salom. Smile cheekes, the faire *Silleus* ſhall be mine.

Phero. Weepe eyes, for *I* muſt with a child combine.

Salom. Well brother, ceaſe your mones, on one con-
Ile vndertake to winne the Kings conſent: (dition
Graphina ſtill ſhall be in your tuition,
And her with you be nere the leiſe content.

    Phero. What's the condition? let me quickly know,
That *I* as quickly your command may act:
Were it to ſee what Hearbs in *Ophir* grow,
Or that the lofty *Tyrus* might be ſackt.

    Salom. Tis no ſo hard a taske: It is no more,
But tell the King that *Conſta:* bid
The ſonnes of *Baba,* done to death before:
And tis no more then *Conſta.* did.
And tell him more that he for *Herods* ſake,
Not able to endure his brothers foe:
Did with a bill our ſeparation make,
Though loth from *Conſta:* elſe to goe.

    Phero. Beleeue this tale for told, Ile goe from hence,
In *Herods* eare the Hebrew to deface:
And I that neuer ſtudied eloquence,
Doe meane with eloquence this tale to grace. *Exit.*

    Salom. This will be *Conſtabarus* quicke diſpatch,
Which from my mouth would leſſer credit finde:
Yet ſhall he not deceaſe without a match,
For *Mariam* ſhall not linger long behinde.
Firſt Iealouſie, if that auaile not, feare
Shalbe my miniſter to worke her end:
A common error moues not *Herods* care,
Which doth ſo firmly to his *Mariam* bend.
She ſhall be charged with ſo horrid crime,
As *Herods* feare ſhall turne his loue to hate:
Ile make ſome ſweare that ſhe deſires to clime,
And ſeekes to poyſon him for his eſtate.
I ſcorne that ſhe ſhould liue my birth t'vpbraid,
To call me baſe and hungry Edomite:

                            With

With patient show her choller I betrayd,
And watcht the time to be reueng'd by flite.
Now tongue of mine with scandall load her name,
Turne hers to fountaines, *Herods* eyes to flame:
Yet first I will begin *Pheroras* suite,
That he my earnest businesse may effect:
And I of *Mariam* will keepe me mute,
Till first some other doth her name detect.
Who's there, *Silleus* man? How fares your Lord?
That your aspects doe beare the badge of sorrow?

Silleus man.

He hath the marks of *Constabarus* sword,
And for a while desires your light to borrow.

Salom. My heauy curse the hatefull sword pursue,
My heauier curse on the more hatefull arme
That wounded my *Silleus*. But renew
Your tale againe. Hath he no mortall harme?

Silleus man.

No signe of danger doth in him appeare,
Nor are his wounds in place of perill seene:
Hee bides you be assured you need not feare,
He hopes to make you yet *Arabia* Queene.

Salom. Commend my heart to be *Silleus* charge,
Tell him, my brothers suddaine comming now:
Will giue my foote no roome to walke at large,
But I will see him yet ere night I vow.

Actus 3.   Scœna 3.

Mariam and Sohemus.

Mariam.

SOhemus, tell me what the newes may be
That makes your eyes so full, your cheeks so blew?

Sohem. I know not how to call them. Ill for me
Tis sure they are: not so I hope for you.

Herod. Mari. Oh, what of *Herod*? *Sohem. Herod* liues!
How! liues? What in some Caue or forrest hid?

E 2   *Sohem.* Nay,

Sohem. Nay, backe return'd with honor. *Cesar* giues
Him greater grace then ere *Anthonius* did.

   Mari. Foretell the ruine of my family,
Tell me that I shall see our Citie burnd:
Tell me I shall a death disgracefull die,
But tell me not that *Herod* is returnd.

   Sohem. Be not impatient Madam, be but milde,
His loue to you againe will soone be bred:

   Mar. I will not to his loue be reconcilde,
With solemne vowes I haue forsworne his Bed.

   Sohem. But you must breake these vowes.

   Mar. Ile rather breake
The heart of *Mariam.* Curfed is my Fate:
But speake no more to me, in vaine ye speake
To liue with him I so profoundly hate.

   Sohem. Great Queene, you must to me your pardon
Sohemus cannot now your will obey: (giue,
If your command should me to silence driue,
It were not to obey, but to betray.
Reiect, and slight my speeches, mocke my faith,
Scorne my obseruance, call my counsell nought:
Though you regard not what *Sohemus* saith,
Yet will I euer freely speake my thought.
I feare ere long I shall faire *Mariam* see
In wofull state, and by her selfe vndone:
Yet for your issues sake more temp'rate bee,
The heart by affabilitie is wonne.

   Mari. And must I to my Prison turne againe?
Oh, now I see I was an hypcorite:
I did this morning for his death complaine,
And yet doe mourne, because he liues ere night.
When I his death beleeu'd, compassion wrought,
And was the stickler twixt my heart and him:
But now that Curtaine's drawne from off my thought,
Hate doth appeare againe with visage grim:
And paints the face of *Herod* in my heart,
In horred colours with detested looke:
Then feare would come, but scorne doth play her part,
                         And

idfaith that fcorne with feare can neuer brooke.
now I could inchaine him with a fmile:
d lead him captiue with a gentle word,
corne my looke fhould euer man beguile,
r other fpeech, then meaning to afford.
lfe *Salome* in vaine might fpend her winde,
n vaine might *Herods* mother whet her tongue:
In vaine had they complotted and combinde,
For I ceuld ouerthrow them all ere long.
Oh what a fhelter is mine innocence,
To fhield me from the pangs of inward griefe:
Gainft all mifhaps it is my faire defence,
And to my forrowes yeelds a large reliefe.
To be commandreffe of the triple earth,
And fit in fafetie from a fall fecure:
To haue all nations celebrate my birth,
I would not that my fpirit were impure.
Let my diftreffed ftate vnpittied bee,
Mine innocence is hope enough for mee.   *Exit.*

   Sohem: Poore guiltles Queene. Oh that my wifh
A little temper now about thy heart: (might place
Vnbridled fpeech is *Mariams* worft difgrace,
And will indanger her without defart.
I am in greater hazard. O're my head,
The fattall axe doth hang vnftedily:
My difobedience once difcouered,
Will fhake it downe : *Sohemus* fo fhall die.
For when the King fhall find, we thought his death
Had bene as certaine as we fee his life:
And markes withall I flighted fo his breath,
As to preferue aliue his matchles wife.
Nay more, to giue to *Alexanders* hand
The regall dignitie. The foueraigne power,
How I had yeelded vp at her command,
The ftrength of all the citie, *Dauids Tower.*
What more then common death may I expect,
Since I too well do know his crueltie:
Twere death, a word of *Herods* to neglect,

What

What then to due directly contrarie?
Yet life I quite thee with a willing spirit,
And thinke thou could'st not better be imploi'd:
I forfeit thee for her that more doth merit,
Ten such were better dead then she destroi'd.
But fare thee well chast Queene, well may I see
The darknes palpable, and riuers part:
The sunne stand still. Nay more retorted bee,
But neuer woman with so pure a heart.
Thine eyes graue maiestic keepes all in awe,
And cuts the winges of euery loose desire:
Thy brow is table to the modest lawe,
Yet though we dare not loue, we may admire.
And if I die, it shall my souie content,
My breath in *Mariams* seruice shall be spent.

Chorus.

T'Is not enough for one that is a wife
  To keepe her spotles from an act of ill:
    But from suspition she should free her life,
And bare her selfe of power as well as will.
  Tis not so glorious for her to be free,
  As by her proper selfe restrain'd to bee.

When she hath spatious ground to walke vpon,
Why on the ridge should she desire to goe?
It is no glory to forbeare alone,
Those things that may her honour ouerthrowe.
  But tis thanke-worthy, if she will not take
  All lawfull liberties for honours sake.

That wife her hand against her fame doth reare,
That more then to her Lord alone will giue
A priuate word to any second eare,
And though she may with reputation liue.
  Yet though most chast, she doth her glory blot,
  And wounds her honour, though she killes it not.

When

When to their Husbands they themselues doe bind,
Doe they not wholy giue themselues away?
Or giue they but their body not their mind,
Reseruing that though best, for others pray?
    No sure, their thoughts no more can be their owne,
    And therefore should to none but one be knowne.

Then she vsurpes vpon anothers right,
That seekes to be by publike language grac't:
And though her thoughts reflect with purest light,
Her mind if not peculiar is not chast.
    For in a wife it is no worse to finde,
    A common body, then a common minde.

And euery mind though free from thought of ill,
That out of glory seekes a worth to show:
When any's eares but one therewith they fill,
Doth in a sort her purenes ouerthrow.
    Now *Mariam* had, (but that to this she bent)
    Beene free from feare, as well as innocent.

Actus quartus: Scœna prima.

Enter Herod and his attendants.

Herod.

HAile happie citie, happie in thy store,
And happy that thy buildings such we see:
    More happie in the Temple where w'adore,
But most of all that *Mariam* liues in thee.
Art thou return'd? how fares my *Mariam? Enter Nutio.*
  Nutio. She's well my Lord, and will anon be here
As you commanded. *Her:* Muffle vp thy browe
Thou daies darke taper. *Mariam* will appeare.
And where she shines, we need not thy dimme light,
Oh hast thy steps rare creature, speed thy pace:
And let thy presence make the day more bright,
And cheere the heart of *Herod* with thy face.

                  It

It is an age since I from *Mariam* went,
Me thinkes our parting was in *Dauids* daies:
The houres are so increast by discontent,
Deepe sorrow, *Iosua*like the season staies:
But when I am with *Mariam*,time runnes on,
Her sight,can make months,minutes,daies of weeke:
An hower is then no sooner come then gon.
When in her face mine eye for wonders seekes.
You world commanding citie,*Europes* grace,
Twice hath my curious eye your streets suruai'd,
And I haue seene the statue filled place,
That once if not for griefe had bene betrai'd.
I all your *Roman* beauties haue beheld,
And seene the shewes your *Ediles* did prepare,
I saw the sum of what in you exceld,
Yet saw no miracle like *Mariam* rare.
The faire and famous *Liuia,Cæsars* loue,
The worlds commaunding Mistresse did I see:
Whose beauties both the world and *Rome* approue,
Yet *Mariam: Liuia* is not like to thee.
Be patient but a little,while mine eyes
Within your compast limits be contain'd:
That obiect straight shall your desires suffice,
From which you were so long a while restrain'd.
How wisely *Mariam* doth the time delay,
Least suddaine ioy my sence should suffocate:
I am prepar'd,thou needst no longer stay:
Whose there,my *Mariam*,more then happie fate?
Oh no,it is *Pheroras*,welcome Brother,
Now for a while,I must my passion smother.

Actus quartus. Scœna secunda.

Herod. Pheroras.

Pheroras.

ALl health and safetie waite vpon my Lord,
And may you long in prosperous fortunes liue

With

With *Rome* commanding *Cæsar*; at accord,
*A*nd haue all honors that the world can giue.

   Herod. Oh brother, now thou fpeakſt not from thy
No, thou haſt ſtrooke a blow at *Herods* loue: (hart,
That cannot quickly from my memory part,
.Though *Salome* did me to pardon moue.
Valiant *Phaſaelus*, now to thee farewell,
Thou wert my kinde and honorable brother:
Oh haples houre, when you felfe ſtriken fell,
Thou fathers Image, glory of thy mother.
Had I defir'd a greater fute of thee,
Then to withhold thee from a harlots bed,
Thou wouldſt haue granted it : but now I fee
All are not like that in a wombe are bred.
Thou wouldſt not, hadſt thou heard of *Herods* death,
Haue made his buriall time, thy bridall houre:
Thou wouldſt with clamours, not with ioyfull breath,
Haue fhow'd the newes to be not fweet but foure.

   Phero. Phafaelus great worth I know did ſtaine
Phereras petty valour : but they lie
(Excepting you your felfe) that dare maintaine,
That he did honor *Herod* more then I.
For what I fhowd, loues power conſtraind me fhow,
And pardon louing faults for *Mariams* fake.

   Herod. Mariam, where is fhe ? *Phero.* Nay, I do not
But abfent vfe of her faire name I make :   (know,
You haue forgiuen greater faults then this,
For *Conſtabarus* that againſt you will
Preferu'd the fonnes of *Baba,* liues in bliffe,
Though you commanded him the youths to kill.

   Herod. Goe, take a prefent order for his death,
And let thofe traytors feele the worſt of feares:
Now *Salome* will whine to begge his breath,
But Ile be deafe to prayers: and blind to teares.

   Phero. He is my Lord from *Salom* diuorſt,
Though her affeꞇtion did to leaue him grieue:
Yet was fhe by her loue to you inforſt,
To leaue the man that would your foes relieue.

F

Herod

Herod. Then halle them to their death. I will requite
Thee gentle *Marsam. Salom. I* meane
The thought of *Mariam* doth fo fleale my fpirit,
My mouth from fpeech of her I cannot weane. *Exit.*

Actus 4.   Scœna 3.

Herod. Mariam.
Herod.

ANd heere fhe comes indeed: happily met
My beft, and deereft halfe: what ailes my deare?
 Thou doeft the difference certainly forget
Twixt Duskey habits, and a time fo cleare.
 Mar. My Lord, I fuit my garment to my minde,
And there no cheerfull colours can I finde.
 Herod. Is this my welcome? haue I longd fo much
To fee my deareft *Mariam* difcontent?
What ift that is the caufe thy heart to touch?
Oh fpeake, that I thy forrow may preuent.
Art thou not *Iuries* Queene, and *Herods* too?
Be my Commandres, be my Soueraigne guide:
To be by thee directed I will woo,
For in thy pleafure lies my higheft pride.
Or if thou thinke *Iudeas* narrow bound,
Too ftrict a limit for thy great command:
Thou fhalt be Empreffe of *Arabia* crownd,
For thou fhalt rule, and I will winne the Land.
Ile robbe the holy *Danids* Sepulcher
To giue thee wealth, if thou for wealth do care:
Thou fhalt haue all, they did with him inter,
And I for thee will make the *Temple* bare.
 Alas. I neither haue of power nor riches want,
I haue enough, nor doe I wifh for more:
Your offers to my heart no eafe can grant,
Except they could my brothers life reftore.
No, had you wifht the wretched *Mariam* glad,

Or

Or had your loue to her bene truly tide:
Nay, had you not defir'd to make her fad,
My brother nor my Grandfyre had not d.de.

Her. Wilt thou beleeue no oathes to cleere thy Lord?
How oft haue *I* with execration fworne:
Thou art by me belou'd, by me ador'd,
Yet are my proteftations heard with fcorne.
Hercanus plotted to depriue my head
Of this long fetled honor that I weare:
And therefore *I* did iuftly doome him dead,
To rid the Realme from perill, me from feare.
Yet I for *Mariams* fake doe fo repent
The death of one: whofe blood fhe did inherit:
I wifh I had a Kingdomes treafure fpent,
So *I* had nere expeld *Hercanus* fpirit.
As I affected that fame noble youth,
In lafting infamie my name inrole:
If I not mournd his death with heartie truth.
Did I not fhew to him my earneft loue,
When I to him the Priefthood did reftore?
And did for him a liuing Prieft remoue,
Which neuer had bene done but once before.

Mariam. I know that mou'd by importunitie,
You made him Prieft, and fhortly after die.

Herod. I will not fpeake, vnles to be beleeu'd,
This froward humor will not doe you good:
It hath too much already *Herod* grieu'd,
To thinke that you on termes of hate haue ftood.
Yet fmile my deareft *Mariam*, doe but fmile,
And I will all vnkind conceits exile.

Mari. I cannot frame difguife, nor neuer taught
My face a looke diffenting from my thought.

Herod. By heau'n you vexe me, build not on my loue.

Mari. I wil not build on fo vnftable ground.

Herod. Nought is fo fixt, but peeuifhnes may moue.

Mar. Tis better fleighteft caufe then none were foud.

Herod. Be iudge your felfe, if euer *Herod* fought
Or would be mou'd a caufe of change to finde:

Yet

Yet let your looke declare a milder thought,
My heart againe you shall to *Mariam* binde.
How oft did I for you my Mother chide,
Reuile my Sister, and my brother rate:
And tell them all my *Mariam* they belide,
Distrust me still, if these be signes of hate.

Actus 4.　　Scœna 4.

Herod.

VVHat hast thou here? *Bu.* A drinke procuring
　　The Queene desir'd me to deliuer it.　(loue,
Mar. Did *I*: some hatefull practise this will proue,
Yet can it be no worse then Heauens permit.
　Herod. Confesse the truth thou wicked instrument,
To her outragious will, tis passion sure:
Tell true, and thou shalt scape the punishment,
Which if thou doe conceale thou shalt endure.
　Bu. I know not, but I doubt it be no lesse,
Long since the hate of you her heart did cease.
　Herod. Know'st thou the cause thereof? *Bu.* My Lord
Sohemus told the tale that did displease.　(I gesse,
　Herod. Oh Heauen! *Sohemus* false! Goe let him die,
Stay not to suffer him to speake a word:
Oh damned villaine, did he falsifie
The oath he swore eu'n of his owne accord?
Now doe I know thy falshood, painted Diuill
Thou white *Inchantres.* Oh thou art so foule,
That *Ysop* cannot clense thee worst of euill.
A beautious body hides a loathsome soule,
Your loue *Sohemus* mou'd by his affection,
Though he haue euer heretofore bene true:
Did blab forsooth, that I did giue direction,
If we were put to death to slaughter you.
A nd you in blacke reuenge attended now
To adde a murther to your breach of vow.
　Mar. Is this a dream? *Her.* Oh Heauen, that t'were no
Ile giue my Realme to who can proue it so:　(more,

1

would I were like any begger poore,
So I for falfe my *Mariam* did not know.
Foule pith contain'd in the faireft rinde,
That euer grac'd a Cædar. Oh thine eye
Is pure as heauen, but impure thy minde,
And for impuritie fhall *Mariam* die.
Why didft thou loue *Sohemus? Mar:*they can tell
That fay I lou'd him, *Mariam* faies not fo.

    Herod. Oh cannot impudence the coales expell,
That for thy loue in *Herods* bofome glowt:
It is as plaine as water, and deniall
Makes of thy falfehood but a greater triall.
Haft thou beheld thy felfe, and couldft thou ftaine
So rare perfection: euen for loue of thee
I doe profoundly hate thee. Wert thou plaine,
Thou fhoul'dft the wonder of *Iudea* bee.
But oh thou art not, Hell it felfe lies hid
Beneath thy heauenly fhow. Yet neuer wert thou chaft:
Thou might'ft exalt, pull downe, command, forbid,
And be aboue the wheele of fortune plaft.
Hadft thou complotted *Herods* maffacre,
That fo thy fonne a Monarch might be ftilde,
Not halfe fo grieuous fuch an action were,
As once to thinke, that *Mariam* is defilde.
Bright workmanfhip of nature fulli'd ore,
With pitched darknes now thine end fhall bee:
Thou fhalt not liue faire fiend to cozen more,
With heauy femblance, as thou coufnedft mee.
Yet muft I loue thee in defpight of death,
And thou fhalt die in the difpight of loue :
For neither fhall my loue prolong thy breath,
Nor fhall thy loffe of breath my loue remoue.
I might haue feene thy falfehood in thy face,
Where coul'dft thou get thy ftares that feru'd for eyes?
Except by theft, and theft is foule difgrace :
This had appear'd before were *Herod* wife,
But I'me a fot, a very fot, no better:
My wifedome long agoe a wandring fell,

                                    Thy

Thy face incountring it, my wit did fetter,
And made me for delight my freedome fell.
Giue me my heart false creature, tis a wrong,
My guiltles heart should now with thine be slaine:
Thou hadst no right to looke it vp so long,
And with vsurpers name I *Mariam* slaine.

Enter Bu:

He: Haue you defign'd *Sohemus* to his end? (guard
Bu: I haue my Lord *Herod*: Then call our royall
To doe as much for *Mariam*, they offend
Leaue ill vnblam'd, or good without reward.
Here take her to her death Come backe, come backe,
What ment I to depriue the world of light:
To muffle *Iury* in the foulest blacke,
That euer was an oppofite to white.
Why whither would you carrie her: *Sould:* you bad
We should conduct her to her death my Lord.

Hero: Wie sure I did not, *Herod* was not mad,
Why should she feele the furie of the sword?
Oh now the griefe returnes into my heart,
And pulles me peecemeale: loue and hate doe fight:
And now hath boue acquir'd the greater part,
Yet now hath hate, affection conquer'd quite.
And therefore beare her hence: and *Hebrew* why
Seaze you with Lyons pawes the fairest lam
Of all the flocke? she must not, shall not, die,
Without her I most miserable am.
And with her more then most, away, away,
But beare her but to prifon not to death:
And is she gon indeed, stay villaines stay,
Her lookes alone preferu'd your Soueraignes breath.
Well let her goe, but yet she shall not die,
I cannot thinke she ment to poifon me:
But certaine tis she liu'd too wantonly,
And therefore shall she neuer more be free.

Actus 4. Scœna 5.

Bu· FOule villaine, can thy pitchie coloured foule
Permit thine eare to heare her caules doome?
And not inforce thy tongue that tale controule,
That muft vniuftly bring her to her toome.
Oh *Salome* thou haft thy felfe repaid,
For all the benefits that thou haft done:
Thou art the caufe I haue the queene betraid,
Thou haft my hart to darkeft falfe-hood wonne.
I am condemn'd, heau'n gaue me not my tongue
To flander innocents, to lie, deceiue:
To be the hatefull inftrument to wrong,
The earth of greateft glory to bereaue.
My finne afcends and doth to heau'n crie,
It is the blackeft deed that euer was:
And there doth fit an Angell notarie,
That doth record it downe in leaues of braffe.
Oh how my heart doth quake: *Achitophel,*
Theu founds a meanes thy felfe from fhame to free:
And fure my foule approues thou didft not well,
All follow fome, and I will follow thee.

Actus 4. Scœna 6.

Conftabarus, Babus Sonnes, and their guard.

Conft: NOw here we ftep our laft, the way to death,
We muft not tread this way a fecond time:
Yet let vs refolutely yeeld our breath,
Death is the onely ladder, Heau'n to clime.   (refigne,
  Babus I. *Sonne.* With willing mind I could my felfe
But yet it grieues me with a griefe vntold:
Our death fhould be accompani'd with thine,
Our friendfhip we to thee haue dearely fold.

Conft:

Conſt. Still wilt thou wrong the ſacred name of friend?
Then ſhould'ſt thou neuer ſtile it friendſhip more:
But baſe mechanicke traffique that doth lend,
Yet will be ſure they ſhall the debt reſtore.
I could with needleſſe complement returne,
Tis for thy ceremonie I could ſay :
Tis I that made the fire your houſe to burne,
For but for me ſhe would not you betray.
Had not the damned woman ſought mine end,
You had not bene the ſubiect of her hate:
You neuer did her hatefull minde offend,
Nor could your deaths haue freed your nuptiall fate.
Therefore faire friends,though you were ſtill vnborne,
Some other ſubtiltie deuiſde ſhould bee:
Were by my life, though guiltles ſhould be torne,
Thus haue I prou'd,tis you that die for mee.
And therefore ſhould I weakely now lament,
You haue but done your duties, friends ſhould die:
Alone their friends diſaſter to preuent,
Though not compeld by ſtrong neceſſitie.
But now farewell faire citie,neuer more
Shall I behold your beautie ſhining bright:
Farewell of _Iewiſh_ men the worthy ſtore,
But no farewell to any female wight.
You wauering crue:my curſe to you I leaue,
You had but one to giue you any grace:
And you your ſelues will _Mariams_ life bereaue,
Your common-wealth doth innocencie chaſe.
You creatures made to be the humane curſe,
You Tygers,Lyoneſſes,hungry Beares,
Teare maſſacring _Hienas_ : nay far worſe,
For they for pray doe ſhed their fained teares.
But you will weepe,(you creatures croſſe to good)
For your vnquenched thirſt of humane blood:
You were the Angels caſt from heaue'n for pride,
And ſtill doe keepe your Angels outward ſhow,
But none of you are inly beautifide,
For ſtill your heau'n depriuing pride doth grow.

Did

Did not the sinnes of many require a scourge,
Your place on earth had bene by this withstood :
But since a flood no more the world must purge,
You staid in office of a second flood.
You giddy creatures, sowers of debate,
You'll loue to day, and for no other cause,
But for you yesterday did deply hate,
You are the wreake of order, breach of lawes.
You best, are foolish, froward, wanton, vaine,
Your worst adulterous, murderous, cunning, proude
And *Salome* attends the latter traine,
Or rather he their leader is allowd.
I do the sottishnesse of men bewaile,
That doe with following you inhance your pride:
T'were better that the humane race should faile,
Then be by such a mischiefe multiplide.
Chams seruile curse to all your sexe was giuen,
Because in Paradise you did offend:
Then doe we not resist the will of Heauen,
When on your willes like seruants we attend?
You are to nothing constant but to ill,
You are with nought but wickednesse indude:
Your loues are set on nothing but your will,
And thus my censure I of you conclude.
You are the least of goods, the worst of euils,
Your best are worse then men : your worst then diuels.

Babus second sonne.

Come let vs to our death: are we not blest ?
Our death will freedome from these creatures giue:
Those trouble quiet sowers of vnrest,
And this I vow that had I Iesue to liue,
I would for euer leade a single life,
And neuer venter on a diuellish wife.

G   *Actus*

Actus 4. Scœna 7.

Herod and Salome.

Herod.

NAy, she shall die. Die quoth you, that she shall:
    But for the meanes. The meanes I Me thinks tis
To finde a meanes to murther her withall,   (hard
Therefore I am resolu'd she shall be spar'd.
    Salom. Why? let her be beheaded. *Her.* That were
Thinke you that swords are miracles like you: (well,
Her skinne will eu'ry Curtlax edge resell,
And then your enterprise you well may rue.
What if the fierce Arabian notice take,
Of this your wretched weaponlesse estate :
They answere when we bid resistance make,
That *Mariams* skinne their fanchions did rebate.
Beware of this, you make a goodly hand,
If you of weapons doe depriue our Land.
    Sal. Why drowne her then. *Herod.* Indeed a sweet de-
Why? would not eu'ry Riuer turne her course   (uice,
Rather then doe her beautie preiudice ?
And be reuerted to the proper sourse.
So not a drop of water should be found
In all Iudeas quondam fertill ground.
    Sal. Then let the fire deuoure her.   *Her.* T'will not
Flame is from her deriu'd into my heart :   (bee:
Thou nursest flame, flame will not murther thee,
My fairest *Mariam*, fullest of desert.   (die:
    Salom. Then let her liue for me. *Herod.* Nay, she sha'l
But can you liue without her ? *Sal.* doubt you that?
    Herod. I'me sure I cannot, I beseech you trie:
I haue experience but I know not what.
    Salom. How should I try? *Her.* Why let my loue be
But if we cannot liue without her sight   (slaine,
                                                 You'e

Youle finde the meanes to make her breathe againe,
Or elfe you will bereaue my comfort quite.

Sal. Oh *I*: I warrant you. *Herod.* What is fhe gone?
And gone to bid the world be ouerthrowne:
What? is her hearts compofure hardeft ftone?
To what a paife are cruell women growne?
She is return'd already: haue you done?
Ift poffible you can command fo foone?
A creatures heart to quench the flaming Sunne,
Or from the skie to wipe away the Moone.

Salo. If *Mariam* be the Sunne and Moone, it is:
For I already haue commanded this. (times.

Her. But haue you feene her cheek? *Sal.* A thoufand
Herod. But did you marke it too? *Sal.* I very well.

Hered. What ift? *Sal.* A Crimfon bufh, that euer limes
The foule whofe forefight doth not much excell.

Herod. Send word fhe fhall not dye. Her cheek a bufh,
Nay, then *I* fee indeed you markt it not.

Sal. Tis very faire, but yet will neuer blufh,
Though foule difhonors do her forehead blot.

Herod. Then let her die, tis very true indeed,
And for this fault alone fhall *Mariam* bleed.

Sal. What fault my Lord? *Herod.* What fault ift? you
If you be ignorant *I* know of none, (that askes
To call her backe from death fhall be your taske,
I'm glad that fhe for innocent is knowne.
For on the brow of *Mariam* hangs a Fleece,
Whofe flendereft twine is ftrong enough to binde
The hearts of Kings, the pride and fhame of *Greece*,
Troy flaming *Helens* not fo fairely fhinde.

Salom. Tis true indeed, fhe layes them out for nets,
To catch the hearts that doe not fhune a baite:
Tis time to fpeake: for *Herod* fure forgets
That *Mariams* very treffes hide deceit.

Her. Oh doe they fo? nay, then you doe but well,
Infooth I thought it had beene haire:
Nets call you them? Lord, how they doe excell,
I neuer faw a net that fhow'd fo faire.

But

But haue you heard her speake? *Sal.* You know *I* haue.

Her: And were you not amaz'd? *Sal.* No, not a whit.

Her. Then t'was not her you heard, her life Ile sauc,
For *Mariam* hath a world amazing wit.

Salo. She speaks a beautious language, but within
Her heart is false as powder : and her tongue
Doth but allure the auditors to sinne,
And is the instrument to doe you wrong.

Heroa. It may be so: nay, tis so: shee's vnchaste,
Her mouth will ope to eu'ry strangers eare :
Then let the executioner make haste,
Lest she inchant him, if her words he heare.
Let him be deafe, lest she do him surprise
That shall to free her spirit be assignde :
Yet what boots deafenes if he haue his eyes,
Her murtherer must be both deafe and blinde.
For if he see, he needs must see the starres
That shine on eyther side of *Mariams* face:
Whose sweet aspect will terminate the warres,
Wherewith he should a soule so precious chase.
Her eyes can speake, and in their speaking moue,
Oft did my heart with reuerence receiue
The worlds mandates. Pretty tales of loue
They vtter, which can humane bondage weaue.
But shall I let this heauens modell dye?
Which for a small selfe-portraiture she drew :
Her eyes like starres, her forehead like the skie,
She is like Heauen, and must be heauenly true.

Salom. Your thoughts do raue with doating on the
Her eyes are eben hewde, and you'll confesse: (Queen,
A sable starre hath beene but seldome seene,
Then speake of reason more, of *Mariam* lesse.

Herod. Your selfe are held a goodly creature heere,
Yet so vnlike my *Mariam* in your shape:
That when to her you haue approached neere;
My selfe hath often tane you for an Ape.
And yet you prate of beautie: goe your waies,
You are to her a Sun-burnt Blackamore :

Your.

Your paintings cannot equall *Mariams* praise,
Her nature is so rich, you are so poore.
Let her be staide from death, for if she die,
We do we know not what to stop her breath :
A world cannot another *Mariam* buy,
Why stay you lingring? countermaund her death.

Sale. Then youle no more remember what hath past,
Sohemus loue, and hers shall be forgot:
Tis well in truth : that fault may be her last,
And she may mend, though yet she loue you not.

Her: Oh God : tis true. *Sohemus* : earth and heau'n,
Why did you both conspire to make me curst:
In cousning me with showes, and proofes vneu'n?
She show'd the best, and yet did proue the worst.
Her show was such, as had our singing king
The holy *Dauid, Mariams* beautie seene:
The *Hittits* had then felt no deadly sting,
Nor *Bethsabe* had neuer bene a Queene.
Or had his sonne the wisest man of men,
Whose fond delight did most consist in change:
Beheld her face, he had bene staid agen,
No creature hauing her, can wish to range.
Had *Asuerus* seene my *Mariams* brow,
The humble *Iewe*, she might haue walkt alone:
Her beautious vertue should haue staid below,
Whiles *Mariam* mounted to the *Persian* throne.
But what auailes it all : for in the waight
She is deceitfull, light as vanitie :
Oh she was made for nothing but a bait,
To traine some haples man to miserie.
I am the haples man that haue bene trainde,
To endles bondage. I will see her yet:
Me thinkes I should discerne her if she sainde,
Can humane eyes be dazde by womans wit?
Once more these eyes of mine with hers shall meet,
Before the headsman doe her life bereaue :
Shall I for euer part from thee my sweet?
Without the taking of my latest leaue.

Sale:

Salo: You had as good refolue to faue her now,
Ile ftay her death,tis well determined:
For fure fhe neuer more will breake her vow,
Sohemius and *Iofephus* both are dead.

   Herod. She fhall not liue, nor will I fee her face,
A long heald wound,a fecond time doth bleed:
With *Iofeph* I remember her difgrace,
A fhamefull end enfues a fhamefull deed.
Oh that I had not cald to minde anew,
The difcontent of *Mariams* wauering hart:
Twas you: you foule mouth'd *Ate*,none but you,
That did the thought hereof to me impart.
Hence from my fight,my blacke tormenter hence,
For hadft not thou made *Herod* vnfecure:
I had not doubted *Mariams* innocence,
But ftill had held her in my heart for pure.

   Salo: Ile leaue you to your paffion: tis no time
To purge me now,though of a guiltles crime.   (*Exit.*

   Herod. Deftruction take thee: thou haft made
As heauie as reuenge,I am fo dull,   (my hart
Methinkes I am not fenfible of fmart,
Though hiddious horrors at my bofome pull.
My head waies downwards: therefore will I goe
To try if I can fleepe away my woe.

Actus 4. Scœna. 8.

Mariam.

AM I the *Mariam* that prefum'd fo much, (breath?
And deem'd my face muft needes preferue my
I,I it was that thought my beautie fuch,
At it alone could countermaund my death.
Now death will teach me: he can pale afwell
A cheeke of rofes,as a cheeke leffe bright:
And dim an eye whofe fhine doth moft excell,
Affoone as one that cafts a meaner light.

                           Had

Had not my selfe against my selfe conspirde,
No plot: no aduersarie from without
Could *Herods* loue from *Mariam* haue retirde,
Or from his heart haue thrust my semblance out.
The wanton Queene that neuer lou'd for loue,
False *Cleopatra*, wholly set on gaine:
With all her slights did proue: yet vainly proue,
For her the loue of *Herod* to obtaine.
Yet her allurements, all her courtly guile,
Her smiles, her fauours, and her smooth deceit
Could not my face from *Herods* minde exile,
But were with him of lesse then little weight.
That face and person that in *Asia* late
For beauties Goddesse *Paphos* Queene was tane:
That face that did captiue great *Iulius* fate,
That very face that was *Anthonius* bane.
That face that to be *Egipts* pride was borne,
That face that all the world esteem'd so rare:
Did *Herod* hate, despise, neglect, and scorne,
When with the same, he *Mariams* did compare.
This made that I improuidently wrought,
And on the wager euen my life did pawne:
Because I thought, and yet but truly thought,
That *Herods* loue could not from me be drawne.
But now though out of time, I plainly see
It could be drawne, though neuer drawne from me:
Had I but with humilitie bene grac'te,
As well as faire I might haue prou'd me wise:
But I did thinke because I knew me chaste,
One vertue for a woman, might suffice.
That mind for glory of our sexe might stand,
Wherein humilitie and chastitie
Doth march with equall paces hand in hand,
But one if single seene, who setteth by?
An if had single or e, but tis my ioy,
That I was euer innocent, though sower:
And therefore can they but my life destroy,
My Soule is free from aduersaries power.) *Enter Doris.*

You Princes great in power, and high in birth,
Be great and high, I enuy not your hap:
Your birth must be from dust : your power on earth,
In heau'n shall *Mariam* sit in *Saraes* lap.　　　(thither,

　Doris. I heau'n, your beautie cannot bring you
Your soule is blacke and spotted, full of sinne:
You in adultry liu'd nine yeare together,
And heau'n will neuer let adultry in.

　Mar: What art thou that dost poore *Mariam* pursue?
Some spirit sent to driue me to dispaire:
Who sees for truth that *Mariam* is vntrue,
If faire she be, she is as chaste as faire.

　Doris. I am that *Doris* that was once belou'd,
Belou'd by *Herod* : *Herods* lawfull wife:
Twas you that *Doris* from his side remou'd,
And rob'd from me the glory of my life.

　Mar: Was that adultry: did not Moses say,
That he that being matcht did deadly hate: ·
Might by permission put his wife away,
And take a more belou'd to be his mate?

　Doris. What did he hate me for : for simple truth?
For bringing beautious babes for loue to him :
For riches : noble birth, or tender youth,
Or for no staine did *Doris* honour dim?
Oh tell me *Mariam*, tell me if you knowe,
Which fault of these made *Herod Doris* foe.
These thrice three yeares haue I with hands held vp,
And bowed knees fast nailed to the ground:
Besought for thee the dreggs of that same cup,
That cup of wrath that is for sinners found.
And now thou art to drinke it : *Doris* curse,
Vpon thy selfe did all this while attend,
But now it shall pursue thy children worse.

　Mar: Oh *Doris* now to thee my knees I bend,
That hart that neuer bow'd to thee doth bow :
Curse not mine infants, let it thee suffice,
That Heau'n doth punishment to me allow.
Thy curse is cause that guiltles *Mariam* dies.

　　　　　　　　　　　　　　　　　Doris.

Doris. Had I ten thousand tongues, and eu'ry tongue
Inflam'd with poisons power, and steept in gall :
My curses would not answere for my wrong,
Though I in cursing thee imployd them all.
Heare thou that didst mount *Gerarim* command,
To be a place whereon with cause to curse :
Stretch thy reuenging arme : thrust forth thy hand,
And plague the mother much: the children worse.
Throw flaming fire vpon the baseborne heads
That were begotten in vnlawfull beds.
But let them liue till they haue sence to know
What tis to be in miserable state:
Then be their neerest friends their ouerthrow,
Attended be they by suspitious hate.
And *Mariam*, I doe hope this boy of mine
Shall one day come to be the death of thine. *Exit.*

Mariam. Oh! Heauen forbid. I hope the world shall (see,
This curse of thine shall be return'd on thee:
Now earth farewell, though I be yet but yong,
Yet *I*, me thinks, haue knowne thee too too long. *Exit.*

Chorus.

THe fairest action of our humane life,
 Is scorniug to reuenge an iniurie :
    For who forgiues without a further strife,
His aduersaries heart to him doth tie.
    And tis a firmer conquest truely sed,
    To winne the heart, then ouerthrow the head.

If we a worthy enemie doe finde,
To yeeld to worth, it must be nobly done :
But if of baser mettall be his minde,
In base reuenge there is no honor wonne.
    Who would a worthy courage ouerthrow,
    And who would wrastle with a worthles foe?

We

We fay our hearts are great and cannot yeeld,
Becaufe they cannot yeeld it proues them poore:
Great hearts are task't beyond their power, but feld
The weakeft Lyon will the lowdeft roare.
   Truths fchoole for certaine doth this fame allow,
   High hartednes doth fometimes teach to bow.

A noble heart doth teach a vertuous fcorne,
To fcorne to owe a dutie ouer-long:
To fcorne to be for benefits forborne,
To fcorne to lie, to fcorne to doe a wrong.
   To fcorne to beare an iniurie in minde,
   To fcorne a free-borne heart flaue-like to binde.

But if for wrongs we needs reuenge muft haue,
Then be our vengeance of the nobleft kinde:
Doe we his body from our furie faue,
And let our hate preuaile againft our minde?
   What can gainft him a greater vengeance bee,
   Then make his foe more worthy farre then hee?

Had *Mariam* fcorn'd to leaue a due vnpaide,
Shee would to *Herod* then haue paid her loue:
And not haue bene by fullen paffion fwaide
To fixe her thoughts all iniurie aboue
   Is vertuous pride. Had *Mariam* thus bene prou'd,
   Long famous life to her had bene allowd.

Actus quintus. Scœna prima.

Nuntio.

WHen, fweeteft friend, did I fo farre offend
Your heauenly felfe: that you my fault to quit
                       Haue

Haue made me now relator of her end,
The end of beautie? Chaſtitie and wit,
Was none ſo haples in the fatall place,
But I, moſt wretched, for the Queene t'chuſe,
'Tis certaine I haue ſome ill boding face
That made me culd to tell this luckles newes.
And yet no news to Herod: were it new,
To him vnhappy t'had not bene at all:
Yet doe I long to come within his vew,
That he may know his wife did guiltles fall:
And heere he comes. Your Mariam greets you well.

Enter Herod.

Herod. What? liues my Mariam? ioy, exceeding ioy.
She ſhall not die. Nun. Heau'n doth your will repell.
   Herod. Oh doe not with thy words my life deſtroy,
I prethy tell no dying-tale: thine eye
Without thy tongue doth tell but too too much:
Yet let thy tongues addition make me die,
Death welcome, comes to him whoſe griefe is ſuch.
   Nunti. I went amongſt the curious gazing troope,
To ſee the laſt of her that was the beſt:
To ſee if death had hart to make her ſtoope,
To ſee the Sunne admiring Phœnix neſt.
VVhen there I came, vpon the way I ſaw
The ſtately Mariam not debas'd by feare:
Her looke did ſeeme to keepe the world in awe,
Yet mildly did her face this fortune beare.
   Herod. Thou doſt vſurpe my right, my tongue was
To be the inſtrument of Mariams praiſe: (fram'd
Yet ſpeake: ſhe cannot be too often fam'd:
All tongues ſuffice not her ſweet name to raiſe.
   Nun. But as ſhe came ſhe Alexandra met,

Who

Who did her death (sweet Queene) no whit bewaile,
But as if nature she did quite forget,
She did vpon her daughter loudly raile.

   Herod. Why stopt you not her mouth? where had she
To darke that, that Heauen made so bright? (words
Our sacred tongue no *Epithite* affords,
To call her other then the worlds delight.

   Nun. Shee told her that her death was too too good,
And that already she had liu'd too long:
She said, she sham'd to haue a part in blood
Of her that did the princely *Herod* wrong.   (glory,

   Herod. Base picke-thanke Diuell. Shame, twas all her
That she to noble *Mariam* was the mother:
But neuer shall it liue in any storie
Her name, except to infamy ile smother.
What answere did her princely daughter make?

   Nun. She made no answere, but she lookt the while,
As if thereof she scarce did notice take,
Yet smilde, a dutifull, though scornefull smile.

   Her. Sweet creature, I that looke to mind doe call,
Full oft hath *Herod* bene amaz'd withall.

   Nun. Go on, she came vnmou'd with pleasant grace,
As if to triumph her arriuall were:
In stately habite, and with cheefull face:
Yet eu'ry eye was moyst, but *Mariams* there.
When iustly opposite to me she came,
She pickt me out from all the crue:
She beckned to me, cald me by my name,
For she my name, my birth, and fortune knew.

   Herod. What did she name thee? happy, happy man,
Wilt thou not euer loue that name the better?
But what sweet tune did this faire dying Swan
Afford thine eare: tell all, omit no letter.

   Nun. Tell thou my Lord, said she. *Her.* Mee, ment she
Ist true, the more my shame: *I* was her Lord,   (mee?
Were *I* not made her Lord, *I* still should bee:

                                 But

But now her name must be by me adord.
Oh say, what said she more? each word she sed
Shall be the food whereon my heart is fed.   (breath.
   Nun: Tell thou my Lord thou saw'st me loose my
Herod. Oh that I could that sentence now controule.
   Nun. It guiltily eternall be my death,
Her: I hold her chast eu'n in my inmost soule.
   Nun: By three daies hence if wishes could reuiue,
I know himselfe would make me oft aliue.
   Herod. Three daies: three houres, three minutes, not
A minute in a thousand parts diuided,   :(so much,
My penitencie for her death is such,
As in the first I wisht she had not died.
But forward in thy tale. *Nun:* Why on she went,
And after she some silent praier had sed:
She did as if to die she were content, .
And thus to heau'n her heau'nly soule is fled. .
   Herod. But art thou sure there doth no life remaine?
Ist possible my *Mariam* should be dead,.   :.
Is there no tricke to make her breathe againe?
   Nun: Her body is diuided from her head.   (art,
Her: Why yet me thinkes there might be found by
Strange waies of cure, tis sure rare things are don:
By an inuentiue head, and willing heart. .
   Nun: Let not my Lord your fancies idlely run.
It is as possible it should befcene,.
That we should make the holy Abraham liue,
Though he intomb'd two thousand yeares had bene,
As breath againe to slaughtred *Mariam* giue.
But now for more assaults prepare your eares,
   Herod. There cannot be a further cause of mone,
This accident shall shelter me from feares:
What can I feare? already *Mariams* gone.
Yet tell eu'n what you will: *Nun:* As I came by,
From *Mariams* death I saw vpon a tree,
A man that to his necke a cord did tie:

Which

Which cord he had defignd his end to bee.
When me he once difcern'd, he downwards bow'd,
And thus with fearefull voyce fhe cride alowd,
Goe tell the King he trufted ere he tride,
I am the caufe that *Mariam* caufeles dide.

    Herod. Damnation take him, for it was the flaue
That faid fhe ment with poifons deadly force
To end my life that fhe the Crowne might haue:
Which tale did *Mariam* from her felfe diuorce.
Oh pardon me thou pure vnfpotted Ghoft,
My punifhment muft needes fufficient bee,
In miffing that content I valued moft:
Which was thy admirable face to fee.
I had but one ineftimable Iewell,
Yet one I had no monarch had the like,
And therefore may I curfe my felfe as cruell:
Twas broken by a blowe my felfe did ftrike.
I gaz'd thereon and neuer thought me bleft,
But when on it my dazled eye might reft:
A pretious Mirror made by wonderous art,
I prizd it ten times dearer then my Crowne,
And laide it vp faft foulded in my heart:
Yet I in fuddaine choler caft it downe.
And pafht it all to peeces: twas no foe,
That robd me of it, no *Arabian* hoft,
Nor no *Armenian* guide hath vfde me fo:
But *Herods* wretched felfe hath *Herod* croft.
She was my gracefull moytie, me accurft,
To flay my better halfe and faue my worft.
But fure fhe is not dead you did but ieft,
To put me in perplexitie a while, .
Twere well indeed if I could fo be dreft:
I fee fhe is aliue, me thinkes you fmile.

    Nun: If fainted *Abel* yet deceafed bee,
Tis certaine *Mariam* is as dead as hee.

    Her: Why then goe call her to me, bid her now

                        Put

Put on faire habite, ſtately ornament:
And let no frowne oreſhade her ſmootheſt brow,
In her doth *Herod* place his whole content.　　　(ſence,
　　Nun: Sheel come in ſtately weedes to pleaſe your
If now ſhe come attirde in robe of heauen:
Remember you your ſelfe did ſend her hence,
And now to you ſhe can no more be giuen.　　　faire,
　　Herod. Shee's dead, hell take her murderers, ſhe was
Oh what a hand ſhe had, it was ſo white,
It did the whitenes of the ſnowe impaire:
I neuer more ſhall ſee ſo ſweet a ſight.　　　(hands;
　　Nun: Tis true, her hand was rare. *Her:* her hand? her
She had not ſingly one of beautie rare,
But ſuch a paire as heere where *Herod* ſtands,
He dares the world to make to both compare.
Accurſed *Salome*, hadſt thou bene ſtill,
My *Mariam* had bene breathing by my ſide:
Oh neuer had I: had I had my will,
Sent forth command, that *Mariam* ſhould haue dide.
But *Salome* thou didſt with enuy vexe,
To ſee thy ſelfe out-matched in thy ſexe:
Vpon your ſexes forehead *Mariam* ſat,
To grace you all like an imperiall crowne,
But you fond foole haue rudely puſht thereat,
And proudly puld your proper glory downe.
One ſmile of hers: Nay, not ſo much a: looke
Was worth a hundred thouſand ſuch as you,
Iudea how canſt thou the wretches brooke,
That robd from thee the faireſt of the crew?
You dwellers in the now depriued land,
Wherein the matchles *Mariam* was bred:
Why graſpe not each of you a ſword in hand,
To ayme at me your cruell Soueraignes head.
Oh when you thinke of *Herod* as your King,
And owner of the pride of *Paleſtine*:
This act to your remembrance likewiſe bring,

　　　　　　　　　　　　　　　　　Tis

Tis I haue ouerthrowne your royall line.
Within her purer vaines the blood did run,
That from her Grandam Sara she deriu'd,
Whose beldame age the loue of Kings hath wonne,
Oh that her iſſue had as long bene li'ud.
But can her eye be made by death obſcure?
I cannot thinke but it muſt ſparkle ſtill:
Foule ſacriledge to rob thoſe lights ſo pure,
From out a Temple made by heau'nly skill.
I am the Villaine that haue done the deed,
The cruell deed, though by anothers hand,
My word though not my ſword made Mariam bleed,
Hircanus Grandchild did at my command.
That Mariam that I once did loue ſo deare,
The partner of my now deteſted bed,
Why ſhine you ſun with an aſpect ſo cleare?
I tell you once againe my Mariams dead.
You could but ſhine, if ſome Egiptian blows,
Or Æthiopian doudy loſe her life:
This was, then wherefore bend you not your brows,
The King of Iuries faire and ſpotleswiſe.
Denie thy beames, and Moone refuſe thy light,
Let all the ſtarres be darke, let Iuries eye
No more diſtinguiſh which is day and night:
Since her beſt birth did in her boſome die.
Thoſe fond Idolaters the men of Greece,
Maintaine theſe orbes are ſafely gouerned:
That each within themſelues haue Gods a peece,
By whom their ſtedfaſt courſe is iuſtly led.
But were it ſo, as ſo it cannot bee,
They all would put their mourning garments on:
Not one of them would yeeld a light to mee,
To me that is the cauſe that Mariams gon.
For though they fame their Saturne melancholy,
Of ſoure behauiours, and of angry moode:
They fame him likewiſe to be iuſt and holy,

And

And iuſtice needes muſt ſeeke reuenge for blood,
Their *Ioue*, if *Ioue* he were, would ſure deſire,
To puniſh him that ſlew ſo faire a laſſe:
For *Ledaes* beautie ſet his heart on fire,
Yet ſhe not halfe ſo faire as *Mariam* was.
And *Mars* would deeme his *Venus* had bene ſlaine,
Sol to recouer her would neuer ſticke:
For if he want the power her life to gaine :
Then Phyſicks God is but an Empericke.
The Queene of loue would ſtorme for beauties ſake,
And *Hermes* too, ſince he beſtow'd her wit,
The nights pale light for angrie griefe would ſhake,
To ſee chaſt *Mariam* die in age vnfit.
But oh I am deceiu'd, ſhe paſt them all
In euery gift, in euery propertie:
Her Excellencies wrought her timeles fall,
And they reioyc'd, not grieu'd to ſee her die.
The *Paphian* Goddeſſe did repent her waſt,
When ſhe to one ſuch beautie did allow:
Mercurius thought her wit his wit ſurpaſt;
And *Cinthia* enui'd *Mariams* brighter brow.
But theſe are fictions, they are voyd of ſence,
The *Greekes* but dreame, and dreaming falſehoods tell:
They neither can offend nor giue defence,
And not by them it was my *Mariam* fell.
If ſhe had bene like an *Egiptian* blacke,
And not ſo faire, ſhe had bene longer liude :
Her ouerflow of beautie turned backe,
And drownde the ſpring from whence it was deriude.
Her heau'nly beautie twas that made me thinke
That it with chaſtitie could neuer dwells
But now I ſee that heau'n in her did linke,
A ſpirit and a perſon to excell.
Ile muffle vp my ſelfe in endles night,
And neuer let mine eyes behold the light,
Retire thy ſelfe vile monſter, worſe then hee

I .   That

That ftaind the virgin earth with brothers blood,
Still in fome vault or denne inclofed bee,
Where with thy teares thou maift beget a flood,
Which flood in time may drowne thee : happie day
When thou at once fhalt die and finde a graue,
A ftone vpon the vault,fome one fhall lay,
Which monument fhall an infcription haue.
And thefe fhall be the words it fhall containe,
Heere Herod lies,that hath his Mariam flaine.

Chorus.

WHo euer hath beheld with fteadfaft eye,
The ftrange euents of this one onely day:
How many were deceiu'd ? How many die,
That once to day did grounds of fafetie lay ?
It will from them all certaintie bereue,
Since twice fixe houres fo many can deceiue.

This morning Herod held for furely dead,
And all the Iewes on Mariam did attend :
And Conftabarus rife from Saloms bed,
And neither dreamd of a diuorce or end.
Pheroras ioyd that he might haue his wife,
And Babus fonnes for fafetie of their life.

To night our Herod doth aliue remaine,
The guiltles Mariam is depriu'd of breath :
Stout Conftabarus both diuorft and flaine,
The valiant fonnes of Baba haue their death.
Pheroras fure his loue to be bereft,
If Saleme her fute vnmade had left.

Herod this morning did expect with ioy,
To fee his Mariams much beloued face :
And yet ere night he did her life deftroy,

And

And furely thought fhe did her name difgrace.
 Yet now againe fo fhort do humors laft,
 He both repents her death and knowes her chaft.

Had he with wifedome now her death delaide,
He at his pleafure might command her death:
But now he hath his power fo much betraide,
As all his woes cannot reftore her breath.
 Now doth he ftrangely lunatickly raue,
 Becaufe his *Mariams* life he cannot faue.

This daies euents were certainly ordainde,
To be the warning to pofteritie :
So many changes are therein containde,
So admirablie ftrange varietie.
 This day alone, our fageft *Hebrewes* fhall
 In after times the fchoole of wifedome call.

FINIS.

The History of the Life, Reign, and Death of Edward II (Wing 313) is reproduced, by permission, from the copy at The Huntington Library. The text block of the copy measures 14 × 23 cm.

102.9 is blemished but should read as follows:

pretending a meer Voyage of Devotion, and had stoln

THE
HISTORY
OF

The LIFE, REIGN, and DEATH

OF

EDWARD II.
King of England,

AND

.L O R D of *I R E L A N D.*

WITH

The Rife and Fall of his great Favourites,

GAVESTON and the *SPENCERS.*

Henry Cary Lord Viscount Falkland

Written by ~~H.~~ F. in the year 1627.

And Printed verbatim from the Original.

his Lordship died in 1663 — Lucius
the celebrated Vice† Falkland was his eldest

Qui nescit Dissimulare, nequit vivere, perire melius,

LONDON:

Printed by *J. C.* for *Charles Harper,* at the Flower-de-luce in
Fleet-street ; *Samuel Crouch,* at the Princes Arms in
Popes-head-Alley in *Cornhil* ; and *Thomas Fox* , at
the Angel in *Westminster-hall.* 1 6 8 0.

THE
PUBLISHER
To the READER.

READER,

THou haſt here preſented to thy View the Life
and Death of *Edward* the Second, one of the
moſt Unfortunate Princes that ever ſwayed the
Engliſh Scepter. What it was that made him ſo, is left
to thee to judge, when thou haſt read his Story. But
certainly the Falſneſs of his Queen, and the Flattery of
thoſe Court-Paraſites, *Gaveſton* and the *Spencers*, did
contribute not a little thereto.

As for the Gentleman that wrote this Hiſtory, his
own following Preface to the Reader will give ſome
ſhort Account, as alſo of the Work it ſelf, together
with the Deſigne and Time of its writing, which was
above Fifty years ſince. And this we think we may
ſay, (and perſwade our ſelves that upon the peruſal
thou wilt be of the ſame opinion) that he was every
every way qualified for an Hiſtorian. And 'bating a
few obſolete words, (which ſhew the Antiquity of the
Work) we are apt to believe thoſe days produced very
few who were able to expreſs their Conceptions in ſo
Maſculine a Stile.

We might eaſily enlarge in our Commendations of
this Excellent Hiſtory; but it needs not; and therefore
we leave it to thee to read and judge.

A 2   THE

TO out-run those weary hours of a deep and sad Paßion, my melancholy Pen fell accidentally on this Historical Relation; which speaks a King, our own, though one of the most Unfortunate; and shews the Pride and Fall of his Inglorious Minions.

I have not herein followed the dull Character of our Historians, nor amplified more than they infer, by Circumstance. I strive to please the Truth, not Time; nor fear I Censure, since at the worst, 'twas but one Month mis-spended; which cannot promise ought in right Perfection.

If so you hap to view it, tax not my Errours; I my self confeß them.

20 Feb. 1627.

H: F.

Henry Cary Lord
Falkland

THE

THE
RAIGN and DEATH
OF
Edward the Second.

EDWARD the Second, eldeſt Son of *Edward* the Firſt and *Elenor* the vertuous Siſter of the *Caſtilian* King, was born at *Carnarvan* * ; and in the moſt reſplendant pride of his age, immediately after the deceaſe of his noble Father, crowned King of *England* †. The principal Leaders of the Rebellious Welſhmen, *Fluellen* and *Meredith,* being taken and executed, the Combuſtions of the *Cambro-Britains* were quieted and ſettled in an uniform Obedience. The *Scots,* by the reſignation of *Baliol,* the execution of *Wallis,* and the expulſion of *Bruce* their pretended King, were reduced to their firſt Monarchy, and brought to an abſolute ſubjection, at ſuch time as he took upon him the Regiment of this then glorious Kingdom. If we may credit the moſt antient Hiſtorians that ſpeak of the Princes and Paſſages of thoſe times, this Royal Branch was of an Aſpect fair and lovely, carrying in his outward appearance many promiſing Predictions of a ſingular expectation. But the judgment, not the eye, muſt have the preheminence in point of Calculation and Cenſure. The ſmootheſt waters are for the moſt part moſt deep and dangerous; and the goodlieſt Bloſſoms nipt by an unkindly Froſt, wither, or produce their fruit ſowre or unwholſome : which may properly imply, That the viſible Calendar is not the true Character of inward Perfection ; evidently proved in the Life, Raign, and Death

*April 25. 1284.

† July 1307.

B   of

of this *unfortunate* Monarch. His Story fpeaks the Morning fair, the Noon-tide eclipfed, and the fad Evening of his Life more memorable by his untimely Death and Ruine. He could not have been fo unworthy a Son of fo noble a Father, nor fo inglorious a Father of fo excellent a Son, if either Vertue or Vice had been hereditary. Our Chronicles, as they parallel not him in his licentious Errours, fo do they rarely equal the Wifdom and Valour of the one that went before, and the other that immediately fucceeded him. Neither was this degenerate Corruption in him tranfcendent from the womb that bare him, fince all Writers agree his Mother to be one of the moft pious and illuftrious pieces of Female-goodnefs that is regiftred in thofe memorable Stories of all our Royal Wedlocks. But the divine Ordinances are infcrutable, and not to be queftioned ; it may elfe feem juftly worthy admiration, how fo crooked a Plant fhould fpring from a Tree fo great and glorious. His younger years difcovered a foftly, fweet, and milde temper, pliable enough to the impreflions of Vertue ; when he came to write Man, he was believ'd over-liberally wanton, but not extreamly vicious. The Royal honour of his Birth-right was fcarcely invefted in his perfon, when Time (the Touchftone of Truth·) fhews him to the world a meer Impofture ; in Converfation light, in Condition wayward, in Will violent, and in Paffion furious and irreconciliable.

Edw. 1's care in educating his Son.

Edward, his valiant and prudent Father, had, by the glory of his victorious Arms, and the excellency of his Wifdom and Providence, laid him the fure foundation of a happy Monarchy ; making it his laft and greateft care to continue it fo in his fucceflion. This caus'd him to employ his beft underftanding and labour for the enabling of his Son, that he might be powerful, fit, and worthy to perfect this great Work, and preferve it. And from this Confideration he leads him to the Scotch Wars, to teach him the right ufe of Arms, which are to

be

be managed as well by difcretion as valour, and the advantage of time and opportunity, which lead humane Actions by the hand to their perfection. Here he likewife inftructs him with thofe more excellent Rules of Knowledge and Difcipline, that he might exactly know what it was, and how to obey before he came to command. Laftly, he unlocks the Clofet of his heart, and lays before him thofe fame *Arcana Imperii* and fecret myfteries of State, which are onely proper to the Royal Operations, and lie not in the road of Vulgar knowledge; yet letting him withal know, that all thefe were too weak to fupport the burthen of a Crown, if there be not a correfpondent worth in him that wears it. With thefe grave Principles the prudent Father opening the way, foon perceives he had a remaining task of a much harder temper; with an unwilling eye he beholds in his Son many fad remonftrances which intimate rather a natural vicious inclination, than the corruption of time, or want of ability to command it. Unlefs thefe might be taken off and cleanfed, he imagines all his other Cautions would be ufelefs and to little purpofe. The pruning of the Branches would improve the Fruit little, where the Tree was tainted in the root with fo foul a Canker. Too well he knew how difficult a thing it was to invert the courfe of Nature, efpecially being confirm'd by continuance of practice; and made habituary by cuftom: yet he leaves no means unattempted; being confident that Wedlock, or the fad weight of a Crown, would in the fenfe of Honour call him in time off to thoughts more innocent and noble. Tendernefs of Fatherly affection abus'd fomewhat his belief, and made him give his diforderly actions the beft conftruction, which fuggefts their progreffion to flow from heat of Youth, want of Experience, and the wickednefs of thofe that fed him with fo bafe impreffions; which, with all thofe fweet and milde intreaties that fpring from the heart of an effential love, he ftrives to reclaim, intermixing withal as great a paternal feverity as might

properly

properly sute the condition of a judicious Father, and the dignity of the Heir apparent of so great and glorious a Kingdom. And to make him more apt and fit to receive and follow his instructions, he takes from him those tainted humours of his Leprosie, that seduced the easiness of his nature, and mis-led his unripe knowledge, too green to master such sweet and bewitching temptations. *Ga-*

Banishes
Gaveston.

veston his Ganymede, a man as base in Birth as in Condi-

Gaveston's
Original
and Cha-
racter.

tion, he commandeth to perpetual Exile. This Syren (as some write) came out of *Gascoign* ; but the Author whom I most credit and follow, speaks him an *Italian* ; not guilty of any drop of Noble blood ; neither could he from the height of his Hereditary hope, challenge more than a bare ability to live ; yet his thoughts were above measure ambitious and aspiring, and his confidence far greater than became his Birthright. Nature in his outward parts had curiously exprest her workmanship, giving him in shape and Beauty so perfect an excellence, that the most curious eye could not discover any manifest errour, unless it were in his Sex alone, since he had too much for a man, and Perfection enough to have equal'd the fairest Female splendour that breath'd within the Confines of this Kingdom. Though in the abilities of the Brain he were short of a deep and solid Knowledge, yet he had Understanding enough to manage his ways to their best advantage ; having a smooth Tongue, an humble Look, and a winning Behaviour, which he could at all times fashion and vary according to the condition of time and circumstance, for the most advantage. The youthful Prince having fixed his wandring eye upon this pleasing Object, and finding his amorous Glances entertained with so gentle and well-becoming a modesty, begins dearly to cherish the growing Affections of this new Forraign Acquaintance ; who applies himself wholly to win him to a deeper Engagement. A short passage of time had so cemented their hearts, that they seem'd to beat with one and the self-same motion ; so that the one seem'd

with-

without the other, like a Body without a Soul, or a Shadow without a Subſtance. *Gaveſton,* the more to aſſure
ſo gracious a Maſter, ſtrives to fit his humour, leaving his
Honour to his own protection, ſeconding his wanton diſpoſition with all thoſe bewitching Vanities of licentious
and unbridled Youth, which in ſhort time, by the fre-
quencie of practice, begets ſuch a confidence, that they
fall from that reſerved ſecrecy which ſhould ſhadow actions ſo unworthy, profeſſing freely a-debaucht and diſ-
ſolute kind of behaviour, to the ſhame and ſorrow of
the grieved King and Kingdom. This haſtened on the
Sentence of his Baniſhment, that thought himſelf then moſt
ſecure in the aſſurance of the Princes favour. The melancholy apparitions of their parting, gave the world a firm
belief that this inchanting Mountebank had in the Cabinet of his Maſters heart, too dear a room and being.
The King knowing ſuch impreſſions are eaſily won, but
hardly loſt, ſtrives to take him off by degrees, and labours to make him wave the memory of that dotage
which with a divining Spirit he foreſaw in time would
be his ruine. But death overtakes him before he could
bring this ſo good a Work to full perfection. The time
was come that exacts the Tribute of Nature, commanding
him to reſigne both his Eſtate and Kingdom. When he
felt thoſe cold fore-running Harbingers of his nearly-
approaching End, he thus intreats his Son and Lords,
whoſe watry eyes ingirt his glorious Death-bed.

> Edward, *the time draws near that calls me to my Grave,*
> *you to enjoy this Kingdom. If you prove good, with happi-*
> *neſs 'tis yours, and you will ſo preſerve it ; if otherwiſe, my*
> *Pains and Glory will be your Diſhonour. To be a King, it*
> *is the gift of Nature ; and Fortune makes him ſo that is by*
> *Conqueſt ; but Royal Goodneſs is the gift of Heaven, that bleſ-*
> *ſeth Crowns with an Immortal Glory. Believe not vainly*
> *that ſo great a Calling is given to man to warrant his diſ-*
> *order. It is a Bleſſing, yet a weighty Burthen, which (if*

Edw. 1's
Dying-
Speech to
the Prince
& Barons.

C   *abuſed)*

abufed) breaks his back that bears it. Your former Er-rours, now continued, are no more yours, they are the Kings, which will betray the Kingdom. The Soveraigns Vice be-gets the Subjects Errour, who practife good or ill by his Ex-ample. Can you in Juftice punish them for that whereof your felf are guilty ? But you, perhaps, may think your felf ex-empt, that are above the Law. Alas, miftake not ; there are Injunctions higher far than are your own, will crave a Rec-koning. To be belov'd, fecures a fweet Obedience ; but fear betrays the heart of true Subjection, and makes your People yours but by Compulfion. Majeftick thoughts, like Elemental fire, fhould tend ftill upwards ; when they fink lower than their Sphere, they win Contempt and Hatred. Advance and cherish thofe of ancient Bloud and Greatnefs : Upftarts are rais'd with Envy, kept with Danger. You muft pre-ferve a well-refpected diftance, as far from Pride, as from too loofe a Bafenefs. Mafter your Paffions with a noble temper ; fuch Triumphs makes the Victor conquer others. See here the Ruines of a dying Scepter, that once was, as you are, a youthful Bloffom. I had not liv'd to fee this fnowy Winter, but that I wean'd my heart from vain Temptations ; my Judgment, not my Eye, did fteer my Compafs, which gave my Youth this Age that ends in Glory. I will not fay, you too too long have wander'd, though my fad heart hath droopt to fee your Errour. The time now fitly calls you home ; em-brace it : for this advantage loft, is after hopelefs. Your Firft-fruit muft make good your Worth ; if that mifcarry, you wound your Subjects Hopes and your own Glory. Thofe wanton Pleafures of wild Youth unmafter'd, may no more touch the verge of your affections. The Royal Actions muft be grave and fteady, fince leffer Lights are fed by their Example : fo great a Glory muft be pure tranfparent, that hand to hand encounters Time and Envy. Caft off your former Conforts ; if they fway you, fuch an unnoble Prefident will fhake your Peace, and wound your Honour. Your wanton Minion I fo lately banisht, call you not back, I charge you on my Bleffing : for his return will haften your deftruction. Such Cankers

may

may not taste your ear or favour, but in a modest and chast proportion. Let true-born Greatness manage great Employments; they are most fit that have a native goodness. Mushroms in State that are preferr'd by dotage, open the Gap to Hate and Civil Tumult. You cannot justly blame the Great ones Murmur, if they command that are scarce fit to serve them; such sudden leaps must break his neck that ventures, and shake that Crown which gives his Wings their motion. And you, my Lords, that witness this last Summons, you in whose Loyal hearts your Soveraign flourisht, continue still a sweet and vertuous Concord; temper the heat of my youthful Successor, that he may prove as good, as great in Title. Maintain the Sentence was by me pronounced; keep still that Viper hence that harbours mischief: if he return, I fear 'twill be your Ruine. It is my last Request; I, dying, make it, which I do firmly hope you will not blemish. I would say more, but, ah, my Spirits fail me.

With this, he fainting, swoons; at length recovers, and sadly silent, longs to hear their Answer. His weeping Son and heavy drooping Barons, do mutually protest a strict Observance, and vow to keep, with truth, this grave Injunction. His jealous Spirit is not yet contented, until they binde it with an Oath, and swear performance. Scarce was it ended, when he mildly leaves the world more confident than he had cause; as a short passage of time made plain and evident. Dead mens Prescriptions seldom tie the living, where Conscience awes not those that are intrusted. *Mortui non mordent*, which gives to humane frailty a seeming uncontrouled power of such Injustice. To trust to Vows or Oaths, is equal hazard; he that will wound his Soul with one, can wave the other. If Vertue, Goodness, and Religion tye not, a Death-bed Charge and solemn Oaths are fruitless. Here you may see it instanc'd: This great King, as wise as fortunate, living, had the Obedience of a Father and a Soveraign; who, scarcely cold in his Mother Earth, was

They swear not to recal Gaveston.

soon

foon loft in the memory both of Son and Subject. His
Funeral-tears (the fruits of form rather than truth)
newly dryed up, and his Ceremonial Rites ended, his
Heir affumes the Crown and Scepter ; while all mens
eyes were fixed to behold the firft Virgin-works of his
Greatnefs : fo many glorious and brave victorious Con-
quefts having given this Warlike Nation life and fpirit fit
for prefent Action. The youthful King being in the bravery of his years, won a belief in the *active Souldier*, that
fo apt a Scholar as he had fhew'd himfelf in the Art Military during the Scotifh Wars, would handfel the Maiden-
head of his Crown with fome Out-ringing Larum that
might waken the Neighbour-Provinces; and make them
know his Power. But his inglorious Aims were bent a-
nother way ; neither to fettle his own, or conquer o-
thers. He had within his breaft an unnatural Civil War
which gains the firft preheminence in his Refolution.
His care is to quiet thefe in a Courfe wholly unjuft, and
moft unworthy his proper goodnefs. Seeing himfelf
now free and abfolute, he thinks it not enough, unlefs his
Will as well as his Power, were equally obey'd. Being
a Son and a Subject, his Conformity had witnefs'd his Obedience ; being now a Soveraign and a King, he expects
a Correfpondence of the felf-fame nature. The fad Re-
ftrictions of his dying Father, fo contrarious to his aims,
trouble his unquiet thoughts ; where the Idea of his abfent love did hold fo firm a footing. With eafe he can
difpence with his own engagement ; but fears the Lords,
whom he conceits too firmly fixt to waver. He dares
not Communicate the depth of his Refolution, being a
fecret of too great weight to be divulged ; he thinks intreaty an act too much beneath him ; and to attempt at
random, full of hazard. In thefe his reftlefs paffions, he
out-runs the *Honey-month* of his Empire ; looking afquint
upon the neceffary Actions of State, that requir'd his more
vigilant care and forefight. This kind of reclus'd behaviour makes him unpleafant to his Lords, and nothing

plaufible

(margin note) The young King troubled at his Oath.

plaufible to the inferiour fort of Subjects, who expect the beginning Acts of a Crown to be affable and gracious; which wins ground by degrees on vulgar Affections, making the way fure to a willing Obedience. But he efteems this as a work of Supererogation; believing the bare Tye of Duty was enough, without confirmation : all his thoughts are entirely fixt upon his *Gavefton*; without him he cannot be, yet how to get him handfomly, without a Scar, is quite without his knowledge. He concludes it in his fecret Revolutions, too great an Injuftice, that confines the King from the free ufe and poffeffion of his neareft and deareft Affection ; and cannot imagine it to be reafon, that his private Appetite fhould fubfcribe to publick neceffity. In thefe kind of imaginary Difputations, he brings himfelf to the height of fuch an inward agitation, that he falls into a fad retired Melancholy; while all men (as they juftly might) wonder'd, but few did know the reafon : Amongft thefe, a Page of his Chamber, one that had an oyly tongue (a fit inftrument for fuch a Phyfician) adventures the care of this difeafed Paffion. This green States-man, with a foreright look, ftrives rather to pleafe, than to advife ; caring not what fucceeds, fo he may make it the Stair of his Preferment. The Court-corruption ingenders a world of thefe Caterpillers, that, to work their own ends, value not at one blow to hazard both the King and Kingdom. The Errour is not fo properly theirs, as their Mafters, who do countenance and advance fuch Sycophants ; leaving the integrity of hearts more honeft (that would facrifice themfelves in his Service in the true way of Honour) wholly contemn'd and neglected : which hath begotten fo many defperate Convulfions, that have (as we may finde in our own Stories) depofed divers glorious Kings from their proper Dignity, and lawful Inheritance. There are too many frequent Examples what mifchief fuch *Parafitical Minions* have wrought to thofe feveral States they liv'd in ; and certainly fuch Revolu-

Falls into the height of melancholy.

The Character and danger of Court-Parafites.

D   tions

tions succeed by a neceſſary and inevitable Juſtice: for where the Royal Ear is ſo guided, there enſues a general Subverſion of all Law and Goodneſs; as you may behold here evidently in this unfortunate King, who willingly entertains this fawning Orator, that thus preſents his Counſel.

A Courtiers Speech to the King, to recal Gaveſtor.

Are you a King (Great Sir) and yet a Subject ? can you Command, and yet muſt yield Obedience ? Then leave your Scepter. The Law of Nature gives the pooreſt their Affections ; are you reſtrained ? It is your own Injuſtice that makes your Will admit this ſeparation : if you command, who dares controul your Actions, which ought to be obeyed, and not diſputed ? Say that your wayward Lords do frown, or murmur, will you for this forbear your own Contentment ? One rough Majeſtick glaunce will charm their anger. Admit great Edward did command Obedience, he then was King, your Sovereign, and your Father; he now is dead, and you enjoy his Power; will you yet ſtill obey and ſerve his ſhadow? His Vigour dull'd with Age, could not give Laws to ſuit your Youth and Spirit; nor is it proper that the Regal Power be made a ſtranger to his own Contentment, or be debarr'd from inward Peace and Quiet. Did you but truely know what 'tis to be a Monarch, you'ld be ſo to your ſelf as well as others. What do you fear, or what is it reſtrains you ? A ſeeming Danger, more in ſhew than ſubſtance. Wiſe men that finde their aims confin'd to hazard, ſecure the worſt before they give them action. You have a Kingdoms Power to back, a Will to guide it ; Can private fear ſuggeſt to ſhake it ? Alas, they cannot, if your ſelf were conſtant : Who dares oppoſe, if you command Obedience ? I deny not, if you be faint or ſtagger, you may be croſt and curb'd by that advantage, that gives their moving-heart ſhew of Juſtice. You underſtand your ſelf, and feel your Paſſions; if they be ſuch as will not brook denial, why do you dally, or delay to right them ? The more you paiſe your doubts, the more they double, and make things worſe

worse than they or are, or can be : appearing like your self;
these clouds will vanish, and then you'll see and know your
proper errour. Will you vouchsafe my trust, I'll fetch him
hither, whose absence gives you such a sad distraction : You
may the while secure his entertainment with such a strength,
may warrant your proceedings. 'Twere madness to ask
leave to act Transgressions, where Pardon may be had when
they are acted. If you do seek consent from your great Ba-
rons; they'll dare deny ; which is nor fault, nor Treason ;
and in that act you foil your hopes and action, which gives
their opposition shew of Justice. But 'tis in vain to plead
the grounds of Reason, since 'tis your Will must give the re-
solution : If that be fixt, there needs no more disputing, but
such as best may bring it to perfection.

When this smooth Physician had prescribed so fit a
Balsamum for so foul a Wound, the King seems infinitely
pleased in his relation ; he had hit his desires in the
Master-vein, and struck his former Jealousie between
wind and water, so that it sunk in the instant : his love-
sick Heart became more free and frolick; which sudden
mutation begat as great a wonder. The Operations of
the Fancy transport sometimes our Imagination to believe
an actual possession of those things we most desire and
hope for; which gives such a life to the dejected Spirits
of the Body, that in the instant they seem cloathed in a
new Habit. Such was the condition of this wanton King,
that in this bare overture, conceits the fruition of his beloved *Damon*, and apprehends this Golden Dream to be
an essential part of his fantastique Happiness. He heaps
a world of promises and thanks on the Relator, letting
him know, he waits but a fitting opportunity to give this
project life and action. It is a politique part of Court-
wisdome, to insinuate and lay hold of all the befitting
opportunities, that may claw the Prince's humour that is
naturally vain-glorious or vicious ; there is not a more
ready and certain way of advancement, if it do shake hands

with

with Modeſty, and appear with an undaunted, impudent boldneſs. He that will be a Courtier, and contains himſelf within the modeſt temperance of pure Honeſty, and not intrude himſelf before he be called, may like a Seamark ſerve to teach other men to ſteer their Courſe, while he himſelf ſticks faſt, unmoved, unpitied. All the Abilities of Nature, Art, Education, are uſeleſs, if they be tyed to the links of Honeſty, which hath little or no ſociety in the Rules of State or Pleaſure, which as they are unlimited, walk in the by-way from all that is good or vertuous.

If this Butterfly had truly laid before his unhappy Maſter, what it had been to break the Injunctions of a dying Father, to falſifie ſuch Vows and Oaths ſo ſolemnly ſworn, and to irritate the greateſt Peers of the Kingdom with ſo unworthy an action, (which had been the Duty of a Servant of his Maſters Honour truely careful) he had felt the Reward of ſuch plain dealing, either with Scorn, Contempt, or Paſſion; whoſe flattering falſehood wins him ſpecial Grace and Favour, and gains the title of an able Agent.

Some few days paſs, which ſeem'd o're long, before the King exacts a ſecond tryal. In the interim, to take away all jealouſie, he enters into the buſineſs of the Kingdom, and with a ſeeming ſerious care ſurveys each paſſage, and not ſo much as ſighs, or names his *Gavaſton*; doubting if in his way he were diſcovered, there might be ſome croſs-work might blaſt his project: He knew how eaſie 'twas (if once ſuſpected) to take away the Cauſe might breed a difference: What could ſo poor a ſtranger do that might protect him againſt or publick Force, or private Miſchief, either of which he knew would be attempted, before the Lords would ſuffer his repriſal? When all was whiſht and quiet, and all mens

The King ſends for *Gaveſton*.

eyes were fixed upon the preſent, he calls his truſty *Roger* to his private preſence, and after ſome Inſtructions throws him his Purſe, and bids him haſte; he knew his Errand.

Errand. The wily Servant knows his Mafters meaning, and leaves the Court, pretending juft occafion, proud of imployment pofting on his Journey. The King having thus far gone, muft now go onward; he knew that long it could not be concealed; fuch actions cannot reft in fleepy filence; which made him think it fit to be the firft Reporter. This makes him fend and call his Council, who foon are ready, and attend his Summons; where he makes known the fury of his Paffions, and tells the way that he had taken to eafe them. So ftrange an act begets as great a wonder; they *unâ voce* labour to divert him, and humbly plead his Fathers laft Injunction, to which their Faiths were tyed by deep Engagement. They urge the Law that could not be difpens'd with, without a publick breach of his prefcription. They fpeak the Vows and Oaths they all had taken, which in confenting would make them falfe and perjur'd. This working nothing, they entreat him he would a while adjourn his refolution; time might happily finde out a way might give him content, and yet might fave their Honours. His jealous fear fufpects this modeft anfwer; a temporizing muft increafe his forrow, while they fo warned might work a fure prevention. Being thus at plunge, he ftrives to make it fure, and win his Will, or loofe his Jurifdiction. Though he were naturally of a fufpicious and timerous Nature, yet feeing now the intereft of his Power at ftake on the fuccefs of this Overture, he lays afide his effeminate difpofition, and with angry Brow, and ftern Majefty, doth thus difcourfe his pleafure.

Acquaints his Council therewith; who labour to divert him.

Am I your King? If fo, why then obey me; left while you teach me Law, I learn you Duty. Know, I am firmly bent, and will not vary. If you and all the Kingdome frown, I care not: You muft enjoy your own affections, I not fo much as queftion or controul them; but I that am your Sovereign, muft be tutor'd to love and like alone by your difcretion. Do

His angry Reply.

not miſtake, I am not now in *Wardſhip,* nor will be chalkt
out ways to guide my fancy. *Tend you the Kingdoms and
the publick Errours* ; I can prevent mine own without Protection. I ſhould be loth to let you feel my Power ; but muſt
and will, if you too much enforce me. If not *Obedience,*
yet your *Loves* might tender a kinde conſent, when 'tis your
King that ſeeks it. But you perhaps conceit you ſhare my
Power ; you neither do nor ſhall, while I command it ; I
will be ſtill my ſelf, or loſs than nothing.

   Theſe words, and the manner of their delivery, bred
a ſtrange diſtraction, in which he flings away with a
kinde of looſe ſcorn ; for their refuſal his valiant heart
had yet his proper motions, which toſt it to and fro
with doubtful hazard. They ſadly ſilent ſit, and view
each other, wiſhing ſome one would ſhew undaunted
Valour, to tye the Bell about the Cats neck that frights
them ; but none appears. They yet were ſtrangers to
their own party, and the Kings conditions. Their late
dead Maſter's ways were ſmooth and harmleſs, as free
from private Wrongs as publick Grievance ; which had
extinguiſht all pretence of Faction, and made them meet
as Friends without aſſurance ; this wrought them with
more eaſe to treat the buſineſs ; each one doth firſt ſurvey
his own condition, which ſingle could do little, and yet
expreſt might cauſe his proper ruine : next they meaſure
the Kings Will and Power, with his Command ; againſt
which in vain were conteſtation, where wants united
ſtrength to make it ſure. Laſtly, they examine what
could at worſt enſue in their conſenting, ſince it was as
poſſible to remove him being here, as ſtop his coming.
The King advertiſed by a private Intelligencer (a fit inſtrument in the body of a State, in the Society and Body
of a Council) of their ſtaggering irreſolution, and finding his Pills had ſo kinde an Operation, lays hold of the
advantage, and would not let the iron cool before he
wrought it. This brings him back with a more familiar
and

and mild look, and begets a difcourfe lefs paffionate, but
more prevailing. Temperately he lays before them the
extremity of his inward trouble, which had fo engroft
his private thoughts, that he had been thereby enforced
to eftrange himfelf from them, and neglected the Rights
due to his Crown and Dignity. He lets them know the
depth of his engagement, which had no aim repugnant
to the Publick Good, nor intention hurtful to their proper Honours; and to conclude, he intreats them, (if
any of them had been truely touch'd with a difeafe of
the fame quality) that they would indifferently meafure
his Condition by their own Sufferings. So fair a Sun-
fhine following at the heels of fo fharp a Tempeft,
wrought a fudden innovation; their yielding hearts feek
to win Grace, rather than hazard his Difpleafure: yet
to colour fo apparent a breach of Faith to their dead
Mafter, they capitulate certain Conditions, which might
feem to extenuate (if not take off) the ftain of their
difhonour; as if matter of circumftance had been a fufficient motive for the breach of an Oath fo folemnly
and authentically fworn. The King refolv'd to purchafe
his peace, (whofe price was but verbal) is nothing fparing to promife all and more than was demanded; which
they credit over-haftily, though they could not be fo
light of belief as to imagine, that he would keep his
Word with the Subject, that wilfully incurs a Perjury a-
gainft his own Father; yet in cafe of neceffity it was by
general confent agreed, rather to fubfcribe, than to endanger the Peace of the Kingdom, by fo unkinde and
unnatural a divifion. The King giving to each of them
particular thanks, (having thus plaid his Mafters prize)
departs wondroufly content and jocund: they feem out-
wardly not difpleafed, that had obtain'd as much as they
could defire; and hoped the end would be fair, if not
fortunate. The eye of the world may be blinded, and
the feverity of humane Conftitutions removed; but fo
great a Perjury feldome efcapes unpunifhed by the Divine

The Coun-
cil confent
to recal
Gavefton.

vine Juſtice, who admits no dalliance with Oaths, even in the Caſe of Neceſſity, as it evidently appears in the ſequel of this Story; where you may behold the miſerable ruine that his principal and efficient cauſe had from this beginning. It had been far more honourable and advantageous to the State, if this young wanton King had point-blank found a flat denial, and been brought to have tugg'd at the arms end; the injuſtice of the quarrel, which might in time have recollected his ſenſes, and brought him to the true knowledge what a madneſs it was, for the looſe affection of ſo unworthy an Object, to hazard his own Dignity, and alien the Love of the whole Kingdom. But it is the general Diſeaſe of Greatneſs, and a kinde of Royal Fever, when they fall upon an indulgent Dotage, to patronize and advance the corrupt ends of their Minions, though the whole Society of State and Body of the Kingdom run in a direct oppoſition; neither is Reaſon, Law, Religion, or the imminency of ſucceeding danger, weight enough to divert the ſtream of ſuch inordinate Affections, until a miſerable Concluſion give it a fatal and juſt Repentance. It were much better, if with a provident foreſight they would fear and prevent the blow before they feel it. But ſuch melancholy Meditations are deemed a fit food for Penitentials, rather than a neceſſary reflection for the full ſtomack of Regal Authority. The black clouds of former Suſpicion being thus vaniſh'd, nothing now wants to make perfect the Royal Deſires, but the fruition of this long-expected purchaſe. The ſmooth Servant that had ſo pleaſingly adviſed, was not leſs careful in the execution of his promiſe. He knew haſte would advance the opinion of his Merit; this makes him ſoon out-run his Journey, and finde the Star of his directions, to whom he liberally relates the occaſion of his coming, which he confirms by the delivery of his Maſters Letter, wherein was drawn to the life the character of his Affection, and the aſſurance of his ſafety

and

and intended promotion. *Gaveston* being ravish'd with
so sweet and welcome a relation, entertains it with as
much joy, as the condemned Prisoner receives his Pardon
at the place and hour of Execution. His long-dejected
Spirits apprehend the advantage of so hopeful an opportunity , and spur him on with that haste, that he hardly
consents to one nights intermission for the repose of this
weary Messenger. No sooner had the Mornings-
Watchman given his shrill summons of the approaching
Day-light, but he forsakes his weary Bed, and hastens
straight to Horseback ; and being not well assured of his
reception in the Kingdom, being a banish'd man by so
Juridical a Sentence, he esteems it too weak an Adventure to expose himself to the hazard of the Road-way,
where he might with ease be intercepted. This leads
him to disguise himself, and seek a secret passage ; which
he as readily findes ; all things concurring to improve his
happiness, if he had had judgment and temper enough
to have given it a right use. Every minute he esteems
ill-lost, till he might again be re-enfoulded in the sweet
and dear embraces of his Royal Master.

   Time, that out-runs proud Fate, brings him at last to
the end of his desires, where the interview was accompanied with as many mutual expressions, as might flow
from the tongues, eyes, and hearts of long-divided Lo-
vers. This pair thus again re-united, the Court puts on
a general face of Gladness, while wiser heads with cause
suspect the issue. They esteem it full of danger, to have
one man alone so fully possess the Kings Affections, who
if he be not truely good, and deep enough to advise
soundly, must often be the cause of Error and Disorder.
This strange piece had neither Nobility of Birth, Ability
of Brain, or any Moral Goodness, whereby they might
justly hope he would be a stay to the unbridled youth of
their Sovereign. A precedent experience during the
Government of their dead Master, had given them a perfect knowledg, that he was more properly a fit instru-

Gaveston returns.

F   ment

ment for a *Brothel*, than to be the Steerſman of the Royal actions : yet there was now no prevention; they muſt hope the beſt, and attend the iſſue.

The King ſlights his Barons.

Edward having thus regained his beloved Favourite, could not ſhadow or diſſemble his Affection, but makes it eminent by the neglects of the State-affairs, and the forgetfulneſs of the civil and ordinary Reſpect due to his great Barons. They wait contemn'd, and cannot gain the threſhold, while this new Upſtart's courted in the Royal Chamber. This kinde of uſage won a ſudden murmur, which calls them off to cloſe and private Meetings; there they diſcourſe their Griefs, and means to right them; they ſift each way might break this fond inchantment, or leſſen this great light obſcured their luſtre. When they had canvaſt all the Stratagems of State, and private workings, they deem'd it the moſt innocent and fair way, to win the King to marry ; the intereſt of a Wife was thought the moſt hopeful inducement to reclaim theſe looſe affections that were proſtituted without or ſenſe or honour ; ſhe might become a fit counterpoiſe to qualifie the Pride of ſuch a ſwelling greatneſs.

They perſwade him to marry.

The major part ſoon jump in this opinion; the reſt are quickly won, that fear'd the ſequel. On this they all together preſent themſelves and their requeſt, and ſhew the reaſons, but touch not the true ground why they deſired it. After ſome pawſe the King approves their motion, yet bids them well conſider it was the greateſt Action of his life, which as it principally concern'd his particular Contentment, ſo did equally reflect on the general Intereſt of the whole Kingdom. If they could find him out ſuch a Wedlock as might adde Strength and Honour to the Crown, and be withal ſuitable to his liking, he would readily embrace it, and value it as a bleſſing. So fair a beginning encourageth them to move for *Iſabel* the French Kings Daughter, one of the goodlieſt and faireſt Ladies of that time. The King readily inclines to

have

have it treated; on which an honourable Embaſſage is
ſent to make the motion. They are nobly receiv'd and
willingly heard that bare this Meſſage, and the Conditions
eaſily reconciled to a full Agreement. This brings them
home with a like noble Company, fully authorized to receive the Kings conſent and approbation.

This Concluſion thus made, ſends our new Lover into *France*, to fetch his Miſtriſs; where he is received like
himſelf, feaſted, and married with a great deal of Joy
and Pleaſure. The Solemnity ended, and a Farewel
taken, he haſtens homewards, returning ſeiſed of a
Jewel, which not being rightly valued, wrought his
ruine. Infinite was the joy of the Kingdom, evident in
thoſe many goodly expreſſions of her Welcome. The
excellency of ſo rare a Beauty could not ſo ſurprize the
heart of this Royal Bridegroom; but that he was ſtill
troubled with the pangs of his old Infirmity: It was in
the firſt *Præludium* of his Nuptials a very diſputable
Queſtion, whether the Intereſt of the Wife, or Favourite,
were moſt predominant in his Affections; but a ſhort
time diſcovers that *Gaveſton* had the ſole poſſeſſion of his
Heart, and Power to keep it. To level their conditions,
and make the terms betwixt them more even, he tyes
this fair bullock in a yoke of the ſame nature, marrying
him to a lovely branch of the houſe of *Gloceſter*, whoſe
noble heart ſtruggled infinitely, yet durſt not contradict
the Kings Injuſtice. He holds his blood diſparag'd by ſo
baſe commixtion. To take away that doubt, the new-
married man is advanced to the Earldom of *Cornwal*, and
hath in his Gift the goodly Caſtle and Lordſhip of *Wallingford*; ſo that now in Title he had no juſt exception;
and for conditions, it muſt be thought enough his Maſter
loved him. To ſhew himſelf thankful, and to ſeem
worthy of ſuch gracious favour, *Gaveſton* applies himſelf
wholly to the Kings humour, feeding it with the variety
of his proper appetite, without ſo much as queſtion or
contradiction: Not a word fell from his Sovereign's
tongue,

The King marries; and marries *Gaveſton* to *Margaret*, Daughter of *Gilb. de Clar.* Earl of *Gloceſter*, by his Wife *Joan* of *Acres*, Daughter to *Edw.1.* Creates him Earl of *Cornwall.*

tongue, but he applauds it as an Oracle, and makes it as
a Law to guide his actions. This kinde of juggling behaviour had so glewed him to his Master, that their
Affections, nay their very Intentions seem'd to go hand
in hand; insomuch that the Injustice of the one, never
found rub in the consent of the other. If the King
maintain'd the party, the servant was ever fortunate, his
voice was ever concurrent, and sung the same Tune to a
Crochet. The discourse being in the commendation of
Arms, the eccho stiles it an Heroick Vertue; if Peace, it
was an Heavenly Blessing; unlawful Pleasures, a noble
Recreation; and Actions most unjust, a Royal Goodness.
These parasitical Gloses so betray'd the itching ear that
heard them, that no Honour or Preferment is conceited

And makes
him chief
Minister of
State. great and good enough for the Relator. A short time in-
vests in his person or disposure all the principal Offices
and Dignities of the Kingdom; the Command of War,
and all Military Provisions, were committed solely to his
care and custody; all Treaties forraign and domestick,
had, by his direction, success or ruine; nothing is concluded touching the Government or Royal Prerogative, but
by his consent and approbation. In the view of these
strange passages, the King appear'd so little himself, that
the Subjects thought him a Royal Shadow without a
Real Substance. This Pageant, too weak a Jade for so
weighty a burden, had not a brain in it self able enough
to manage such great Actions; neither would he entertain those of ability to guide him, whose honest freedom
might have made him go through-stitch with more reputation. He esteems it a gross oversight, and too deep a
disparagement, to have any creature of his own thought
wiser than himself; he had rather his Greatness (than
hazard such a blemish) should lie open to the malice of
time and fortune. This made him chuse his Servants as
his Master chose him, of a smooth fawning temper, such
as might cry ayme, and approve his actions, but not dispute
them. Hence flew a world of wilde disorder; the sacred

cred Rules of Juſtice were ſubverted, the Laws integrity
abuſed, the Judge corrupted or inforc'd, and all the
Types of Honour due to Vertue, Valour, Goodneſs, were
like the Pedlers pack, made Ware for Chapmen. Neither was it conceiv'd enough thus to advance him beyond
proportion, or his birth and merit, but he muſt carry all
without diſputing. No one may ſtand in his way, but
taſtes his power. Old Quarrels are ript up, to make his
ſpleen more extant.

The grave Biſhop of *Cheſter*, a man reverend for years, *Gaveſton*
impriſons
the Biſhop
of *Cheſter*.
and eminent for his Profeſſion and Dignity, is committed,
and could be neither indifferently heard or releaſed, upon the meer ſuppoſition that he had been the cauſe of his
firſt Baniſhment. Theſe inſolencies, carried with ſo great
a height, and expreſt with ſo malicious a liberty, were
accompanied with all the remonſtrances of a juſtly-grieved
Kingdom. The ancient Nobility, that diſdain'd ſuch an The King-
dom re-
ſent it.
equal, accuſe the injuſtice of the time that makes him their
Superiour. The grave Senators are griev'd to ſee the
places, due to their worths, poſſeſs'd by thoſe unworthy
and unable. The angry Souldier, that with his blood had
purchas'd his experience, beholds with ſorrow, Buffoons
preferr'd; while he, like the ruines of ſome goodly Building, is left to the wide world, without uſe or reparation. The Commons, in a more intemperate faſhion,
make known their griefs, and exclaim againſt ſo many
great and foul Oppreſſions. The new-made Earl both ſaw
and knew the general diſcontent and hatred, yet ſeeks
not how to cure or ſtop this miſchief; his proud heart
would not ſtoop or ſink: his greatneſs, which might
perhaps have qualified the fury, with an ill-adviſed confidence out-dares the worſt of his approaching danger,
and is not ſqueamiſh to let the Kingdom know it. The
ſlumbring Barons, ſtartled with the murmur that ecchoed
nought but fear and quick confuſion, at length awake,
and change their drowſie temper, condemning their long
patience, that was ſo far unfit their Bloud and Greatneſs.

G

Lincoln,

Lincoln, *Warwick*, and *Pembrooke*, whofe noble hearts
difdain'd to fuffer bafely, refolve to cure the State,
or make the Quarrel fatal. This Mufhrome muft be
cropt, or Arms muft right the Kingdom. Yet before
they will attempt by force, they'll feel their Soveraign's pulfes ; who, drown'd in fenfual pleafure, dreams
not of their practice. This Refolution leads them
to the Court, where with fome fute they gain admittance; where to the King brave *Lincoln* thus dif-
cours'd their Grievance.

Lincoln's
Speech to
the King.

*See here (my Liege) your faithful though dejected fer-
vants, that have too long cry'd ayme to our Afflictions ; we
know you in your felf are good, though now feduced ; the
height is fuch, we fear a coming Ruine. Let it not taint
your ear to hear our forrow, which is not ours alone, but all
the Kingdoms, that groan and languifh under this fad burden. One man alone occafions all this mifchief ; 'tis one
mans pride and vice that crufheth thoufands : we hope you
will not bouljter fuch a foul diforder, and for one poor worth-
lefs piece, betray a Kingdom. The Heavens forbid fo
great and fond injuftice. You are your own, yet we believe
you ours ; if fo, we may what you forget, remember. Kings
that are born fo, fhould preferve their Greatnefs ; which
Goodnefs makes, not all their other Titles. Your noble Father dying, bound our Honours ; yet we fubfcribed a breach
at your intreaty : You promis'd then a fair and grave proceeding ; but what fucceeds ? the worft of bafe Oppreffion.
So long as we had hope, our tongues were filent ; we fate
and fighed out our peculiar Sufferings : But when we fee fo
fond and lewd progreffion, that feems to threaten You and
all your Subjects, you cannot blame us if we feek to right
it. Would your unpartial eye furvey the prefent State of this
late glorious Kingdom, you there fhall fee the Face of Shame
and Sorrow. No place is free ; both Court and Country
languifh ; all men complain, but none finde help or comfort.
Will you for him, not worth your meaneft favour, confent*
                                                        the

the Ruine of so brave a Nation? Alas, Sir, if you would, we may not bear it ; our Arms that guard your Life, shall keep your Honour. 'Tis not unjust, if you your self enforce it ; the time admits no respite: For God's sake, Sir, resolve us ; since you must part with him, or us, then chuse you whether.

The King amazed with this strange Petition, believes it backt with some more secret practice: He knew their Griefs were just, yet loath to right them ; He hop'd this Tempest would o'reblow, he might advise his Answer: But when he saw them fixt to know his pleasure, he then believes it was in vain to struggle. He knew their strength that had combin'd to seek it ; and saw he was too weak for contradiction. This made him yield he should be once more banisht. Though his wretchless improvidence had laid him open to this advantage, yet he was still Master of his antient King-craft, which made him smoothly seem to pass it over , as if he well approv'd this Sequestration, which he resolves to alter as he pleased, when he had made the party sure might back his actions ; till then, he slubbers o're his private Passion. The Lords, whose innocent aims had no end but Reformation, depart content, yet wait upon the issue. A second time this Monster is sent packing, and leaves the Kingdom free from his Infection. *Ireland* is made the Cage must mewe this Haggard, whither he goes as if to Execution. With a sad heart he leaves his great Protector, vowing revenge if he may live to act it. This weak Statesman here gives a sure testimony of the poverty of his Brain, that in the time of his Prosperity and Height had not made sure one forreign Friend, to whom he might have had a welcome access in time of his expulsion. But he had handled matters so, that he was alike hateful here and abroad, insomuch that he believes this barbarous Climate his surest refuge. But he being gone, all things seem'd well reconciled ; the State was

quiet,

Gaveston banished the second time, and sent into *Ireland.*

quiet, and mens hopes were fuitable to their defires, which feem'd to promife a quick and fpeedy Reformation. But the vanity of this belief vanifht away like a fhadow, and the intermiffion was little lefs intemperate than the former agitation. This wilie Serpent continues fo his forreign Correfpondence, that the King was little better'd by his abfence; which made it evident, that Death alone would end his practis'd mifchief. Their Bodies were divided, but their Affections meet with a higher Inflammation. The intervacuum of their abfence hath many reciprocal paffages, which interchangeably flie betwixt them. The King receives not a Syllable, but ftraight returns with golden intereft. Infinitely are they both troubled with their divifion, but far more with the affront of the prefuming Barons, that had extorted it by force, yet with intreaty. The King efteem'd this kinde of proceeding too great an indignity to be pocketted; yet fince it had the pretence of his Safety and the general Good, there was not apparent Juftice enough to call it to an after-reckoning. But alas, that needed not; for his effeminate weaknefs had left him naked of that Royal refolution, that dares queftion the leaft diforderly moving of the greateft Subject. He was conftant in nothing but his Paffions, which led him to ftudy more the return of his left-handed Servant, than how to make it good, effected. He lays afide the Majefty of a King, and thinks his Power too flender; his Sword fleeps like a quiet harmlefs Beaft, while his Tongue proves his better Champion. He fends for thofe that had been the principal Agents in the laft Sentence, and treats with them feverally; knowing that Hairs are pluckt up one by one, that are not mov'd by handfuls; encountring them thus fingle, hand to hand, what with his hypocritical Entreaties and mildew'd Promifes, he foon gets from their relenting hearts a feveral Confent anfwerable to his defires. When by untying the Bundle he

. had

had difunited the ftrength of their Confederacy, he then
with confidence makes it a general Propofition; which
takes fo, that the repeal of *Gavefton's* banifhment pafs'd
currant without exception.

Again re-
called.

The Kings intent and the approbation of the Lords
is fcarcely known, before (like an Irifh Hubbub, that
needs nothing but noife to carry it) it arriv'd in *Ireland.* Upon the wings of Paffion, made proud by the
hope of Revenge and a fecond Greatnefs, he flies fwiftly
back to the Fountain of his firft Preferment. Once
more the breach is foder'd; and this True-loves Knot
enjoys his firft Poffeffion. But there wanted yet that
deep reach and provident forefight that fhould have
given it affurance. The King had neither enabled himfelf to carry things in their former height by main
ftrength, neither had he wrought his diforder'd Affections
to a conformity, or a more ftayed temper. His female
Mercury leffens not his former Ambition, but returns
the felf-fame man; onely improved with the defire of revenge, which was naked of the means to act it : fo that
it was quickly perceiv'd that the Kingdom muft feel a-
nother fit of her Convulfion. The mutual Corruptions
of thefe two, went with an equal improvidence; which
gave the Lords their advantage, and them too late a caufe
of repentance.

Immediately on his reception, the King falls into a
more dangerous Relapfe of his former Dotage; which
fo fully ingrofs'd him, that all Difcourfe and Company
feem'd harfh and unpleafant, but fuch as came from the
mellow tongue of his *Minion,* who invents many new Enchantments to feed and more engage his frenzie. All
the diffolute Actions of licentious Youth are acted *Cum
Privilegio.* This bred fuch a Grief and Diftemper in
the forrowing heart of the Subject, that a general Cloud
of Sadnefs feem'd to fhadow the whole Kingdom. Thofe
former ftrict Admonitions were not powerful enough to
bridle this Diftemper, not fo much as for a fair in-come;

the

the one becomes at the firſt daſh more fond, the other more inſolent : thoſe whom before he onely ſcorn'd, he now affronts with publick hatred , letting them know his ſpleen waits but advantage. He fills his Soveraigns ears with new ſuſpition, and whets him on to act in bloud and miſchief.

It is a Diſpute variouſly believ'd, what Climate hatch'd this Vulture. I cannot credit him to be an *Italian,* when I obſerve the map of his Actions ſo far different from the diſpoſition and practice of that politick Nation : They uſe not to vent publickly their ſpleens, till they do act them. He that will work in State, and thrive, muſt be reſerved ; a downright way that hath not ſtrength to warrant it, is cruſht and breaks with his own weight, without diſcretion. Thoſe that are in this trade held their Crafts-maſters, do ſpeak thoſe faireſt whom they mean to ruine, and rather truſt cloſe work than publick practice. Wiſe men made great, diſguiſe their aims with Vizards, which ſee and are not ſeen, while they are plotting. Judge not by their ſmooth looks or words, which hath no kindred with the hearts of *Machiavilian* States-men. Who truſts more to his will than wit, may act his Paſſion ; but this mans malice is within protecti-on. Where miſchief harbours cloſe and undiſcovered, it ruines all her Rubs without ſuſpition ; a Pill or Po-tion makes him ſure, that by plain force might have out-liv'd an Army : ſuch ends thus wrought, if once ſuſpe-cted, a neat State-lye can parget o'r with Juſtice. But thoſe antient times were more innocent, or this great Favorite more ignorant. He went on the plain way of corrupted fleſh and bloud, ſeeking to enchant his Ma-ſter, in which he was a perfect Work-man ; and the con-tempt of his Competitors ; in which he was as wilful as fearleſs : but in the managing of his proper greatneſs, there he appears like himſelf, a meer Impoſture, going on with a full carreer, not ſo much as viewing the ground he went on.

The

The Royal Treasure he exhausts in Pride and Riot; the Jewels of the Crown are in the Lumbard; that same goodly Golden Table and Tressels of so great and rich a value, he surreptitiously embezzles; and nothing almost left, that might either make Money, or improve his Glory. No man may now have the Kings ear, hand, or Purse, but he's the Mediator; his Creatures are advanc'd, his Agents flourish, and poorest Grooms become great Men of Worship. The King hath nothing but the name, while his Vicegerent hath the benefit and execution. All that appertains unto the Crown and Royal Dignity are wholly in his Power, so that he might justly be thought the Lessee, if not the Inheritor of the Prerogative and Revenue. The sense of Grief and Duty that had long contested in the Lion-hearts of the Nobility, are now reconciled. These strange presumptions had banish'd all possibility of a longer sufferance; They vow to make this Monster shrink, and let his Master know it. On this, well and strongly attended, they wait upon the King, and not with mild or fair Intreaties, they boldly now make known their Wrongs, and call for present Justice. *Edward* with a steady eye beholds their looks, where he sees registred the Characters of a just Indignation, and the threatning furrows of ensuing danger. He stands not to dispute the quarrel, lest they should tear the object of their anger from his elbow: without all shew of inward motion, he tells themselves had power to act what was most fitting, to whom he had assign'd the care should keep his Person, and assure the Kingdom. They beyond their expectation finding the wind in that door, give not his inconstant thoughts time to vary, but command their Antagonist off to a third Banishment. He deprived of heart and strength, is enforced to obey, having not so much liberty, as to take a solemn Farewel. Now is he sent for *Flanders*; the Jurisdiction of the Kings Dominions are esteem'd no fit Sanctuary to protect so loose

Abuses the King and Kingdom.

Gaveston banished the third time; goes into Flanders.

a

a Livet. They leave him to prey and practice on the *Dutch*, whofe Caps fteel'd with Liquour, had reeling Craft enough to make him quiet.

This paffage bred a fuppofition that he was now for ever loft : the King made fhew as he were well contented ; and men were glad to fee this ftorm appeafed, that feem'd to threaten an inteftine ruine. This Happinefs was but imaginary, but it is made perfect by one more real ; *Windfor* prefents the King an Heir apparent ; which happy News flies fwiftly through the Kingdom, which gives it welcome with a brave expreffion. The Royal Father did not tafte this Bleffing with fuch a fenfe of Joy as it deferved. Whether 'twas his mifgiving Spirit, or the abfence of his loft Jewel, he fadly filent, fighs out the relation ; fuch a deferving Joy could not win fo much as a fmile from his melancholy Brow, grown old with trouble. The appearance of his inward agitation was fuch, that the greateft enemies of his Dotage were the moft compaffionate of his Sufferings. Such a mafculine Affection and rapture was in thofe times without prefident, where Love went in the natural ftrain, fully as firm, yet far lefs violent. If the circumftances of this paffionate Humour, fo predominant in this unfortunate King, be maturely confidered, we fhall finde them as far fhort of poffibility, as reafon ; which have made many believe, that they had a fupernatural operation and working, enforc'd by Art, or Witchcraft. But let their beginning be what it will, never was man more immoderately tranfported, which took from him in this little time of his third abfence, the benefit of his Underftanding and Spirits fo fully, that he feems rather diftracted than inamour'd, more properly without Reafon, than ability to command it. In the circumference of his Brain he cannot finde a way to lead him out of this Labyrinth, but that which depended more of Power than Wifdome. Bridle his Affections he could not, which were but bare embryons

without

Edward of Windfor, afterwards Edw. the 3. Born, 13 Oct. 1312.

without poffeffion ; alter them he cannot, where his
eye meets not with a fubject powerful enough to engage
him : what then refts to fettle this civil difcord, but
reftitution ? which he attempts in fpight of oppofition.
Gavefton comes back ; the King avows, and bids them
ftir that durft, He would protect him. Princes that *Gavefton* a-
gain re-
turns.
falfifie their Faiths, more by proper inclination than a
neceffary impulfion, grow not more hateful to forreign
Nations, than fearful and fufpected to their own Subjects. If they be tainted with a known Guilt, and juftifie it, 'tis a fhrewd prefumption of a fick State, where
the Head is fo difeafed. A habit of doing ill, and a
daring Impudence to maintain it, makes all things in a
Politique Wifdome lawful. This Pofition in the end
cofens the profeffor, and leaves him in the field open to
fhame and infamy: And it ftands with reafon ; for if
Vertue be the Road-way to Perfection, the corruption
of a falfe Heart muft certainly be the path to an unpitied ruine.

The enraged Barons feeing great *Cornwal* return, are The Barons
take up
Arms.
fenfible of their difhonour, and think it too great a
wrong to be difpens'd with ; yet they will have the fruit
of their revenge through-ripe, before they tafte it. He
appears no Changeling, but ftill purfues the ftrains of
his prefumption. The actions of Injuftice feldom leffen.
Progreffion is believ'd a moral Vertue. He that hath a
Will to do ill, and doth it, cannot look back but on
the Crown of mifchief. This makes him not difguife
his conceptions, but fhew them fully ; having withal
this excellent Vertue, that would be never reconciled
where he once hated. The Lords obferving his behaviour, think time ill loft in fo weighty a bufinefs ; they
draw their forces together, before the King could have a
time to prevent, or his abufer to fhun it.

The gathering together of fo many threatning Clouds
prefag'd the Storm was a coming ; *Gavefton* labours to
provide a fhelter, but 'twas too late ; the time was loft

I   that

that fhould affure the danger : All that he could effect by his own ftrength, or the Royal Authority, he calls to his affiftance, (but fuch was the general diftafte of the Kingdom, he could not gain a ftrength might feem a party.) The Court he knew would be a weak Protection againft their Arms, whofe Tongues had twice expell'd him. This made him leave it, and with fuch Provifion as fo fhort a time could tender, commit himfelf to *Scarborough*-Caftle. This Piece was ftrong, and pretty well provided, but prov'd too weak againft fo juft a Quarrel. His noble Enemies being inform'd where they fhould finde him, follow the track, and foon begirt this Fortrefs. He feeks a Treaty; they defpife Conditions, knowing he none would keep, that all had broken. All hope thus loft, he falls into their power from whom he had no caufe could hope for mercy. The Butter-flies, companions of his Sun-fhine, that were his fortunes friends, not his, forfake his Winter, and bafely leave him in his greateft troubles. The tide of Greatnefs gain'd him many Servants; they were but hangers on, and meer Retainers, like Rats that left the houfe when it was falling. The Spring adorn'd him with a world of Bloffoms, which dropt away when firft they felt this Tempeft. Forfaken thus, this Cedar is furpriz'd, and brought to know the end of fuch ambition. The Prey thus tane, fhort work concludes his ftory, left that a Countermand might come to ftop their Verdict: *Gaverfeed* is made the fatal place that facrific'd his life to quench their fury.

Thus fell the firft glorious Minion of *Edward* the Second; which appearing for a time like a Blazing-ftar, fill'd the world with admiration, and gave the Englifh caufe to blame his fortune, that liv'd and died, nor lov'd, excus'd, or pitied. In the wanton Smiles of his lovely Miftrifs, he remembers not that fhe was blinde, a Giglet, and a Changeling; nor did he make himfelf in time a Refuge might be his Safeguard. If fhe had prov'd unconftant,

Seize *Gavefton at Scarborough*-Caftle;

and behead him.

conftant, fuch a Providence had made the End as fair as
the Beginning. But thefe fame towering Summer-birds
fear not the Winter, till they feel it; and then benumb'd,
they do confefs their Errour. Height of Promotion
breeds Self-love; Self-love, Opinion; which underva-
lues all that are beneath it. Hence it proceeds, that
few men, truely honeft, can hold firm Correfpondence
with fo great a Minion; his ends go not their ways, but
with Crofs-capers, which cares not how, fo thefe attain
perfection. Servants that are confin'd to truth and
goodnefs, may be in fhew, but not in truft; their Agents.
He that will act what Pride and Luft impofeth, is a fit
Page to ferve fo loofe a Mafter. Hence it proceeds,
that ftill they fall unpitied; and thofe they chufe for
Friends, do moft fupplant them. To fecure an ill-ac-
quired Greatnefs that is begot with envy, grows in hatred; as it requires judgment, claims a goodnefs to keep
it right, and grave direction. Thofe that are truely
wife, difcreet, and vertuous, will make him fo that purfues their counfel; upon which Rock he refts fecure
untainted. But this is Country-Doctrine Courts refent
not, where 'tis no way to thrive; for them are honeft.
A Champion-Confcience without bound or limit; a
Tongue as fmooth as Jet that fings in feafon, a bloudlefs
Face that buries guilt in boldnefs; thefe Ornaments are
fit to cloath a Courtier: he that wants thefe, ftill wants
a means to live, if he muft make his Service his Revenue.
He that a Child in Court grows old, a Servant expecting
years or merit fhould prefer him, and doth not by
fome by-way make his fortune, gains but a Beard for all
his pains and travel; unlefs he'll take a Purfe, and for
reward, a Pardon. Though many rife, it is not yet concluded they all are of fo bafe corruption which would
produce a fudden Ruine. The greater Peers by birth
inherit fit place in this Election. The Kings favour, or
their interceffion, may advance a deferving Friend or
Kinfman; extraordinary Gifts of Nature, or fome Excellency

cellency in knowledg may prefer him that enjoys them;
all thefe beams may fhine on men that are honeft.   But
if you caft your eye upon the grofs body of the Court,
and examine the ordinary courfe of their gradation, it
will plainly appear, that twenty creep in by the back-
gate, while one walks up by the ftreet-door.   But leaving thofe to their fortune, and that cunning conveyance
muft guide their Deftiny ;   when the fad tidings of
this unhappy Tragedy came to the Kings ears, his vexations were as infinite as hopelefs, and his Paffion tran-
fports him beyond the height of forrow, which leads
him to this bitter Exclamation.

The King's
Exclama-
tion on the
news, vow-
ing revenge.

*Could they not fpare his Life, O cruel Tygers ? What
had he done, or how fo much offended ? He never fhed
one drop of harmlefs blood, but faved thoufands. Muft
he be facrificed to calm their anger ? 'Twas not his fault, but
my affection caufed it ; which I'll revenge, and not difpute
my forrow. They, if I live, fhall tafte my juft difpleafure, and dearly pay for this their cruel errour. Till now
I kept my hand from blood and fatal actions ; but henceforth I will act my Paffions freely, and make them know I
am too much provoked. Blood muft have blood, and I will
fpend it fully, till they have paid his wandring Ghoft their
forfeit. And thou, O fweet Friend, whom living I fo
loved, from thy fad Urn fhalt fee thy wrong requited.
Thy Life as I mine own did dearly value, which I will
loofe, but I'll repay their rigour.*

This faid, he withdraws him to his melancholy
Chamber, and makes himfelf a Reclufe from the Day-
light. His manly tears bewray his inward forrow, and
make him feem to melt with height of Paffion; He
could not fleep, nor fcarce would eat, or fpeak but
faintly ; which makes him living dye with reftlefs torment. His lovely Queen (not forry that this bar was
taken away, which ftopt the paffage betwixt her Huf-
bands

bands Love and her Affections) is truely penſive at this ſtrange diſtraction, which ſeem'd without the hope of reconcilement. His nearer Friends amazed to ſee his Paſſion, reſolve to ſet him free, or looſe his favour; boldly they preſs into his Cell of darkneſs, and freely let him know his proper errour. They lay before him, how vain a thing it was to mourn or ſorrow for things paſt help, or hope of all redemption: His greatneſs would be loſt in ſuch fond actions, and might endanger him and eke the Kingdom : If he but truely knew what deſperate murmurs were dayly whiſper'd by his vain diſtemper, he would himſelf appear to ſtay the danger, and to excuſe the Barons act, ſo hateful : they touch upon the Earls intemperate carriage, which threatned them and all the Kingdoms ruine : they ſhew his inſolence and misbehaviour, which having Honour ſo far above his birth, and Wealth above his merit, was ne're contented. Laſtly, they tell him plainly, unleſs he would reſume more life and ſpirit, they fear'd the Subject would make choice of one more able.

The unworthy touches of his Minion, though but ſparingly given, nipt him to the Soul; but when he heard the Tenour of their laſt Concluſion, it rows'd him up, for fear of Depoſition. This brings him forth in ſhew and look transformed, but yet reſolv'd not to forget this Treſpaſs. The Operations in his heart were not ſo great and weighty, but that his Lords were full as cloſe and wary. So fair a warning-piece gave them their Summons, in time to make a ſtrength might keep them ſure. They cannot now recoyl, or hope for favour; their Arms muſt make their Peace, or they muſt periſh. Theſe circumſtances made them preſerve ſo well a reſpected diſtance, that well the King might bark, but durſt not bite them : He was reſolv'd, 'tis true, but not provided, and therefore holds it wiſdome to be ſilent; the time he hop'd would change, and they grow careleſs ; when they ſhould know ſuch wrongs are not

K   forgotten.

Henry Lacy, Earl of *Lincoln,* dies, 1310.

forgotten.　But now brave *Lincoln,* one of the principal Pillars of the Barons Faction, follows his adversary to the grave, but with a milde and fairer fortune. This reverend piece of true Nobility was in Speech and Conversation sweet and affable , in resolution grave and weighty; his aged temper active and valiant above belief , and his Wisdome more sound and excellent in inward depth than outward appearance. When those pale Harbingers had seized his vital Spirits, and he perceived the thought of Life was hopeless, he gives *Thomas* of *Lancaster,* his Son-in-Law, this dying Legacy.

His dying-Speech to *Tho.* Earl of *Lancaster,* his Son-in-Law.

My Son, (quoth he) *for so your Wedlock makes you, bear and observe these my last dying Precepts. Trust not the King; his Anger sleeps, but dyes not ; he waits but time, which you must likewise tender, else in the least neglect be sure you perish. Make good my place among the Lords, and keep the Kingdom from foul Oppression, which of late is frequent. Your Soveraign cares not how the State be guided, so he may still enjoy his wanton Pleasures ; have you an eye to those that seek to wrong him : be not deceived with his sugar'd language ; his heart is false, and harbours Blood and Mischief. Keep your selves firm and close ; being well united you are secure, he will not dare to touch you. If he again fall on a second Dotage, look to it in time, 'twill else be your confusion. His Minions Death lies in his heart concealed, waiting but time to act revenge and terrour : he shadows o're, but cannot hide his Malice, which fain would vent it self, but yet it dares not. If I had lived, he must have changed his copy, or one of us had felt a bitter tryal ; yet still beware you take not light occasion, or make the publick ends for private Passion. He is your Sovereign, you must so obey him, unless the Cause be just enforc'd your moving. If he himself do swerve or raise combustion, the Kingdoms good must give your Arms their warrant : short time will let you know your own condition ; however, do not trust the sleepy Lion. I knew his*

ways,

ways, and could as well foreftal them; but now I muft re-
figne it to your wifdom. Of this be fure (remember my
Prediction) if he relapfe, and make a new Vice-gerent,
which fhall leap o're your heads, and you endure it, The
King, You, or the Kingdom muft perifh. *My wearied*
Soul would fain embrace his freedom, and now my Spirits
yield to Death and Nature. Commend me to my noble
Friends and Fellows, and fay, Old Lincoln liv'd and died
their Servant.

Lancafter, whofe noble heart was before-hand feafon'd,
receives willingly thefe grave Inftructions, and like a
good Steward, locks them up in the clofet of his heart,
till time call'd upon him to give them life and action;
and yet he fuffers not this goodly Tree to fall, before
affured : He vows obfervance, and as truely keeps it ; but
erring in the time, it wrought his Downfal. Beginning
Evils are eafily fupprest, which grown to ftrength, if
cleans'd, are cur'd with danger : Twigs may be broken,
younger Plants removed ; but if once they grow Trees,
their Fall is fatal. Things ftanding thus, and all mens
minds in fufpence what would be the iffue between the
enraged King and *jealous* Lords, the indifferent friends
of either Party that fear'd this unkinde Divifion would
fhake the Peace and Tranquillity of the Kingdom, pro-
pounded divers Overtures of reconcilement ; which are
neither readily accepted, nor abfolutely refufed. The
Kings Meditations were more fixed on Revenge than
Conference ; yet feeing into the Quality of the time,
and into the fufpected Affections of the Kingdom, is
won at length to admit of a Treaty.

The Barons truely rellifhing the Tickle-terms they
ftood on, which were pinn'd to the mutability of popular Faction, were not eftranged from the thoughts of
Peace, though they would not feek it. Interceffion and
importunacy of the Mediators, brings it at length to
the upfhot ; where there was fuch an inveterate fpleen,
and

and so great an antipathy in Wills, it is not thought fit to hazard this great Work on a private discussion, where Recapitulations of old Wrongs, or the apprehension of new Indignities, might shake the Foundation. The High Court of Parliament, the gravest Senate of the Kingdom, that had an over-ruling Power to limit the King, and command the Subject, is deemed the most Honourable place of this Enterview, where a business of so great weight would be gravely discours'd; which might assure the end, and make it more authentical. Whereupon it is immediately call'd, and in short space assembled at *London*; where, after many interchangeable Expostulations diversly handled by the pregnant Wits and nimble Tongues of either Party, a settled Agreement is concluded, and many excellent Laws are enacted, which both the King and Peers are sworn to maintain and keep inviolate. By these discreet means the violence of this great Fire is rak'd up in the Embers, which in aftertimes breaks out with greater rage and fury: whatsoever the hidden Resolutions were, the Kingdom now seem'd in a fair way to settle Peace and Quiet. But a new and unexpected Accident varies this Conceit before it was cold, and calls them from private Actions, to maintain the Honour and Revenue of the Kingdom.

Edward the First, that brave and valiant Monarch, had thrice with his victorious Arms run through the Bowels of *Scotland*, and brought that stubborn Nation (that deny'd him Fealty and Homage) into an absolute Subjection. Their last precedent King, *Robert le Bruce*, had tryed the height of his fortune, and with a fruitless opposition won no more than the loss of his Kingdom, and his own Expulsion. The Conqueror finding himself quitted of this Obstacle, takes upon him the Regiment of this Kingdom, with a double string to his Bow; the one of antient Title, the other of Conquest. The Nobility of *Scotland*, and all the inferiour Ministers of State, seeing the great Effusion of Bloud
spent

(marginal notes)
A Parliament called.

The *Scots* adhere to *Bruce*, 1313.

spent in this Quarrel, which continued, feemed to threaten a general devaftation of their Country, fubmit themfelves to the *Englifh* Government, and are all folemnly fworn to obey it. *Edward* thus in poffeffion, confirms it, by feizing the property of all the Royal Jurifdiction into his own hand, removing fuch Officers as were not agreeable to his will and liking, and giving many goodly Eftates and Dignities to divers of his faithful Servants that had valiantly behaved themfelves in this Service. The Form of Government by him eftablifhed, was peaceably obey'd, and continued during his Life ; neither was it queftioned in the beginning Government of his unhappy Succeffor. But the wary *Scots*, more naturally addicted to a Phœnix of their own Nation, feeing into the prefent diffentions and diforders of the Kingdom, thought it now a fit time to revolt to their old Mafter, who like a crafty Fox harbours himfelf under the *French* Kings protection (the antient receptacle and Patron for that Nation.) No fooner is he advertifed that the gate was open and unguarded, and that his well-affected Subjects wifhed his return, but back he comes, and is received with a full applaufe and welcome. All Oaths, Obligements, and Courtefies of the *Englifh*, are quite cancell'd and forgotten ; and this longloft Lion is again re-invefted in the Royal Dignity. Affoon as he had moor'd himfelf in a domeftique affurance, he then like a provident Watchman begins to raife a ftrength that might oppofe all forreign Invafion, which he forefaw would thunder from the Borders. This Martial Preparation flyes fwiftly to the King and Council of *England*, where it appears like a great Body upon a pair of Stilts, more in bulk than the proportion of the ftrength that bare it. The Pillars of the State, which wifely forefaw how great an inconvenience it would be to fuffer fuch a Member to be diffever'd, that in the conteftation with *France* would make the War a Mattachine, or Song of three parts, perfwade

L   their

their Sovereign it was not proper for his Greatnefs to
fuffer fuch an unworthy fubverfion of his Fathers Conftitutions, and to loofe the advantage of fo fair a part
of his Revenue.

Edward, that had ontflept his native glory, had yet a
juft compunction of this difhonour, which feem'd to
rob him of a portion of his Inheritance, purchafed at
too dear a value. He lays by his private rancour, and
fettles himfelf to fupprefs this fudden and unlookt-for
Commotion, waking from that fenfual Dream, which
had given him fo large a caufe of Sorrow. Scarcely
would he give his intentions fuch an intermiffion, as
might attend the levy of his Army, which he had fum-
moned to be ready with all fpeed and expedition. The
jealous Lords ftartled with this Alarum, conceiting it
but fome trick of State to catch them napping, they
fufpect thefe Forces, under pretence of publick action,
might be prepared to plot a private mifchief. The
King they knew was crafty, clofe, and cunning ; and
thought not fit to truft too far to Rumour. This
makes them ftand upon their guard, and keep Affem-
blies, pleading for warrant the felf-fame ground of rifing.
But when their Spies in Court had given them knowledge
that all was fure, they need not fear their danger, and
that they dayly heard the Northern clamour that ecchoed
loudly with the *Scotifh* motions, they draw their Forces
to the King's ; who thus united, in perfon leads them to
this hopeful Conqueft. But forehand-reckonings ever
moft mifcarry ; he had thofe hands, but not thofe hearts
which fought his Fathers fortune.

Scarce had he paft and left the *Englifh* Borders, but
he beholds an Army ready to affront him, not of dejected Souls, or Bodies fainting, but Men refolv'd to
win, or dye with Honour. Their valiant Leader hear-
tens on their Courage, and bids them fight for Life,
Eftate, and Freedome, all which were here at ftake ;
which this day gains, or makes hereafter hopelefs.

The King
goes in per-
fon againft
the *Scots,*
1314.

Edward,

Edward, that expected rather submission, or some honest Terms of agreement, finding a Check given by a Pawn, unlook'd for, plays the best of his game, and hopes to win it.   He contemns their condition and number, slighting their Power; and in the memory of his Father's Conquests, thinks his own certain.   But the success of Battles runs not in a Bloud, neither is gained by Confidence, but Discretion and Valour.   No one thing hurts more in a matter of Arms, than Presumption : a Coward that expects no mercy, is desperate by compulsion ; and the most contemptible Enemy proves most dangerous, when he is too much undervalu'd.   You may see it here instanc'd, where a rabble multitude of despised Blue-caps, encounter, rout, and break the Flower of *England* : *Eastriveline* doth yet witness the fatal memory of this so great Disaster.   There fell brave *Clare* the Earl of *Gloucester,* the valiant *Clifford,* and stout *Mawle,* with above Fifty Knights and Barons.   This bloudy day, which had spilt so great a shower of Noble bloud, and cropt the bravest Blossoms of the Kingdom, sends the King back to *Barwick* with a few straggling Horse, whose well-breath'd speed out-run the pursuing danger. So near a Neighbourhood to so victorious an Enemy, is deemed indiscretion, where the Prize was believ'd so richly worth the Venture.   This sends away the melancholy King jaded in his hopes, and dull with his misfortune.   If we may judge by the Event, the Condition of this man was truely miserable ; all things at home, under his Government, were out of rule and order ; and nothing successful that he undertook by forraign Employment : but where the Ground is false, the Building cannot stand ;   He planted the foundation of his Monarchy on Sycophants and Favorites, whose disorderly Proceedings dryed up all that sap that should have fostered up the springing Goodness of the Kingdome, and made him a meer stranger to those Abilities that are proper to Rule and Government.   Kings ought

The King defeated at *Banocksbourn* near *Striveling.*

ought to be their own Surveyors, and not to pafs over the whole care of their Affairs, by Letter of Atturney, to another mans Protection: fuch inconfiderate actions beget a world of mifchief, when there are more Kings than one, in one and the felf-fame Kingdom; it eclipfeth his Glory, and derogates from his Greatnefs; making the Subject groan under the unjuft Tyranny of an infolent oppreffion. No man with fuch propriety can manage the griefs and differences of the Subject, as the King, who by the Laws of God, Men, and Nature, hath an intereft in their Heart, and a fhare in their Affections. When they are guided by a fecond hand, or heard by a Relator, Money or Favour corrupts the Integrity, and over-rules the courfe of Juftice, followed at the heels with Complaint and Murmur, the Mother of Difcontent and Mifchief.

The unexpected return of the General of this illfucceeding Enterprize, filled the Kingdom with a welldeferved Sorrow, and is welcom'd with a News as ftrange, though not fo full of danger. *Poydras*, a famous Impoftor, a Tanners Son, and born at *Exeter*, pretends himfelf, with a new ftrain of Lip-coufenage, to be the Heir of *Edward* the Firft, by a falfe Nurfe chang'd in his Cradle for the King now reigning. All Novelties take in the itching ears of the Vulgar, and win either belief or admiration. This Tale, as weak in truth as probability, was fortunate in neither, only it exalts this imaginary King to his Inftalment on *Northampton*-Gallows, where he ends the hour of his melancholy Government with as ftrange a Relation, which fuggefts, That for two years fpace, a Spirit, in the likenefs of a Cat, had attended him as the chief Groom of his Chamber, from whom in many fecret Conferences he had received the truth and information of this Myftery, with affurance it would bring him to the Crown of *England*. It was as great a fault in the Mafter to believe, as for the Servant to abufe; yet the defire of the

Poydras of *Exeter* pretends himfelf King, and the King a Changling.

His ftrange Confeffion.

one

one to change his Tanfat for a Kingdom, was not much out of fquare; nor the Lying of the other, fince he continued but his trade which he had practis'd from the beginning. It is a foul offence and overfight in them that have not Devils of their own, to hunt a-broad and feek where they may gain them by purchafe. If it be a myftery of State to know things by Prediction of fuch vertuous Minifters, methinks they were much better kept, as this Tanner kept his, rather as an houf-hold-Servant, than a Retainer; which may in time bring them to a like Preferment: Such Agents may feem Lambs, but in the end they will be found as favage as Tygers, and as falfe as the Camelions. Till now our wanton King had never felt the true touch of a juft grief; but mens misfortunes alter their impreffions; he inwardly and heartily laments his own difhonour, yet ftrives to hide and conceal his Sorrow, left thofe about him might be quite dejected. It was a bitter Corrofive to think, how oft his Royal Father had difplaid his victorious Colours, which knew not how to fight un-lefs to conquer: How often had he over-run this Neigh-bour-Nation, and made them take fuch Laws as he impofed? How many times had he overthrown their greateft Armies, and made them fue they might be-come his Subjects? The memory of this doth vex his Spirits, and makes him vow Revenge and utter Ruine. He calls to Council all his Lords and Leaders, and lays before them the antient Glory of the Kingdom, the late Misfortune, and his proper Errours, and laftly his defire to right his Honour. They glad to hear the King in the fenfe of fo general a difgrace touch'd with fo noble a ftrain, do fpur it on before it cool'd, or the *Scots* fhould grow too proud of their new Glory. The former Lofs had toucht fo near the quick, that there is now a more wary Refolution: Difpatches are fent out for a more exact and full provifion; a mature Confi-deration is thought neceffary before it come to action:

M *York*

York is made the Cabinet for this grave Council, there the King soon appears, attended by all the bravest and ablest Spirits of the Kingdom. The act of the first conference tends to the security of *Berwick*, the street-door of the North, and principal Key of the borders. This care with a full provision is committed to the Fidelity and Valour of Sir *Peter Spalden*, who undertakes the

charge, being plentifully furnisht, and promiseth defence against the united Power of *Scotland*. This unfortunate King was as unhappy in Council as in Action. A short time shews this unworthy Knight to the world false and perfidious. *Robert le Bruce*, that had this Strength as a mote in his eye, conceived it by force almost impregnable; this made him seek to undermine it by corruption, and aloof off to taste the palate of this new Governour.

The Hook was no sooner baited, but the Trout falls a nibbling; ready Money, and a specious promise of an expectant Preferment, makes this Conspiracy perfect, which at one blow sells the Town, with all its warlike Provisions, and the treacherous Keeper's Reputation and Honour. The Pope, who with a pious and a truely compassionate eye beheld the misery of this Dissention,

and the unnatural effusion of so much Christian Bloud, seeks to reform it; and to this effect sends over two of his Cardinals to mediate a Peace, and to compose, if it might be, the differences in question. They being arrived in *England*, come down into the North to the King, by whom they are with great Ceremony, according to the fashion of those Religious Times, received and welcomed. They discourse to him the occasion of their Employment, and encline him with many excellent and vertuous motives to embrace a Peace with *Scotland*. The greenness of the Disgrace, and the late Wound yet bleeding new, kept him in a long demurrer. Yet the holy and milde prosecution of these holy Fathers won him at length to their Mediation, with a proviso that he were not too far prejudiced in Interest and Honour. With this Answer they take their leave, and prosecute their Journey for *Scotland*; but with an example full of barbarous Inhumanity, they are in the way surpriz'd and robbed. Infinitely is the King incens'd with this audacious act, which threw so foul a stain upon the whole Nation ; which causeth a strict inquisition for the discovery of these Malefactors, which are soon known and taken. *Middleton* and *Selby*, both Knights, expiate the offence with their shameful Execution. The persons of Embassadours amongst the most savage Nations are free from rapine ; but being cloathed in the habit of Religion and such a Greatness, and going in a work so good and glorious, certainly it was an act deserv'd so severe a punishment. Immediately at the heels of this, follows another Example less infamous, but far more full of danger. Sir *Josline Denvile*, having wasted his estate, and not able to lessen the height of his former expences, gets into his society a Regiment of Ruffians, terming themselves Out-laws : with these he infests the North with many outragious Riots ; insomuch that no man that had any thing to loose, could be secure in his own house from Murder, Theft and Rapine. A little time had brought this little Army, rowling like a Snow-ball, to the number of 200 ; all the diseased flux of the corrupted humours of those parts flye to this Imposthume. An Attempt so impudent and daring flyes swiftly to the Kings knowledg. Report, that seldom lessens, makes the danger far greater than it deserv'd : The Royal ear conceits it little better than a flat Rebellion, whose apprehension felt it self guilty of matter enough to work on. This made an instant levy, and as ready a dispatch for the suppression of the flame, while it but burnt the suburbs. Experience soon returns, the Fear is found greater than the Cause ; the principal Heads and Props of this Commotion are surprized, and fall under the severity of that Law, whose protection they in this enterprize had absolutely disclaimed.

Who ate robbed at *Derlington.*

Sir *Gilbert de Middleton* and Sir *Walter de Selby* executed for the same.

Sir *Josline Denvile* with certain Ruffians infest the North.

claimed. Thofe that more narrowly examin'd the depth
of this Convention, believ'd it but a mafque for a defigne more perillous.   The intemperate and indifcreet
Government had alien'd the hearts of this People ; there
was a general face of Difcontent over the whole Kingdome ; the Ulcers fefter'd dayly more and more.; the
Scotifh difafter is afcribed to the Regal weaknefs, and
all things feem'd to tend to quick confufion.   If this un-
advifed and ill-grounded diforder had tafted the general
inclination in a more innocent and juftifiable way , it
was conftantly believed the King had fooner felt the
publick Revolt of the whole Kingdom : But this work
was referved till a farther time, and the operation of
thofe that had the opportunity of effecting it with more
power, and a fairer pretence of Juftice. It is a very
dangerous thing when the Head is ill, and all the Members fuffer by his infirmity. Kings are but men, and
Man is prone to Errour; yet if they manage their di-
ftempers with Wifdome or Difcretion, fo that they lye
not open to publick view and cenfure, they may be
counted faults, but not predictions : but when the heart
is gangren'd, and the world perceives it, it is the fatal
mark of that infection, which doth betoken ruine and

The Cardi-
nals return.
deftruction.   The Cardinals are now come back, the
hopes of Peace are defperate;the *Scots* are on the Sunny-
fide of the hedge, and will have no Conditions but fuch
as may not be with Honour granted. *Edward* inflam'd,
will have no farther Treaty ; this makes them take their
leave, and haften homeward. Their Loffes liberally
are requited, and many goodly Gifts beftow'd at parting. Being come to *Rome*, they inform his Holinefs of
the fuccefs of their journey ; who takes ill the contu-

The Pope
Excommu-
nicates the
Scotch King
and King-
dom.
macy of the perfidious *Scots,* and excommunicates both
that King and Kingdom. But this thunderbolt wrought
a fmall effect ; where Honefty had fo little an acquaintance, Religion muft needs be a great ftranger. The
lofs of *Barwick,* and the difgrace of his firft Overthrow,
                                                        calls

calls the King to adventure a Revenge, which he thinks he had too long adjourned. He makes it a difputable queftion, whether he fhould befiege *Barwick*, or invade *Scotland*; but the confideration thereof is referr'd till the moving of the Army, which is advanc'd with all fpeed poffible. Men, Arms, and Money, with all fuch other Provifions as were as well fit to continue the War as begin it, are fuddenly ready in full proportion. The Army attends nothing but the King's Perfon, or fome more lucky General to lead it. In the knowledg he loofeth no time; but appears in the Head of his Troops, and leads them on, making an armed hedge about *Barwick*, before his enemies had full knowledg of his moving. The Council of War thought it not expedient to leave fuch a thorn in the heel of fo glorious an Army. The *Scots* thought it too great a hazard to attempt the breach of fo ftrong a body, fo excellently intrencht and guarded; the memory of former paffages made them entertain this War with lefs heat, but with a more folid judgment. *Barwick* they knew was ftrong by Art and Nature, and fully provided to hold the *Englifh* play, till Want and the Seafon of the Year did make them weary. This made them leave the roadway, and continue the War more by Difcretion than Valour. But during thefe paffages, the Divine Juftice fends down the other three fatal executioners of his wrath, Plague, Dearth, and Famine; no part is free, but hath his portion of one or all of thefe fo cruel Sifters. To make this mifery more perfect, the wylie *Scots* taking the advantage of the King's fruitlefs encamping before *Barwick*, like a land-flood over-run the naked Borders, and boldly march forward into the Country, with Fury, Blood, and Rapine. The ftuff that fhould ftop this breach, was abfent with the King, fo that they finde no rub in their eruption. The ArchBifhop of *York*, a Reverend Old man, but a young Souldier, able enough in his element, but ignorant in the

King Edw. befieges Barwick.

A great Dearth, which lafted three years.

The Scotch over-run the Borders.

The ArchBifhop of York oppofeth them.

N   Rules

Rules of Martial Discipline, resolves to oppose this unruly devastation; he straightways musters up his Congregations, and gives them Arms, that knew scarce use of Iron. Soon had his example collected up a multitude, in number hopeful; but it was composed of men fitter to pray for the success of a Battle, than to fight it. With these, and an undaunted Spirit, he affronts his Enemies, and gives them an encounter; making *Milton* upon *Swale* more memorable by the blood of this Disaster. His Victorious and Triumphing Enemies christned this unhappy Conflict in derision, *The white Battle.* Many Religious-men, with loss of their Lives, purchas'd here their first Apprentiship in Arms; and found that there was a dangerous difference betwixt fighting and praying. The intent of this grave Bishop was certainly noble and worthy; but the act was inconsiderate, weak, and ill-advised. It was not proper to his Profession, to undertake a Military Function, in which his hope in reason answer'd his experience; neither did it agree with the Innocency and Piety of his Calling, to be an actor in the effusion of Blood, though the quarrel were defensive, but by compulsion. But questionless he meant well, which must excuse his action. Too great a care improperly exprest, doth often loose the cause it strives to advantage. In all deliberations of this nature, where so many Lives are at stake, there should be a deep foresight even in matter of circumstance; and the quality as well of our own, as of our adversaries, duely considered; else with a dangerous errour we leave the success to the will of Fortune, who in nothing is more tickle and wanton, than in the event of Battles, which are seldom gain'd by multitude, the Mother of Confusion. To be a General, is an act of greatness, and doth require a great and perfect Knowledge, ripe by Experience, and made full by Practice. It is not enough to dare to fight, which is but Valour; but to know how and when, which makes it perfect.

Marginal note: and is beaten at *Milton* upon *Swale*.

Discretion

Difcretion and Judgment fometimes teach advantage, which make (the weight being light) the fcale more even. I will not deny, but the moft expert Leader may have all thefe, and yet may loofe a Battle; fince (as all things are) this great defigne is guided by a Divine Providence; and many Accidents may happen betwixt the Cup and the Lip, while things are in action. But he that hath a well-grounded and warrantable reafon for his Engagement, may lofe the day, and yet preferve his Honour. Wife-men do cenfure Errours, not Events of Actions, which fhew them good or bad, as they be grounded. The News of the Defeat of this Spiritual Army, like the voice of a Night-raven, had no fooner croakt his fad eccho in the King's ear, but he ftraight raifeth his Army, weaken'd with Famine, and leffen'd with Sicknefs. The prigging *Scots* feeing his going off, judge his Retreat little better than a plain flight; which gave them heart to fet upon the fag-end of his Troops, which they rout and break, to the aftonifhment of the whole Army. This done, they return, and think it honour enough they had done the work they came for. The King doubles his pace homewards; inftead of Triumph, glad he had got loofe from fo imminent a danger. This blank return fill'd the Kingdom with a fretting murmur, and forreign Nations thought their Valour chang'd, who had fo oft before o'recome this Nation. Mated with grief, oppreft with fhame and forrow, *Edward* exclaims againft his wayward Fortune, that made his Greatnefs, like the Crab, go backward; while he feeks to improve, the opinion of his worth he impairs, and grows ftill leaner; and when he fhuns a taint, he findes a mifchief. Sadly he now refolves no more to tempt her; he lays afide his Arms, for harms to feed his humour. His Vanities (companions of his Greatnefs) had flept out the night of thefe combuftions; he now awakes them, with a new affurance they fhould poffefs their former manfion. His wandring eyes now ravage through

The King leaves Barwick.

through the confines of his great Court, made loose by
his example. Here he feeks out fome Piece, or Copper-
metal, whom by his Royal ftamp he might make currant. He findes a fpacious choice, being well-attended,
but 'twas by fuch as made their tongues their fortunes;
Vain-glory here found none to cure it, and the fick
heart ne're felt the touch of Wormwood. The Agents
were compos'd of the juft temper, as was the fpring
that gave their tongues their motion; fuch an harmo-
nious Confort fits the Organ, that lov'd no flats nor
fharps, or forc'd divifion. No language pleas'd the
King, (the Servants know it) but that which was as
fmooth as Gold new burnifht. Old antient truth was,
like a thread-bare Garment, efteem'd a foul difgrace
to cloath a Courtier. Sincerity was no fit Mafter for
thefe Revels, nor honeft Plainnefs for a feat in Council.
This made this King, this Court, and glorious Kingdom,
fall by degrees into a ftrange confufion. The Infidelity of Servants cloathed in hypocrifie, betrayes the Mafter, and makes his mifery greater or lefs dangerous,
according to the qualities of their employments. It is
an excellent confideration for the Majefty of a King, in
election, to reflect on Goodnefs, Truth, and Ability, for
his attendance, more than the natural parts, or thofe
that are by Art and Cunning made pliable to his Difpofition. The firft prove the props of Greatnefs, the
other the inftruments of Danger and Diforder; which
makes the Mafter at beft pitied, but moft commonly
hated and fufpected. Neither is it fafe for the Royal
ear to be principally open to one mans information, or
to rely folely on his judgment. Multiplicity of able
Servants that are indifferently (if not equally) countenanced, are the ftrength and fafety of a Crown, which
gives it glory and luftre. When one man alone acts
all parts, it begets a world of errour, and endangers
not only the Head, but all the Members.

Edward could not but know, that a new Prefident

over

over his Royal actions, muſt make his Subjects his but
at a ſecond hand ; yet he is reſolv'd of a new choice,
of ſuch a Favourite as might ſupply and make good the
room of his loſt beloved *Gaveſton* ; hence ſprung that
fatal fire which ſcorcht the Kingdom with inteſtine
Ruine. He was put to no great trouble to ſeek a forreign Climate ; he had variety of his own, that might be
eaſily made capable enough for ſuch a looſe employment. He had a ſwarm of Sycophants that gap'd after
greatneſs, and cared not to pawn their Souls to gain
promotion ; amongſt theſe his eye fixt on *Spencer*, a
man till then believ'd a naked States-man ; he was young,
and had a pleaſing aſpect ; a perſonage though not
ſuper-excellent, yet well enough to make a formal Minion.

*Spencer ta-
ken into fa-
vour.*

The Ladder by which he made his aſcent, was
principally thus : he had been always conformable to
the King's Will, and never denied to ſerve his appetite in every his ways and occaſions ; which was vertue
enough to give him wealth and title. Some others think
this feat was wrought by Witchcraft, and by the Spells
of a grave Matron, that was ſuſpected to have a Journey-
man Devil to be her Loadſtone : which is not altogether improbable, if we behold the progreſſion ; for
never was Servant more inſolently fortunate, nor Maſter unreaſonably indulgent. Their paſſages are as much
beyond belief, as contrary to the Rules of Reaſon.
But leaving the diſcourſe of the Cauſe, the King applauds his own Workmanſhip, and doats infinitely on
the Non-age of this Impoſture, which ſeeing the advantage, labours to advance it ; and though in his own
nature he were proud, harſh, and tyrannous, yet he
cloaths himſelf in the habit of Humility, as obſequious
to his Maſter, as ſmooth and winning to his Acquaintance ; knowing that a Rub might make the Bowl fall
ſhort while it was running : Heat of Blood, and height
of Spirit, conſult more with Paſſion than Judgment ;

where

where all fides are agreed, quick ends the bargain. *Spencer* muſt riſe, the King himſelf avows it ; and who was there durſt croſs their Sovereigns pleaſure ? The reſolution known, like flocks of Wild-geeſe, the ſpawn of Court-corruption fly to claw him. The great ones that till now ſcarce knew his Off-ſpring, think it an ho-nour to become his Kinſmen : The Officers of State, to win his favour, forget their Oaths, and make his Will their Juſtice. Lord, how the Vermin creep to this warm Sun-ſhine, and count each Beam of his a ſpecial Favour ! Such a thing is the Prologue of a beginning Greatneſs, that it can Metamorphoſe all but thoſe that hate it. The King, though he were pleaſed with this new ſtructure, yet his inward revolutions were not alto-gether free from agitation. He beheld the Lords and Kingdom now quiet, and the *Scotch* Tragedy worn out of memory ; he was not without cauſe doubtful, whe-ther this new Act might not cauſe a new Diſtraction : He calls to minde the ground of his firſt troubles, and found it had with this a near reſemblance ; He looks upon the ſullied State ſcarce cleanſed, and fear'd this leap might cauſe a new pollution. Theſe thoughts, like miſty vapours, ſoon diſſolved, and ſeem'd too dull to feed his Love-ſick fancy. His hatred to the *Barons* bids him freely venture ; that in their moving he might ſo op-preſs them, which on cool blood might ſeem too great Injuſtice. *Gaveſton*'s Death lay in his heart impoſtum'd, not to be cur'd, but by a bloody iſſue. From this falſe ground he draws his proper ruine, making Phantaſms ſeem as deeds were acted. Such Caſtles in the Air are poor Conceptions, that ſell the Skin before the Beaſt be killed. The *Barons* were no Children, he well knew it ; the hope was little might be got with ſtriving, where all the Kingdom was ſo much diſtaſted ; but he priz'd high his own, contemning theirs, which wrought their Death, and after his Misfortune. Being reſolv'd to coun-tenance his Will with more haſte than adviſement, He

honours

honours the subject of his choice with the *Lord Chamberlain's* place, professing freely he thought him worthy, and would maintain him in it. This foreright jump going so high, made all men wonder, and soon suspect him guilty of some secret vertue. Scarce had this new great Lord possession of the White-staff, but he forgets his former being, and sings the right Night-crow's tune of upstart Greatness, and follows his Predecessors pattern to the life, but with a far more strength and cunning. He was not born a stranger or an alien, but had his Birth and breeding here, where he is exalted ; and though he had not so much depth to know the Secrets, yet understands the plain-Song of the State, and her progressions, which taught him his first Lesson, That Infant-greatness falls where none support it: From this principle, his first work is employ'd to win and to preserve an able party. To work this sure, he makes a Monopoly of the Kings ear, no man may gain it but by his permission; establishing a sure intelligence within the Royal Chamber ; not trusting one, but having sundry Agents, who must successively attend all motions. By this he wedgeth in his Sentinels at such a distance, that none can move, but he receives the Larum. The first request he makes his Sovereign (who ne're denied him) was, that he would not pass a *Grant,* till he survey'd it ; for this he makes a zealous care the cover, lest by such Gift the Subject might be grieved, the King abused. This stratagem unmaskt, gave perfect knowledge, who ever leapt the Horse he held the Bridle, which rein'd his foes up short, while friends unhors'd them ; and raised as he pleased all such as brib'd or sought him. To mix these serious strains with lighter objects, he feeds the current of his Sovereign's Vices with store of full delights, to keep him busied, whilst he might act his part with more attention. He quarrels those whom he suspects too honest, or at the least not his more than their Masters, and quickly puts them off, that

Spencers po-
licy.

that there may be entry for such as he prefers, his proper creatures; so that a short time makes the Court all of a piece at his Commandment. Those whom he fear'd in State would cross his workings, he seeks to win by favour or alliance; if they both fail, he tenders fairly to lift them higher by some new promotion, so he may have them sure on all occasions; and with these baits he catcht the hungry Planets. Such as he findes too faithful for surprisal, these he sequesters, mounting his Kindred up to fill their places. The *Queen*, that had no great cause to like those Syrens, that caus'd her grief, and did seduce her Husband, he yet presumes to court with strong professions, vowing to serve her as a faithful Servant. She seeing into the quality of the time, where he was powerful, and she in name a Wife, in truth a Hand-maid, doth not oppose, but more increase his Greatness, by letting all men know that she receiv'd him. To win a nearer place in her opinion, he gains his Kindred places next her person; and those that were her own, he bribes to back him. The Court thus fashion'd, he levels at the Country, whence he must gain his strength, if need enforc'd it. Here he must have an estate, and some sure refuge; this he contrives by begging the Custody of divers of the principal Honours and Strength of the Kingdom. But these were no inheritance which might perpetuate his Memory, or continue his Succession. He makes a Salve for this Sore; and to be able to be a fit Purchaser of Lands, by the benefit of the *Prerogative* he falls a selling of *Titles*, in which it was believ'd he thriv'd well, though he sold many more Lordships than he bought Mannors; by this means yet he got many pretty retiring places for a younger Brother, within the most fertil Counties of the Kingdom. This for the Private, now to the Publick; he makes sure the principal Heads of Justice, that by them his credit might pleasure an old Friend, or make a new at his pleasure. If in this number any one held him at

too

too fmart a diftance, prizing his integrity and honour before fo bafe a traffique, he was an ill Member of State, and either filenc'd, or fent to an *Irifh* or *Welfh* Employment. It is enough to be believ'd faulty, where a difputation is not admitted. The Hare knows her ears be not horns, yet dares not venture a Tryal, where things muft not be fentenc'd as they are, but as they are taken. The Commanders that fway moft in Popular Faction, as far as he durft or might without combuftion, he caufeth to be conferr'd on his Friends and Kindred; and above all things, he fettles a fure Correfpondence of Intelligence in all the quarters of the Kingdome, as a neceffary leading prefident : he fills the peoples ears with rumour of forreign danger, to bufie their brains from difcourfing Domeftick Errours; and fends out a rabble of fpying *Mercuries*, who are inftructed to talk liberally, to tafte other mens inclinanations, and feel the pulfes of thofe that had moft caufe to be difcontented. For the antient Nobility, which was a more difficult work to reduce to conformity, laying afide the punctilio's of his greatnefs, he ftrives to gain them as he won his Mafter ; but when he found them fhy and nice to make his party, he flights them more and more, to fhew his Power, and make them feek to entertain his favour. And to eclipfe their Power by birth and number, he findes the means to make a new Creation, which gave the Rabble-Gentry upftart Honours, as Children do give Nuts away by handfuls ; yet ftill he hath fome feeling of the bufinefs. Laftly, he wins the King to call his *Father* to the Court, who with the fhoal of all his Kin are foon exalted, while he makes all things lawful that correfpond his Will, or Mafters Humour. He thus affuming the adminiftration of the Royal affairs, his Mafter giving way to all his actions, the *incenfed Lords* grown out of patience, appoint the rendevouz of a fecret Meeting at *Sharborough*, where they might defcant their griefs with

The Barons incenfed.

P   more

more freedom, yet with such a cautelous Secrecy, that this *Harpy* with his *Lyncean* eyes could not perceive their anger.   Assoon as they were met, *Thomas* of *Lancaster*, the most eminent of this Confederacy, in a grave discourse lays before them the Iniquity of the time, the Insolency of this new *Ganymede*, and the Kings intemperate wretchlesness, which made the Kingdom a prey to all manner of Injustice. *Hereford* adviseth, that they should all together petition the King, that he would be pleased to look into the Disorders, and grant a Reformation. *Mowbray*, *Mortimer*, and the rest, soar a higher pitch, which *Clifford* thus expresseth.

Clifford's Speech.

   My Lords, *It is not now as when brave* Lincoln *lived, whom* Edward *fear'd, and all the Kingdom honoured. Nor is this new Lord a* Gavelton, *or naked Stranger, that only talkt, and durst not act his Passions. We now must have to do with one of our own Country, which knows our ways, and how to intercept them : See you not how he weaves his webs in Court and Country, leaving no means untryed may fence his greatness? And can you think a verbal Blast will shake him, or a set Speech will sink his daring Spirit ? No, he is no fantastick* Frenchman, *but knows as well as we where we can hurt him: his Pride is such, he'll ne're go less a farding ; but he must fall a key, or we must ruine. Women and Children make their tongues their Weapons ; true Valour needs no words, our wrongs no wrangling. Say this unconstant King hear our Petition, admit he promise to redress our Grievance ; this sends us home secure and well-contented, until the Plot be ripe for our destruction. If you will needs discourse your cause of Grievance, be yet provided to make good your errour ; a wise man gets his guard, then treats Conditions, which works a Peace with ease and more assurance. All Treaties vain, our Swords must be our warrant; which we may draw by such a just compulsion : those ready, then attempt your pleasure, and see if words can work a Reformation.*

I

*I am no tongue-man, nor can move with language ; but if
we come to act, I'll not be idle : Then let us fall to Arms
without disputing ; We'll make this Minion stoop, or dye
with honour.*

This rough Speech, uttered with a Souldier-like liberty, by one so truly noble and valiant, inflam'd the
hearts of such as heard them. They concur all in a general approbation, and thereupon they fall to present Levies.
Mortimer, a brave young active Spirit, with his Retinue,
gains the *maiden-head* of this great Action. He enters
furiously upon the possession of the *Spencers,* spoiling and
wasting like a profest enemy. This outrage flies swiftly to the owners, and appears before them like *Scoggins
crow,* multipli'd in carriage. They assoon make the King
the sharer of their intelligence, and increase it to their
best advantage. *Edward* sensible of so audacious an
affront, thought it did yet rather proceed from private
spleen than publick practice ; which made him in the
tenderness of the one, and malice to the other, by Proclamation thus make known his pleasure, That the Actors
of this misdemeanour should immediately appear perso-
nally, and shew cause, whereby they might justifie their
Actions, or forthwith to depart the Kingdom, and not to
return without his special Licenfe. When the tenour
of this Sentence was divulged, and come to the knowledge of *the Confederate Lords,* they saw their interest
was too deeply at stake to be long shadow'd. In the obedience of such a doom, the *primitiæ* of their Plot must receive a desperate blemish. They therefore resolve, as
they had begun, so to make good and maintain the
quarrel ; they reinforce their Forces, and draw them into a body strong enough to boulster out their doings,
and to bid a base to the irresolute wanton King and his
inglorious Favourite, whose Platforms were not yet so
compleat, as that they durst adventure the Tryal of so
strong a Battery. Yet the more to justifie their Arms
(which

The Barons
take Arms.

Mortimer
spoils *Spen-
cer's* Posses-
sion.

The Kings
Proclama-
tion there-
on.

(which in the best conſtruction ſeem'd to ſmatch of Rebellion) they ſend unto the King a fair and humble
Meſſage, the Tenor whereof lets him know, that

The Barons
Meſſage to
the King.

*Their intentions were fair and honeſt; and that the Arms
thus levied, were to defend his Honour, and not offend
his Perſon. The Sufferings of the Kingdom were ſo deep
and weighty, that all was like to run to preſent ruine, unleſs he would be pleas'd to cure this Feaver. In all humility they deſire he would ſequeſter from his preſence, and
their uſurpt authority, thoſe Inſtruments which acted this
diſorder, and that their doings might receive a teſt by a fair
Tryal. To this if he give way, they would attend him
with all the expreſſions of a Loyal Duty; but if his heart
were hardned for denial, they then intreat his pardon that
would not be Spectators of the general miſchief which drew
too ſwiftly on by this Diſtemper.* The King receiving ſo
peremptory a Meſſage, thinks this fair gloſs a kind of
By-your-leave in ſpight of your teeth. He ſaw readily
how the Game went, and was loath to ſtrike the Hive,
for fear the Swarm ſhould ſting him. Dearly he doted
on his *Minion,* yet conceiv'd it fitter he ſhould a little
ſuffer, than they both ſhould ruine, which probably
might ſoon enſue if they prevailed. He had no power
provided to withſtand them, nor was he ſure that time
would make it ſtronger; the *Lords* were well belov'd,
their quarrel pleaſing, while he had nothing but the
name of King, might hope aſſiſtance. Now he condemns bitterly his improvidence, that had not ſecur'd his
work before he acts it. *Spencer,* that ſaw himſelf thus
quite foreſtalled, and his great foreſight in a manner
uſeleſs, ſince thoſe whom he had made were but a handful, and thoſe of the poorer ſort of weaker ſpirits, that
ſtow themſelves in tempeſts under Hatches, knew 'twas
too late to think of oppoſition; and therefore perſwades
his irreſolute *Maſter* to ſubſcribe to the preſent neceſſity:
yet ſo, that theſe angry Hornets might not be their own
Carvers. He knew, or at leaſt believ'd, his faults were
not

not yet Capital, yet could not tell what conftruction
might be given, if thofe which were his enemies were
admitted to be his fole Judges; and therefore made rather choice to be at the mercy of a Parliament, than
at their difpofing. He was not without hope to be able
to make an able party in this Affembly, where at worft
he knew he fhould be fentenc'd, rather by fpleen than
fury. This refolution by the King approved, an anfwer
is return'd to the Lords : *That his Majefty having ex-*
amin'd the contents of their Petition, found therein a fair
pretext of Juftice and reafon; and that if their allegations
were fuch as were by them pretended, himfelf would with as
much willingnefs as they could defire, joyn in the act of
Reformation. But for as much as private Paffion maskt it
felf fometimes under the vail of publike grievance, and parti-
cular ends had the pretext of general Reformation, he thought
it expedient to make this rather a Parliamentary *work than*
the act of his Prerogative, *or their inforcement ; which was*
more for their proper Honours, and the good of the whole
Kingdom : which refolution if they thought fit to entertain,
he wifht them to lay down their Arms, which were the
marks rather of an intended violence, than a real defire of
Juftice ; that done, in the knowledg of their approbation, he
would fpeedily caufe his Summons to be fent out for the calling
together of this great *Affembly.* The reception of this
anfwer was not difpleafing to the *Barons*, who defir'd
thofe might be the Judges that had equally fmarted with
the ftripes of this affliction; yet they conceiv'd it not
wifdom to disband their Forces on a bare fuppofition ;
which could not be yet continued, without too much
charge, and too great jealoufie. To reconcile this, they
divide themfelves, every one retaining to himfelf a
guard fufficient to affure his Perfon ; and fo difpofe the
reft, that they might be ready on the leaft Item. Things
ftanding thus, the *Writs* and Proclamations for Election
are fent out, in which there was as much time won as
might be taken without fufpition. Now is there ftiff

labouring on all fides (though not vifibly, yet with under-hand working) to caufe a major part in this Election; which the *Lords* wifely forefeeing (as the main fpring that muft keep all the wheels in their right motion) had be-forehand fo provided for, that the engines of the adverfe Party ferv'd rather to fright, than make a breach in the rule and truth of this Election. The fubjects fenfible of the diforders of the Kingdom, and feeing into the advantage which promis'd a liberty of Reformation, make choice of fuch as for their wifdome and integrity deferv'd it; rejecting fuch as fought it by corruption, or might be in reafon fufpected. This made the undertakers fall fhort and wide of the Bow-hand.

The day of appearance being come, the jealous *Lords* would not rely fo much on the *King*'s good Nature, but that they come up like themfelves, bravely attended with feveral Crews of lufty Yeomen, that knew no other way to win their Landlords favour, but with Fidelity and Valour. Thefe, for diftinction, and that they might be known all Birds of a feather, are fuited in *Caffocks* with a *white guard athwart*; which gave this the name of *the Parliament of white Bends.* *Spencer* feeing the Retinue of his Adverfaries, makes himfelf a Rampire of all his Servants, Friends and Kindred. The *jealous Citizens*, that fometime look beyond their Shop-board, feeing fuch a confluence from all parts of the Kingdom, and fo ill-inclin'd, had a kinde of fhivering phantafie, left while thefe ftrong Workmen fell a *hammering*, the *Corporation* might become the *Anvil.* The *Mayor*, to prevent the worft, doubleth the Guards, and plants a ftrong Watch to keep the Gates and Suburbs. Now according to the ufual Cuftome, the *Speaker* is prefented, and the *King* himfelf doth thus difcourfe his pleafure, which they attend e're they begun this *Seffion.*

My Lords, and you the Commons of the Nether-Houfe!

I

The Barons appear with a ftrong Guard.

The King's Speech to the Parliament.

I have at this time call'd you hither, to crave your aid,
advice, and best assistance. I am inform'd my Subjects
are abus'd, and that the Kingdoms welfare dayly suffers;
such actions I maintain not, nor will suffer. Sift out the
depth of this, and finde the Authors; which found, I'll
punish as your selves think fitting. A Kingdomes weight
depresseth so his Owner, that many faults may scape his
eye unquestion'd; your Body is the Perspicil that shews
him what errours be, and how he may prevent them; which
leads both King and Subject to a settled quiet. Be not
too curious in your inquisition, which wastes but time, and
feeds diseased Passion; nor may you make those faults that
are not, which savours more of Envy than of Justice.
Actions of State you may not touch but nicely, they walk
not in the Road of vulgar Knowledge; these are high
Mysteries of private workings, which fore-right eyes can
never see exactly. You cannot blindfold judge their form or
substance. As all times are believ'd, these may be guilty;
yet let your Judgments make them so, not private Fancy,
which is the Nurse that suckles up confusion. So grave a
Senate should not be the meeting where men do hunt for
News to feed their malice. Nor may you trench too near
your Soveraigns actions, if they be such as not concern the
Publick: You would not be restrain'd that proper freedom,
which all men challenge in their private dwellings: My
Servants are mine own, I'll sift their errours, and in your
just complaint correct their Vices. Seek not to bar me of a
free election, since that alone doth fully speak my Power:
I may in that endure no touch or cavil, which makes a
King seem lesser than a Subject. I know those I affect are
more observed, and Envy waits their actions, if not Ha-
tred; 'twere yet Injustice they for this should suffer, or for
my Love, not their own Errours, perish. What one among
you would not be exalted, or be to me as he whom now you
aim at? Reason and Nature tye me to their limits, else
might you share it in a like proportion.
Ambition, that betrays poor Mans Affections, stares al-
ways

ways upwards, sees nothing beneath it, till striving to
o'rethrow some lofty Steeple, it stumbling falls in some foul
Saw-pit. Perhaps the Court is guilty of some Errours, the
Countrey is not free from worse Oppressions; yet these are
wav'd, as acts unfit your knowledge, which rob and tear
the poor distressed Commons, who must be still possest; my
greater Agents are the contrivers of this publick mischief,
while you by these make good your proper greatness. This
should not be, if you conceit it rightly; 'tis far from
Justice and a due Proportion, one man should fall, and
thousands stay unpunisht, that are more guilty far of foul
transgression. If you would sift, and with impartial dealing sweep from the Kingdom such unjust Oppressors, it
were a work of goodness worth your labour; would leave
to after-times a brave Example. But these Assemblies
think those acts improper, which may reflect upon the proper freehold of those that are most nice, and apt to censure.
I now desire (it is your Soveraign speaks it) you will reform this kinde of strange proceeding; prejudicate not any
till you finde him faulty, nor shoot your darts at one, where
more are guilty. In such a number diversly affected, there
are, I fear, too many thus affected, that this advantage
fits their private rancour, making the Publick Good the
stale and subject, which aims unvail'd at nought but Innovation. These busie-brains, unfit to be Law-makers, let
graver Heads restrain by their discretions; else I must
make them know and feel my Power. I will support and
still assist your Justice, but may not suffer such a fond
distemper. Your Priviledge gives warrant, speak in freedome; yet let your words be such as may become you;
if they flye out to taint my Peace or Honour, this Sanctuary may not serve to give Protection; if so, some
discontent, or ill-affected Spirit may challenge Power to
vent a Covert Treason. But your own Wisdomes, I
presume, will guide you to make this such, that I may
often call you. What more is fit, or doth remain untouch'd; you still shall understand in your progression,

wherein

wherein let Vertue lead, and Wisdome rule your tem-
per.

The King having ended, the several *Members* of this
goodly Body draw together; where notwithstanding
this grave admonition full of implicite direction, they
fall roundly to their business. For forms-sake, they a
while discourse the *petty Misdemeanors* of the Kingdom, to
make a fairer introduction into the *main end* of their
Assembly. A few *Balls* being tost and bandied to and
fro, they begin to crack the Nut where the Worm lay
that eat the Kernel. No sooner was the Vote of the
House discover'd, but informations fly in like Points, by
dozens; no business is discours'd which toucht the dishonour of the King, the grief of the Kingdom, or the oppression of the Subject; but straight flies upward, and
makes a noise that all had one beginning. The general
thus far questioned, the particulars come to a reckoning;
wherein *Spencer* is pointblanck charg'd with *Insolency,
Injustice, Corruption, Oppression, neglect of the publick, and
immoderate advancement of his own particular.* Those few
faint friends he had gotten into this number, more to
express their own abilities, than with a hope of prevailing, hearing these thundering aspersions, rise up to
justifie, or if that fall short, to extenuate the faults of
their glorious Patron; but their *Oratory* prov'd, just like
the *Cause* they strive to defend, full of apparent falshood.
Those nimbler spirits that haunt the Ghosts of corrupted
greatness, seek not to *Undermine* this great Building,
whose structure had so hasty and rotten a Foundation,
but prove in reason, justice, and necessity, that it ought
to be *Demolished* , since it was the Spring that polluted
all the lesser Fountains. The places of *Judicature* being
still *marted*, the Purchaser must *sell* his Judgements;
which was a commerce fit for those that had the worst, and
were most diffident. The *Simoniacal* trading for *Spiritual* promotions, as it dishonoured the dignity, so it must

The Com-
mons
Charge a-
gainst *Spen-
cer.*

R   exalt

exalt such as knew better how to *share* their Flocks than
feed them.   *Bartring* of *Honour* for private lucre, would
ruine the glory of *antiquity* in *blood*, and in another age,
as prodigal as this, make *Lords* as common as *Drovers.*
Possession of so many great *Offices*, as it was an injury to
those of more deserving, so might it in time become a *Mo-*
nopoly for every new-made *Upstart.*   Setling the strengths
and Military Provision in the command of *One* so much *in-*
sufficient, must open the way to foraign loss, or domestick mischief. Planting of the principal Officers of
the Common-wealth by *one* mans corrupt distribution,
must bring all to his guidance, and the Kingdom to confusion. Admission of the Royal ear to *one Tongue* only,
ties all the rest, and resembles the Councel-chamber to
a School where Boys repeat their Lessons. These passages discours'd and *Aphorism'd* at large in the House ; at
the private *Committee*, divers fouler suspitions and aggravations are treated with a greater freedom ; which being
again with their several proofs reported before the
whole Body, by the general doom he is pronunced *guilty.*
This *daring favourite* seeing the violence of the Tide, begins to fear it ; and letting his Anchor fall, hulls out the
full Sea in the Royal Harbour, he strikes his top-sail, yet
contemns the Winds that cause the Tempest, and quarrels
with their Power must be his Judges. This takes away all
hope of reconcilement, and more inflam'd their hearts that
did pursue him. They know he now must fall, or they
must ruine. Lions may not be toucht, till they be sure,
lest breaking loose, they tear those Gins that catch them.
This consideration begets a solemn *Messenger*, well attended with divers Seconds, to make a full relation both
of their *Verdict* and whole Proceedings.

The *Spen-*
cers banish-
ed. The *Lords* being prepossest by their own knowledg, of
all the actions of this *false Impostor*, after a *Conference* and
grave discussion, pronounce their Sentence, *That the*
Spencers, Father and Son, should both be forthwith sent
to live in Exile. This done, a grave Declaration is
made

made by both Houses, and prefented to the *King,* expref-
fing the Tenour of their doom, and reafons moved them
to it. The *King,* as weak in his diftractions, as wilful
in advantage, fees now there was no ftriving, unlefs he
would adventure his own hazard by fuch denial. No
time is now left for difpute; he *ratifies* the Sentence,
and prefent execution fwiftly follows Judgment. Immediately are thefe two great *Courtiers* carryed with more
attendants than they car'd for, unto the Port of *Dover,*
and ftraightways fhipt, to feek fome other Fortune.
The *Son* is no whit dejected, but bears up bravely:
He knew his *Mafter's* Love, and fcorn'd their Malice.
Parting, he takes a filent farewel full of rancour, which
vows revenge, and hopes to live to act it. The aged
Father, whofe Guilt was lefs, and forrow greater, deferv'd in Juftice Pity and Compaffion; his fnowie
Winter melts in tears, and fhews his inward grievance;
bitterly he taxeth his Sons Pride, and his own Vanity,
exclaiming againft the rigour of his fortune, that had
in the laft act of his age caft him fo cruelly from his
Inheritance, and at the very brink of the grave eftrang'd
him from his Birth-right. He confeffeth the improvidence of his errour, which being rais'd by *by-ways,*
fought to keep it. Laftly, he wifheth his behaviour
had been fuch, that in this change might give him help
or pity; but it is the infeparable companion of Greatnefs fraudulently gotten, not by Defert or Vertue, it
prefers falfhood, and a kinde of fhifting juggling, before
a winning truth or goodnefs, which draws with it a firm
affurance. Of all others, it is the moft erroneous fond
opinion, which conceits Affections may be won and
continued in a fubordinate way. They are the proper
Operations of the Soul, which move alone in their own
courfe, without a forc'd compulfion. Other ways may
ferve as temporary provifions, but he that by a juft
defert, and credit of his own worth, hath won the
Love of good men, hath laid himfelf a fure foundation:

The Son
turns Pi-
rate.

tion: This makes his Honour his own, and the Succession permanent to his continuing praise and glory.
These *imperious* Servants thus removed, the elder, in
obedience of his Doom, makes a forreign Climate witnefs his Submission. The *younger*, of a more impatient
and turbulent fpirit, makes the fpacious Sea the centre
of his dwelling. He would not truft to any other Nation, fince his own Climate fo unkindly left him. The
King, yet fcarcely weaned from his forrow, makes yet
fair weather to the parting *Barons*; He thanks them for
their care and great difcretion, which he would ftill ac-
knowledge and remember. Thus *Kings* can play their
parts, and hide their Secrets, making the Tongue the inftrument of fweetnefs, when that the Heart is full of
bitter Gall and Wormwood: They knew he juggled,
yet applaud his Goodnefs, and give him back an Anfwer juftly fuiting; their Tongues feem'd twins, their
Hearts had both one temper, which at the length occafioned all their ruine. And thus with the Enacting
of fome few ragged Laws, He diffolves this Meeting.
Now is the loft *Chamberlain* furrowing up the watery
fides of angry *Neptune*, wafting about the skirts of his
firft dwelling: falling fhort in the poffibility of revenge
of thofe he hated, he vows to make the harmlefs Merchant feel it. What by furprize, and what by purchafe,
he had made himfelf ftrong at Sea, and well provided;
with which he fcowres the Coaft, and robs all comers,
making a prize of all he rifled. Sometimes he flips into
the private Harbours; and thence brings out the Ships
were newly laden: fuch work to thofe that trade by Sea,
breeds ftrange amazement. A *Piracy* fo ftrong and
daring, foon makes the terrour great, the clamour greater; the Councel-table's covered with Petitions, the
Royal ear is cloy'd with exclamations; all ftill enforce
that Trade muft fink and founder, unlefs the *King* the
fooner did prevent it. *Edward* well knew their griefs,
and did believe them; but faw withal it was his *Spencer*

                                                    caufed

caufed them, whom he too well affected to purfue with
danger. He thinks it reafon to eafe *his* grievance ere
he right the *Subject*; let them expect and bite upon the
bridle, that they may tafte the errour of their Judgment. Neceffity in time would make them feek their
quiet, the means whereof he thinks not fit to motion;
yet ftill he thunders out his fhew of anger, and gives
directions that fhipping fhould be rigg'd and mann'd,
well-furnifh'd to bang this Pyrate off from his oppreffion, whom he would take, or lofe the Royal Navy; yet
under-hand he countermands thefe Precepts, pretending
prefent want for fuch provifion as might make good at
full this Expedition; which fhould be done fecurely,
though delay'd... While thus the rage grows out of
this diforder, all Plaints prove fruitlefs; there was no
provifion. The flock of Merchants all appear before
him, letting him know the ftate they ftood in; *Their*
Stocks, his Cuftome muft impair and minifh, unlefs fome
prefent courfe reprefs this Pyrate. The *King* gave Anfwer, *He laments and pitied their Lofs, his Wants, and*
private Dangers, which in the inftant was of fuch a na-
ture, that he had caufe to fear his proper fafety. The
Malecontents, that fifh in troubled waters, were plotting
new Combuftions to act their malice; he underftood their
workings ftrong and cunning, which he was forc'd to ftop
with hafte, or loofe the Garland. This *was the caufe he*
could not yet go onward to help their griefs, which fhortly
he intended; till which, he wifht their grave Deliberations
could fall upon. fome way might ftop the current, and take
off Spencer *from fo curft proceeding, which he believ'd he*
acted by enforcement, rather than Will to wrong his fellow-
Subjects. The *Citizens,* as naturally talkative as fufpicious, parting from the *King* forget their Loffes, and
fall to a liberal difcourfing upon the *King's* words,
what the *Plot* of this great Treafon might be. They
were not without a kinde of jealous fufpicion, left the
City might fhare in the fufferance, if it came to be acted.

The Mer-
chants peti-
tion the
King againft
him.

The Kings
Anfwer.

S   A

A little time brought this news to be the common difcourfe of every Barbers fhop and Conduit. To make
the fufpition more authentical, the *King* makes a ftrong
Guard about his Perfon, fending forth directions to his
friends and all his well-affected fubjects, that they fhould
enable themfelves with the beft ftrength they could, and
to be ready on occafion upon an hours warning. To

The King writes to the Lords. lull the watchful *Lords* afleep, he addreffes unto them
his particular Letters, full of humanity and gentlenefs,
*defiring as he moft repofed on their loves and fidelity, fo
that they would (if the neceffity required) be ready to af-
fift him againft a crew of difordered perfons, who were fe-
cretly contriving both the ruine of Himfelf, the antient Nobility, and the Kingdom; their Plot was not yet ripe, and he
conceiv'd it in the reafon of State, fit to have the Birds flufh
before he caught them.* The *Lords*, that in the firft rumour
fufpected it had fome reflection on their particular, or a
meer noife without ground or fubftance; on the receipt
of this Letter alter their opinion, and believe there was
fome real caufe of this fufpition. They knew the *King*
was wretchlefs, dull, and fleepy, and did not ufe to wake
but when it thunder'd; they think him fhort in depth
of fo much judgment, as with a Jigg of State might catch
them naked. His Letter feem'd a character of truth, but
not of cunning; this kept them free from boubt, but not
from danger.

The Barons Anfwer. They fend back an anfwer gracioufly received; *themfelves, their ftrengths and ftates fhould wait his Pleafure.*
Thefe paffages thus fpent, the *Citizens*, that like no laws
but thofe of profit, do lay their heads together, to finde
out a way how to difpofe things, fo that they might
trade with fafety. A cunning Enginier (one of the
Kings own making) avows there was no means but one
to make things fure, which was, to move the *King* to call
the *Spencers* home, and reconcile them. The fequel was
not fearful, fince this Tryal would make them know
themfelves, and be more quiet; if not, they yet might
be

be in diftance where they might be furpriz'd if they offended. This Propofition findes confent and liking in
the grave Brain of the deep Corporation : in ftead of
punifhment fo well deferved, the *Thief* muft be prefer-
red, to free the paffage; yet to excufe their errour, they
faw the *King* had an itching inclination that way, and
were not without a hope that *Spencer* being by their
means recalled, would, of a profeft enemy, become a
fure friend to the City. This gave them heart to draw
up their Petition, and immediately to prefent it to the
King; who having that he lookt for, in outward fhew
feem'd nothing well contented. *He bids them examine
well the nature of their Petition, which run in a direct line
in oppofition againft a Parliamental fentence, and would
incenfe the reconciled Barons, againft whofe ftrength
he could not well oppofe, but it muft hazard him and all
the Kingdom. Yet if their wifdomes did think fit, in their
affur'd affiftance he would venture, fince he prefer'd their
good before his private. Though Spencer had tranfgreft
his will and pleafure, yet their intreaty fhould difpenfe his
errour, in hope he would become a new-made Subject.* They
cry *God blefs your Grace*; revoke your Judgment, you
fhall command our lives to back your goodnefs. *Edward* thus far on his way, caufeth a *Declaration* to be
made, containing the *requeft* of his faithful fubjects, and
beloved Royal *Chamber* of *London*, at whofe importunate intreaty he thought fit, out of his grace, and tendernefs of the general good, to recal the *Spencers*, who
had given fufficient caution for their future good abear-
ing. This known, foon brings them back to grace and
favour: their petty thefts at Sea muft have a fure way
to trade in; they muft return to fhave and rob the Kingdom, 'twas thought more fit, than they fhould rob the
Merchants. 'Tis ftrange to fee what fhift this poor *King*
made to work his own undoing. But when Religion's loft,
and Virtue banifht, and men begin to trade with flights
and falfhood, the end proves fatal, and doth lead them
blind-

The *Londo-
ners* Peti-
tion for
Spencers
return.

The *Spen-
cers* return.

blindfold into the ways that work their own deſtruſtion. The actions of a Crown are exemplar, and muſt be perfect, clean, upright, and honeſt; their *errours* die not with them, but are *regiſter'd* in the ſtory of their *Lives* with Infamy or Honour: which conſideration may, in juſtice beget a ſincerity and cautelous reſpect from acting under the pretence of policy, thoſe ſtratagems which ſeem, but are not fruit of Royal goodneſs. A like care muſt be had in the limitation of affections, ſo that they enforce him not to thoſe ways, which at one blow take from him his Judgment and his Honour. The *power Majeſtick* is or ſhould be bounded; and there is a reciprocal correſpondence, which gives the *King* the obedience, the ſubject equal right and perfect juſtice, by which they claim a property in his actions; if either of theſe fall ſhort, or prove defective by wilful errour, or by ſecret practice, the State's in danger of a following miſchief. The *Spencers* thus return'd, are reinveſted into their former high and wonted greatneſs: the burnt Child fears the Fire; they know their danger, and not attend the Storm until they feel it. Their *Maſters Plot* they ſecond, and cloſely gain a ſtrength for preſent Action: That done, they appear with confidence, and by main ſtrength ſeek to cruſh thoſe of the adverſe faction. Sir *Bartholomew Baldſmere* is the firſt that taſts the Prologue; they ſeize upon his *Caſtle* of *Leedes* without or Law or Title; he ſues to have his own, but is rejected. Their peremptory return, and the abrogation of that Law that ſent them packing, was provocation enough; there needed not a ſecond motive to enflame the angry *Barons*: but when they underſtood the unjuſt oppreſſion of their confederate, and the daily levies that were underhand made, they then conceive it time to look about them. They finde the fruit of dalliance, and viſibly ſee into the *Kings Plot*, which had abus'd them; condemning their credulity and coldneſs, that had not ſpoil'd the brood while it was hatching. The *King*, who

Sir *Barthol.*
Baldſmere's
Caſtle
ſeiſed.

who had fo oft been catcht, was now more wary; and
refolving to be aforehand with his bufinefs, prepares his
Forces. He knew his Arms, not Tongue, muft plead his
Quarrel; another errour in his Guard, he fufpects, would
make him liable to a more curft proceeding. His *Favou-*
rite, that had his Spies in every corner, is foon inform'd
the Potion was a brewing would give him Phyfick, if
he did not prevent it : the gathering Clouds portend a
fudden Darknefs, which threaten fhowers of Bloud and
Civil Mifchief. He thinks his Guilt above the Rate of
Favour, and vows to wade in Bloud, or die, or vanquifh;
To fuffer ftill, and not to act, he counts it weaknefs;
which makes him ftrive to be the firft Invader. He
wins the *King* to march with thofe ftrong Forces their
forefight had prepar'd, being foon united. The firft
Exploit feizeth the two *Mortimers,* that with an unadvi-
fed fecurity had plaid over their old Game anew on his
Poffeffions. Their Strength was great enough for an
Incurfion, but far too weak to cope with fuch an Army.
Their Refolution was to give the Larum, and then retreat to knit with their Confederates ; but they were intercepted ere they fear'd it, and made the *Tower* the
Prize of their Adventure.

- Thus fometimes it falls out, who acts Injuftice, is
catcht in the fame Net himfelf was weaving. The Lords
with this Report are ftrangely ftartl'd ; they fee themfelves foreftall'd in their own Working ; Arms now
they know muft be their Warrant, or elfe their Lives
muft pay a bitter Forfeit. Their Forces were not yet
fully ready, yet they march on, refolv'd to wait the *Kings*
approach at *Burton.* Time, that runs fwift to Mifchief,
flow to Goodnefs, at length conjoyns their Strength and
feveral Levies; which were not great, and yet believ'd
fufficient to give a Canvas to the Royal Army ; which, as
their Curriers told them, was not mighty. Soon are they
brought to view each others Countenance ; where
Friend againft Friend, and Son againft the Father, Bro-

The King takes Arms.

Seizes the two Morti-niers.

The Barons rife.

T   ther

ther againſt the Brother, ſtood embattl'd : ſuch miſchief
follows ſtill a Civil Diſcord. The *Kings* Force far ex-
ceeds in ſtrength and number, which made the Terms of
hazard far unequal. The adverſe part perceiving well
the danger which they were in, if they abide the Tryal,
condemn their own belief, and Servants falſhood, who
had ſo far fallen ſhort in their diſcovery. But now a
ſecond Deliberation is entertain'd, which adviſeth them
to decline the Battle, and to make a Retreat, till they
were re-enforced. This Reſolution taken from the
preſent ſuſpition, was not more diſhonourable than dangerous : it gave confidence to their Enemies, and de-
jeĉted their own Party, willing rather to try their hands
than their heels, where the peril ſeem'd indifferent : But
the Reaſons given in excuſe were grave and weighty.
The Earl of *Lancaſter* had ſent Sir *Thomas Holland* to
raiſe his Northern Friends and Tenants ; who was marching up ſtrongly and well provided ; ſo that if they
could have adjourned the Battle off to his arrival, it
would have made the Terms more hopeful, if not equal.
It is in the Rule of War eſteem'd a weakneſs to affront
an Enemy for a ſet Battle, with too great diſproportion
in number ; but to recoyl without a marvelous, diſcreet,
and orderly proceeding, is no more than laying the diſ-
heartned Troops to a preſent ſlaughter ; the Experiment whereof was here apparent. The *Lords* riſe, but
ill, and in diſorder, more like a Flight than a diſcreet Retiring. *Valence* Earl of *Pembrooke,* that did command in
chief under the *King,* ſees this Confuſion, and ſtraight
lays hold of ſuch a fair advantage. He chargeth hotly
on the Reer, which ſtraight was routed ; the *Barons*
make a head, but are forſaken ; which makes them flie to
ſeek their proper ſafeguard : With much ado they get
to *Pontefret,* whither the broken Troops at length repair for ſuccour. *Holland* intruſted, performs the work
he went for, and marcht with ſpeed, hoping to give a
Reſcue ; but when he ſaw that their Affairs were deſperate,

The Barons
beaten, fly
to *Pontfreĉt.*

rate, he thinks it his beſt play to change his *Maſter,* and leads his Troops to get the *Kings* Protection. As it deſerv'd, it gains a gracious welcome. Thus all things tend to their Confuſion ; one miſchief ſeldom comes, but many thunder. The deſpairing *Barons* finding themſelves hotly purſu'd, repair to Council, where many ways are mov'd, and none embraced, ſave that ſame *fatal* one which wrought their Ruine. They leap, like Fiſhes, from the Pan that ſcorcht them, into the raging Flames that ſoon conſum'd them. The Caſtle of *Donſtanborough* was believed a ſtrength tenable, until their Friends do raiſe a ſecond Army, or they at worſt might treat ſome fair Conditions : they march to gain this hold, but are prevented. Sir *Andrew Harcklaye* meets them at *Borough-briggs,* and guards the Paſſage ; *Hereford* and *Clifford* ſeek to force it, and like inraged Lions here act Wonders : twice had their angry Swords made the way open, but freſh Supplies oppreſt them ſtill with number, till wearied, not o'ercome, they yield to Fortune, and by a glorious Death preſerve their Honour. When theſe brave *Arches* fell, the *Building* totter'd ; though *Mowbray* made a while a brave reſiſtance, till his Heroick Bloud, not Valour, fail'd him. The ſurprizal of *Lancaſter,* and many other noble *Knights* and *Barons,* perfects this Overthrow, and ends theſe Civil Tumults.

The Prey thus ſeiz'd, the *Spencers* long to taſte it ; and, like to furious Tygers, act their Paſſions : They give not their incenſed *Maſter* time to deliberate on that Work which was ſo weighty, which had the Lives of ſuch great *Peers* in balance. They whet on, and exaſperate the *Kings Revenge,* that needs no inſtigation. Soon is the Work reſolv'd, where deep Revenge hath maſter'd humane Judgment, and Reaſon doth ſubſcribe to private Malice.

Valence, a ſtout and noble Gentleman, hating ſuch a barbarous Cruelty, ſeeks to divert it, and mildly thus intreats the Royal favour.

Valens' Speech in favour of the Lords.

To

To win a Battle (*Sir*) it is glory; to use it well, a far
more glorious Blessing. In heat of Blood to kill, may taste
of *Valour*, which yet on cooler terms may touch of Murder.
Laws were not made to catch offences, but to judge them;
which are dispens'd with where the cause is weighty, else
none may live where many are delinquent.

Celestial Powers have blest you with a Conquest, and do
expect to see how you will use it. For your own Goodness
sake, make known your Vertue; be like to him that gave you
this great Blessing, and then your Mercy will exceed your
Justice. The savage beasts but kill, to kill their hunger;
and will you act in blood to please your fancy? the Heavens forbid the Royal Heart should harbour a thought that
justly may be deemed cruel. Your Sword victorious is im-
brew'd with Honour, let it not savage where is no resistance:
to spill where you may save, obscures your Glory; to save
where you may spill, proclaims your Goodness. I'll not
excuse their faults, or plead their merits, which both are
lesser far than is your Mercy; let not such branches so untimely wither, which may in time be your defence and shelter. Kings are but men, that have their fates attend them,
which measure out to them, what they to others. Blood is
a crying Sin that cries for vengeance, which follows swiftly
those that vainly shed it. Black Apparitions, fearful
Dreams, affright them whose guilty Souls are stain'd with
deeds of darkness. Oh let your purer thoughts be unpolluted, that they may live to shew your Grace and Vertue,
and After-ages speak your worth in Glory.

The *King* had scarce the patience to hear out the
Conclusion of a Theme so contrarious to his resolution
and humour; yet weighing the Integrity and well-de-
serving of the man that spake it, to justifie himself, and
to give him satisfaction, with an angry brow he makes
The Kings Reply. this sudden Answer. *Valence, but that I know you truely
love me, your words do touch too near your Soveraigns
Honour. Shall I, seduced by a female pity, compassion those
that*

that do attempt my ruine ? such actions may be goodness,
no discretion : how many times have I declin'd my Power,
to win them home by mercy, not by justice ? what hath my
mildness won but flat Rebellion, which had it took, where
then had been their virtue ? Say I should spare their Lives
and give them freedom, each slight occasion colours new
eruption, and I may then too late repent my kindness.
When my poor Gaveston *was tane, where was their mercy ?*
They made their Arms their Law, their Swords their
Justice: He had no guilt of Treason or Rebellion, his great-
est fault was this, his Soveraign lov'd him; and shall I
spare those that for my sake wrought his ruine ? No, blood
must have blood, their own Law be their Tryal; let justice
take her course, Ile not oppose it. The deeds of Charity must
so be acted, that he that gives, be not abus'd by giving.
Who saves a Viper that attempts to sting him, if after stung
deserves nor help nor pity. What could they more have
done than they have acted, unless to kill the King they so
much hated; and shall I pardon these sought my destructi-
on, and make them fit to act a new Rebellion ? If it be vir-
tue, 'tis a poor discretion. No, I will make them sure, that
their example may others teach the just reward of Treason.
Dead men do neither bark nor bite the Living.

 Instantly he flings away, and to the general grief of
the whole Army signeth a dispatch for present execution,
without so much as the exception of any one particular
of all the great ones whom this last conflict had thrown
at his mercy. *Lancaster* is beheaded at *Pontefret,* and
two and twenty others, of noble blood and great eminency, in other places of the Kingdom; so that there was
scarce a *City* of any note, but was guilty of this bloody
Massacre. So many excellent lives, so ingloriously
lost, had been able to have commanded a victorious Army
while it had triumpht in some forrain conquest. *Thomas*
of *Lancaster,* a man good and virtuous, though unfortunate, kept faithfully the death-bed promise he made

Lancaster
beheaded,
and 22
more.

V

his

his father *Lincoln*; but erring in the time and manner, he tasted his prediction. The *King*, that was before so apparently guilty of many *puny* vices, by this act loseth all their memory, and dyes himself in grain with the true colour of a cruel Tyrant. The reaking blood of so many brave subjects so untimely spilt, had a quick and bitter reckoning, to the final destruction of him and all the Actors. In the operations of so great a weight, though the colour of justice seem a Warranty; yet mercy should have preceded rigour; since they were not all alike guilty. In point of extremity, it is more safe and Honorable to do less than we may, rather than all we may; the one makes known our goodness, the other the cruelty of our nature, which with a loathed fear thrusts a zealous and true love out of possession in the hearts of those, that behold and observe our actions. Had these *Lords* been of a disposition equally cruel, *Spencer* had not liv'd to triumph in their misery, nor they to taste his malice; for it is clear, when they had him at their mercy, that they sought not blood, but reformation; and assuredly in this their last act, which was rather *defensive* than otherwaies, their intentions towards the *Crown* were innocent. In all respects (saving the levy of their Arms, which was done onely to support it with more Honour) as things fell out afterwards, it had been happy for the *King* if he had lost this Battel, and they had prevailed; for winning it was the beginning of all his ensuing misery, of which the fundamental cause (as appeareth in the sequel) originally sprung; that this bridle being taken away, he fell to those dissolute actions, and injurious kind of oppression, that his Government became hateful, and his Name odious; which wrought in time the general revolt of the whole Kingdom. Fear, and the suspition of the following danger, kept both him and his familiars in a better temper: for though they were fully as vicious, yet they were less confident, and more

reserved,

referved ; which, this *barricado* taken off, finds neither
bound nor limit.

Certainly, in the Regiment of a Kingdom, It is a difcreet and wife confideration in Court and Council to
maintain a divided faction, yea, and interchangeably fo
to countenance them, that the one may be ftill a fit Coun-
terpoife to the other. The King by this means fhall be
ferved with more fincerity and diligence, and informed with more truth and plainneff. Where one particular man or faction is alone exalted and onely trufted,
his words, be they never fo erronious, finde feldom
contradiction, and his unjuft actions pafs unqueftion'd ;
all men under him feeking to rife by him, fing the fame
tune, the Flock ever bleats after the voice of the Bell-
weather; which ftands with a politick wifdome, fince
in oppofition they purchafe but difgrace and ruine. By
thefe means the *Royal* ear is abufed, and the *Minions* acts
are more daring and infolent, who cares ever more how
to conceal cleanly, than to be fparing in doing the actions of injuftice; by this the judgment of the *King* is
impaired, the Honour of the Crown abufed, the Common-wealth fuffers daily more and more, which by degrees aliens and eftrangeth the heart of the fubject. The
greater the heighth is, the ftronger is the working to preferve it, which for the moft part is attended with thofe
fame State-actions of impiety and injuftice; hence fpring
murmur and hatred, exafperated by a continuing Oppreffion which ends for the moft part in a defperate conclufion.
Though the fury of this victorious *King* had fo fully acted his *Tragedy,* yet the *Mortimers* were fpared; but it
was rather out of forgetfulnefs than pity, whofe deaths
had been more available than all thofe which in fo great
hafte had tafted his fury. Some think that the *Queens* interceffion got the refpite of their execution; mainly followed by *Spencer,* who in that act irreconciliably loft her favour ; by the fubfequent effect it feems probable enough ;
but howfoever it was wrought, it appears he was referved

Good Policy
to maintain
a divided
Faction in
Court and
Council.

ſerved to be one of the fatal executioners of the divine juſtice, which taught his perſecutor that ſame antient Roman Law of *Talionis*; and gave his unfortunate *Maſter* ſo ſad a cauſe of a juſt Repentance. The King-dom after theſe bloody Hurly-burlies and ſtrong Convulſions, begins now to be a little ſetled, onely it was fill'd with grief and expectation where theſe aims would end that ran on with ſuch violence. The principal Pillars of the common good being taken away, and thoſe that remain'd being frighted and diſhearined, gave ſuch a liberty to the now great *Officers*, that the whole intereſt of the State was believed little better than the fruits of an abſolute Conqueſt. All men ſuffer baſely, yet no man dares oppoſe or queſtion't. The King ſecur'd, approves his *Spencers* actions, and makes the Regal *Power* the Servants warrant. Hence ſprings the inſolency of unjuſt oppreſſions, and thoſe unlawful ways to drain the ſubject, which leave no means might fill the Royal Coffers. The grieved Kingdom languiſht with theſe burdens; the great Ones ſuffer baſely, courting his vices, which like a tree oregrown, of immenſe greatneſs, ſhadow'd their growth, and did ſuppreſs their merit. They fawn upon the time, and view each other as Ships ſalute at Sea, whoſe Voyage differs; they were become ſtrangers to themſelves and to their fellows, which ſtop the paſſage to ſo juſt a quarrel. The private end was now the thing in faſhion, the publique was forſa-ken as a monſter. The *Commons*, whoſe home-bred looks are the true *Index* of all that dwells within, and honeſt plainneſs, do more than murmure out theſe oppreſſions. They gape to catch the turning tide, and would have moved, but find no one would give them heart or leading. Oft do they make attempts, but yet diſcreetly, to try if they could finde a ſtaff to lean to; but 'twas in vain, the Law was ſuch a terrour, that he that ſtirs and ſticks was ſure of drowning. Now do the Learned *Sages* ſee their errour, that hung themſelves

in

in Chains fo great and many, making a Lime-twig for each feveral feather; now do they blame thofe Laws themfelves enacted, not like a Watch, but as a Paper-Army, to keep the good ftill in the worft condition; as if the multiplicity had been the glory, where Laws are made to catch, not eafe the fubject. If that great volume of the Law draw forth his engines, what fubject can untoucht efcape his rigour ?

Spencer, that knew himfelf thus hated, and that the general cry proclaim'd his bafenefs, finks not his height, nor would go lefs a farding; but makes his mifchief like himfelf, ftill foul, but greater; with reafon yet fufpects and fears the fequel. His *Miftris* fate on thorns, which made her ftartle; he knows the Wheel would turn, almoft with touching. This calls his Wits toge-ther, and puts them on the rack for a Confeffion, what was the way might beft affure this danger. The *King's* weak humour, naturally wanton, he makes more vi-cious, and apparent guilty, hoping to make him alike hateful, that in the Change they both might run one fortune. A pretty Policy, that makes it lawful to wound his *Mafter*, that thereby he may fcape the hand of juftice, or at the leaft may make the hazard equal ! The King he knew was too indulgent, but not tender, or of a heart enough to work the fafety of his Servants, as he obferv'd in the Cafe of his Predeceffor *Gavefton*, and his own late experience. To give him a more re-al engagement, and pin himfelf faft by neceffity, he egges him on to all thofe actions that were more than moft odious in practife, and hateful in the eye of the fubject; feeding him in the mean time with a vain be-lief that the Kingdom was generally ill-affected, and fought his depofition; which there was no better way to reprefs, than by holding them fhort, and making feve-rity rather than paternal love the Hand-maid of his Scepter. In all the actions of State, whatfoever carried a fair glofs, or prov'd well, he takes it upon his proper

Spencer's Policy.

X care

care and diligence; if the success were ill, or not prosperous, it must be esteemed either the will, weak advice, or fortune of his *Master*; in all complaints that spake unjust oppression, he seemed to share the grief, but made the cause the *Kings*, not his which must obey him; he guilds his proper actions o're with shews of kindness, sullying the Royal with his grossest errours, who sat and slept, or winkt at these disorders. This was the substance of his first conceptions; but yet this was too weak to make a ground-work on which he might rely his false proceedings. Time daily chang'd, and new occurrents happen might win another faction to pursue him; for to prevent this fear, he fetcht a Compass, and leaves the beaten way of blood and malice; such of the great ones as were yet remaining, and out of reason might be most suspected, or did but cross his way, by private practice he sends to feed the Worms and kiss their Mother, who knew not her own Children so transformed. When that the Blossomes dropt away (the Gardens glory) the season being sweet, and mildly pleasant, all men admir'd, but quickly knew the reason; some unkind hand had tainted that which fed them. This was too much, but yet he wades in deeper. His Brain is subtle, cunning, wary; an active stirring Wit, a quick invention, an heart grown proud in mischief, full of falshood, that dwelt within a conscience knew no bounder; from these he hammers out another project that works upon the *King* as well as subject. This hath two *forms*, though of a different temper, yet both resembl'd nearly in dependance. The *first* must keep the Crown in fear, the Kingdom busied with forraign danger or domestick trouble; The *second* holds it still in want, the Coffers empty, to keep the subject poor as they supply it; security in one might keep him careless, and peace with plenty make the other wanton. From these, being marshal'd with a sound discretion, he thinks the way was easie to assure his greatness within

his

his breſt alone was lockt the ſecrets of the prime Plots of State and waighty buſineſs; the Councellors, that were but meerly Cyphers, knew but the ſtrains of flight and vulgar motions; he ſat alone at Helm, and ſteer'd the Compaſs, which fancies in his thoughts a vain impulſion; he muſt be ſtill employ'd, or all would ruine; if in the agitations of the *King* or Kingdom puzzl'd with motions of the preſent danger, he could aſſure each party from theſe Harpyes, it needs muſt adde much to his faith and wiſdome, and make his ſtation far more ſtrong and ſure; the reſty mindes that kick at preſent greatneſs, may then turn *Craven*, and approve his judgment; he that conceits he could command the Planets, doubts not to make ſuch trifles light and eaſie. His principles thus laid, he falls to action; with a looſe ſcorn he continues the *French* correſpondence, ſlighting their Treaties and deſire of Friendſhip; the Marriage of a Siſter was not powerful to ſet things right betwixt theſe Warlike Nations; there was no open War, but private grudges, which made the State uncertain, robb'd the Merchant; heart-burning on all ſides, while both ſtrain courteſie who ſhould begin to ſet the balance even! The Scots that were not ſure, but yet were quiet, he irritates afreſh for new combuſtions; but this was done with ſuch a neat conveyance, that all men ſee the Smoke, yet feel no Fire. And to the *Lords* at home that ſtood ſpectators, he pares off from his greatneſs ſome few chippings, and gives them here and there to feed their longings; that they might thus be ſtill, if not contented, he gives away his female Kindred for new Friendſhip, and makes the Portion great, though nothing yet in Title; which turn'd the world backward in appearance; while *January* and *June* were dancing *Trenchmore.* Thoſe *fixed ſtars* that mov'd not with this *Comet*, but kept aloof, and did preſerve their diſtance, theſe he contemns and ſcorns with ſuch proud uſage, that they may ſeek his grace, or ſeem

to

to threaten some jealous danger to his fearful *Ma-*
ster.

  Great Impositions daily are divulged, and some imposed are not fully levied, to make the *Commons* fear,
not feel their ruine. No circumstance is left, that but
induced, to make the *Soveraign* fear, the subject hate him.
The *King*, whose Arms ne'er thriv'd but in the conflict
which winning loft his Honour, caused his downfal,
was in the memory of his former unfortunate proceedings
sufficiently aw'd; and being now given over to the sen-
suality of his delights, entertains quickly the least apprehension of fear, if his supervisor did present it so,
that this part of his work was no great difficulty; and
the *second* was not more uneasie. The Royal *Treasure*
is profusely spent without Accompt or Honour, being
but the *fountain* that served to water the *drought* of himself, his herd of hungry Kindred, and the swarm of
Flesh-flies that became his creatures. The antient *Plate*
is without the art of Arithmetick multiplied into a world
of *little pieces*; the *Jewels* of the *Crown* do leap beyond
the Sea, and are ta'n Prisoners till they pay their ransome; the *Revenue Royal* being now grown weary, by
Proclamation would exchange his Landlord; the Prerogative, the type of Soveraignty, forgets his Patron,
and cleaves to the fingers of some musty Farmor. This
want was great in shew, but more in substance; which made
the *Surgeon* seek to gain a plaister: the Poverty of these
Institutions answer not the Work-mans expectation, for
the Remedy began to seem as fearful as the Disease;
These profuse prodigalities, in stead of a counterfeit,
brought in such a real necessity of such a height, that
without a speedy supply it must beget a desperate hazard. Many several projections are made, but they fall
wholly short, and like Pistols charg'd with Powder, make
a noise, but hit not that they aim at; the hope was
dead, unless the old and right *way Parliamental* did give
it life and spirit. *Spencer* knew well enough that such

Assem-

Aſſemblies was like a *Ringworm* on the neck of greatneſs;
a *Court* that in the bulk of high Corruption would breed a
Palſie, or a *Hectick* Feaver; the ſubject here he knew
would ſee his inſide, which ſingle durſt not quinch,
much leſs encounter. He doubts the *King* would hardly be ſupply'd, unleſs he were expos'd to try their mercy; yet there's no other means, he muſt adventure.
This thus reſolv'd, he leaves it not at random, or doth
reſign his ſtate alone to Fortune; but wiſely makes the
way before he run it. With a reſerved ſecrecy he hides
the Platform, till that his practice might receive perfection. He hurries forth ſtrange news of *forraign* dangers to draw the peoples eyes from private workings;
he makes a ſhew as if all things went currant, and ſha-
dows o're the Royal wants with plenty, yet cloſely
wills his friends and thoſe his creatures to get them
place betimes in this great Meeting. All ſuch as were
the *Kings* entirely, theſe he inſtructeth with the ſelf-
ſame Counſel, and courts all ſuch as he believes are Powerful to advance his ends, or elſe procure him danger;
and to let all the world know he ſtood right in his
Maſters affections, he gets his *Father*, *himſelf*, and Sir
Andrew Harclay, a Chip of the ſame Block, made *Earls*
of *Wincheſter*, *Briſtow*, and *Carlile*; *Baldock* a mean man
altogether unworthy, unleſs it were for being a diſciple
of ſo virtuous a Patron, is made Lord *Chancellour* of
England. The ſolemnity of this goodly *Creation* ended,
and the *Plot* now ripe for execution.

The bruit of a *Parliament* flies through the Kingdom, A Parlia-
ment called.
and is follow'd at the heels with *Writs* for preſent Ele-
ction. The time limited for appearance was ſhort,
which ſpeedily drew this great *Body* together, bleeding
with the freſh memory of the loſs of ſo many of his
brave and glorious Members. All Ceremonies are laid
aſide, or handled briefly, ſo that the time now ſerves
to fall upon the buſineſs. Their pulſes being felt aloof
off, and their temper tryed, there was a full diſcovery

that

that the *major* part was sure, the rest were heartless. Then comes the *King's* Demand, with fair pretences, which pleads the greatness of his charge and present uses; and shews he had on the strength of his Revenue maintain'd the *Scotish* Wars without assistance, which had exhausted so the Royal Treasure, that now He is enforc'd to try his Subjects. This motion is soon seconded by such apt Scholars, as learnt to get the *King's* or *Spencer's* favour; others, that had a hope to share the booty, speak it great reason to assist their *Sovereign*. The *Commons* justly grieved with their Oppressions, would fain have made a head to stop this current; but 'twas in vain, here was too weak a Party, and wants a heart to put it to a tryal; this swayed the *King* the

They give the King the fixth Peny.

sixth peny of the *Temporalty*; and ends this Meeting. When the knowledge of this Grant came into the *Country*, it bred a general Murmur, and quite estrang'd their loves from their subjection, cursing those times that caused so sad a burden. Upon the neck of this (if we may give credit to those *Historians*, that all agree and publish this relation) were many fearful and pro-

Prodigious Sights.

digious *Sights*, which maz'd the people; amongst which this one was most remarkable; the *Sun* for six hours space shew'd himself in perfect *Blood*, and sanguin'd over. The ensuing times that retain'd it in their Memory, and applied it as a Prediction of the sequel, believ'd it did foreshew the King's destruction, which followed swiftly; others conceit it as a *Wonder* shew'd from *Heaven*, as a sure Token of the just Displeasure for the loss of the Noble Earl of *Lancaster* and his Adherents; whose Blood implored Justice and sharp Vengeance. Thus in amazement Man becomes a Prophet.

The *Scotch* invade the *Englifh* Borders and *Ireland.*

The *Scots*, that love not rest, delight in prigging; and considering the Distractions of the *English*, thought it a fit time to fall to action; and with a double blow to vent their malice; one strikes upon the Borders, which
they

they boldly enter, but are repuls'd with little loss or damage ; the other doth invade their Neighbour-*Irish*, where they receive with grief a worser welcome. *Bruce*, the *Kings* Brother, General of this Army, and all his Troops, are killed and broken ; scarce one was left to carry back the News of this Disaster. The *King*, resenting this new provocation, and all the former mischiefs they had wrought him, resolves once more to tempt his *froward* Fortune ; but 'twas not his own Valour, *Spencer* mov'd it, that had his aim beyond his *Master's* meaning ; he knew this was the way to waste that Treasure, which else might breed a fearless fulness : if it succeeded well, the gain and honour would be his share, as well as his that won it, since his advice had father'd first the action : admit it should prove ill, he then was guiltless, it must be deem'd alone his *Soveraign's* Fortune, whose Destiny was such to be still luckless ; however yet, it would keep him so in action, he might at all times yield the groaning Subjects a short account how he had spent their Money. Upon this, a Summons is sent out to call together all the Captains and Men of war ; Provisions are dayly made to wait upon so constantly a resolved Journey : The former Misfortune had taught him to undertake this action strong and soundly ; the *black Ox* had trod upon his foot, that well he knew the danger. The *King's* intentions known, brings him together all the remaining bravery of the Kingdom ; they knew that there was Money store to pay the Souldier, which gives him life to fight, and seek occasion. The cream of all this strength must guard his Person, the other fill the Rere, and make the Vantguard ; with these he marcheth forward and invadeth *Scotland*, making that Nation justly fear the sequel. But whether it were the Infidelity of those about him, the Will of him that is the Guide of Battles, or the proper destiny of this unfortunate *King*, this great Preparation produced no effect answerable to the

Are repulst.

Their General slain.

The King invades Scotland.

the general expectation; he is enforc'd to retire without doing any one act worthy his Memory, or the greatness of such an Expedition. The wary *Scots*, that had kept themselves in their *Strengths* and places of Advantage, seeing the Storm almost past, follow aloof off, and in a watch'd opportunity set upon the tail of his Army, surprizing all his Stuff and Treasure. This loss sends him home to entertain a *defensive* War, which came from the Coast he least expected; whether justly, or to transfer the guilt of his own unhappiness upon the treachery or falshood of another. The new-made Earl of *Carlile* is accused, condemned, and put to a shameful execution. The grounds against him were *probable*, not certain; howsoever, he was believed to have attempted, like *Judas*, the sale of his *Master*, which must be taken a *sole* motive of the inglorious *retreat* of this so brave an Army. The *principal* reason that may lead us to the opinion that he was guilty, may be taken from the *solemnity* of his Tryal, and the *severity* of the Sentence; which upon so grave and full a hearing depriv'd him both of Life and Honour in a ceremonious way, whereof till this there appears no former president. His old friend *Spencer*, whose ends he had faithfully serv'd, left him at plunge; being as it seems well content now he had (as he thought) rooted his own greatness, to be free of his Ambition, which he fear'd might rather supplant than support it. A common course of such as rise by their own or other mens corruption; they love a while their *props*, but after fear them; when with some *Dog-trick* they pick some fain'd occasion, private or publick, for to send them packing. If you survey it well, it stands with reason: for such as to serve their ends would act in baseness, in the least change may do so for another that in appearance must succeed his fortune: besides, where the reward seems shorter than the merit, fills one with grief, the other with suspition; which two can never long hold correspondence; and *Kings* them-

themſelves that do abet the *Treaſon,* do ſeldome love, but always fear the *Traytour.* But now old quarrels ſleep, here comes a new one that uſher'd on the way to *Edwards* ruine.

The French King *Lewis* being dead, *John* next ſucceeds him; a Prince youthful and hot, full ripe for action. He privately informed of the ill uſage of his *Siſter,* and that the *King* was wholly led by his proud *Minion,* whoſe actions witneſs'd he was ill-affected to hold firm Peace but with his own conditions, thinks it fit time to break the *League* which had ſo weak aſſurance. On this he makes an attempt upon the *Frontiers* of *Guien,* and ſends a ſolemn *Meſſage* he would no more continue Peace with *England.* *Edward,* that had not yet digeſted his *Scotiſh* Pills, was much diſpleaſed to hear ſo curſt a Declaration from a *Brother.* *Spencer,* the *ſpring* that gave this difference motion, did little dream it would be his deſtruction; he wiſht theſe *Princes* might fall out and quarrel, but yet not ſo, that it ſhould come to action. He deem'd it not amiſs his Soveraign *Maſter* ſhould hear of War from *France,* but not to feel it. The *French* were of another minde; they ſaw us beaten, and diſcontent within our ſelves, full of confuſion; which gave them hope the time would fitly ſerve them to reunite this *Piece* to her *firſt Honour.* Thus *Kings* play faſt and looſe with their advantage; affinity and *Oaths* are weak reſtrictions; where *Profit* holds the Plough, *Ambition* drives it.

Edward piercing narrowly into the danger, taxeth bitterly the infidelity of his *Brother,* and begins to examine his own condition, whereby he might accordingly order his affairs, either to entertain the War, or embrace Peace, the hopes whereof were not yet deſperate. He findes himſelf in the affections of his own fear'd and hated; his Coffers emptied by the *Scotiſh* ſurprizal, and the *ſinews* of his late Parliamentary ſupplying *ſhrunk* in his Proviſion and prodigality; a ſecond ſupply, unleſs

The French King breaks his Peace with England.

Z   con-

conditional, was doubtful ; the Kingdom was grown too wife, to be again anticipated in election : and *laftly,* he calls to minde the *feverity* of that misfortune that waited fo his *Military* actions, that the fubjects were diffident of fuccefs where he was either *General,* or a party. In this diftraction, while he remains irrefolute, he feeks the advice of his *Cabinet Councel,* the Clofet of his fecrets; he thinks him alone worthy to communicate the depth of his mifery, and to give the refolution.

The King
advifeth
with *Spen-
cer.*

Spencer, that had his underhand *aims,* out of a virtuous modefty appears not till he is call'd; which fucceeding as he knew out of courfe and neceffity it muft, pleads

Spencer's
Anfwer.

his own difability in an affair fo great and weighty, defiring his Majefty that his *Father* and the *Chancellour* might be admitted into this deliberation, whofe maturity of years and ripenefs in knowledg might be rely'd on with more affurance. The reafon of this *reply,* in fhew full of wifdom and care, had a *Plot* with two faces, like the old defcription of *Janus*; the one lookt upon his *father* and faithful *Friend,* whom by this means he thought to advance in credit; the other was more to countenance his own particular, which had a part to play, that muft be (as he thought) his *Mafter-piece.* No word of his founds harfhly, nor found contradiction in his Soveraigns ear, who made his tongue a guide to lead his actions; they are freely admited, and fall to confultation, where the condition of the prefent affairs is fully open'd, and fundry propofitions made to reconcile them : but thefe all prove defective in fome material point or other, that according to the pack, *Spencer* might hit the nail on the head, and by their applaufe make his project more folid and autheutical.

Ever fince the breach that hapned between him and the Queen concerning *Mortimer,* there had been a ftrong heart-burning, and many diftaftful expreffions of the ill inclination fhe bare him. He knew her to be a Woman of a ftrong Brain, and ftout Stomack, apt on all occafions

fions to trip up his heels, if once fhe found him reeling; and was not without fome difcreet fufpicion, that fhe was as well contriving inward practice, as fhe had been clofely forward in the inftigation of her Brother. To make her fure, and to pare her nails before fhe fcratcht him, he thinks occafion had prefented him with a fit opportunity, which he intended not to loofe without a tryal; from which ground he thus expreffeth his conceptions,

Things ftanding as they do (Royal Sir) there is but one way left to right them ; but how that way may like you, that I know not. You are not fit for War, if you confider your proper weaknefs, bare of Strength or Money: to feek, not fue for Peace, is no difhonour, but fhews a pious Will to perfect Goodnefs. A Servants care, I not deny, may work it ; but this will ask Inftruction, Time and Leafure, which your condition cannot fitly limit. Such Treaties, for the moft part, fo are fettled; but 'tis with long difpute, and many windings, by which we muft grow worfe, and they ftill ftronger. If they once finde that we purfue it hotly, they'll raife their height to win their own conditions, which may be far unfit your ftate and greatnefs. I know you love the Queen too much to fpare her, and I am loath to touch the ftring fhould caufe it: But fince great Works are fitteft for great Actors, I wifh to her alone this brave employment ; her Wifdome and her Love fo well united, will work (I doubt not) Peace as you defire; fo fair a Pleader cannot be denied in that requeft, which chiefly made her Wedlock. And fince I am all yours, vouchfafe your Pardon, if I in reafon difcourfe it farther: Admit that he deny, her journey fort not, you ftill are where you were, with fome advantage: If he refufe your Love, you may his Sifter, which is then with him, where he fo may keep her till things are reconcil'd, and quarrels ended. Reafon of State muft mafter your Affections, which in this act will tell you, 'tis unfitting fhe fhould be here, that may

inform

He advifeth the Queen be fent to France.

inform her Brother from time to time of all your secret Counsels. Say that your Love and her Obedience tye her, and keep the Scale still even; 'tis a hazard which wise men dare not trust in female weakness: admitting that her Goodness do assure it, this cannot warrant yet her silent Servants, who may be sent with her perhaps of purpose; or after brib'd to sift and shew your workings. Councels are seldome so reserv'd, but that they glimmer some little light that leads to their intentions ; which if they fly to those they touch unacted, finde swift prevention, ere their worth be valued. These things consider'd, I do speak it freely; 'tis fit the Queen alone should undertake it ; which lessens well the charge of your great Houshold, and brings you Peace; or makes you elfe a Freeman from those domestick Cares that shake your quiet.

This Act ended, *Baldocke* the Chorus, who equally hated the Queen, seconds it with a learned approbation ; and the old Roost-cock in his Country-language, which was the only tongue he was guilty of, tells the King briefly, he should be sure of Peace at home or abroad. The King with an attentive ear hears this relation, and could not but believe his *Spencer* spake it; nor did he dote so much upon his Wedlock, but he could be contented well to spare her, whose eyes did look too far into his Pleasures. But yet his wandring Soul had strange impressions, which struck him deeply with a sad prediction, and made him faintly yield, but yet delay it.

This Overture being come to the Queens ear, and withal the knowledge how this Gipsie had marshall'd his cunning practice, and had prescrib'd the way for her escape, which she herself intended, and in her private thoughts had laboured with the best powers of her understanding ; she seem'd wondroufly well-pleas'd, and offers to undertake, and to assure the bufinefs. Their several ends, far wide of one another, do kindly
meet

She offers to go.

meet and knit in the firſt Prologue ; where Craft encounters Cunning, it ſometimes happens one and the
ſelf-ſame Hood doth fit the head-piece of divers Actors,
diverſly affected ; hence it proceeds the Plot's more
ſurely acted, when each ſide doth believe his proper
iſſue : There is not ſuch a Cut-throat for a Coz'ner, as
that which in his own trade doth croſs-bite him : The
Bee gets Honey where the Spider Poyſon ; and that
may kill Phyſicians, cures their Patients. Such are the
qualities of Stateſmens actions, that labour to contrive
anothers miſchief, and in their own way finde their own
deſtruction. Love and Jealouſie, that equally poſſeſt the
Queen, being intermixed with a ſtronger deſire of Revenge, ſpurs her on to haſten on this Journey. She
ſaw the King a ſtranger to her bed, and revelling in
the wanton embraces of his ſtoln pleaſures, without a
glance on her deſerving Beauty. This contempt had
begot a like change in her, though in a more modeſt
nature, her youthful Affections wanting a fit ſubject to
work on, and being debarr'd of that warmth that
ſhould have ſtill preſerv'd their temper, ſhe had caſt her
wandering eye upon the gallant *Mortimer*, a piece of
maſculine Bravery without exception ; had thoſe his
inward Gifts been like his outſide, he had not been
behinde-hand in reception, but with a Courtly, brave
reſpect, full meets her Glances. A ſilent Rhetorick,
ſparkling Love, findes quick admittance ; ſuch private
trading needs few words or brokage : but his laſt Act
had mew'd him in the *Tower*, where he was faſt from
ſight of his great Miſtriſs Love, that makes ſome men
fools, makes others wary : Had *Mortimer's* deſigne been
known, his head had paid for't ; which *Spencer's* malice long and ſtrongly aim'd at, but that the Queen had
begg'd a ſolemn reſpite, which *Edward* would not
break at his intreaty. The Cage of his reſtraint was
ſtrong, and guarded ; yet 'twas too weak to cloyſter
his Ambition, which did ſuſpect, but never fear'd his

She caſts a wandering eye on Mortimer.

Mortimer in the Tower.

A a Free-

Freedome; which he attempts, but yet was not fo fure;
that he durft truft it. In the mean time, with a fweet
Correfpondencie; and the interchange of many amorous Letters, their hearts are brought together, and their
feveral intents perfectly known ; hers, to profecute her
Journey ; his, to purchafe his Freedome, and to wait
upon her, or elfe to loofe his Life if it mifcarry. It
was a ftrange Adventure in the Queen, in this inqui-
fitive and dangerous time, to hazard her Honour under
the fidelity of a Meffenger; but fhe was well belov'd,
paid liberally, and was not more careful in her election,
than wary in the employment ; which makes things
difficult in themfelves, prove facile and eafie. No fooner had fhe knowledg of the Plot for his efcape, but by
all her beft means fhe confirms and ftrengthens it, and
in the mean time advances her own affairs by all ways
poffible : She courts her Adverfary with all the fhews
of perfect reconcilement. But new delays interpofe ;
the King had certainly fome inward motive that prefag'd his ruine, and that this Wife of his muft be the
Actor ; which brought him flowly on to fet her forward. *Spencer*, that by his own could judge her Cunning, fufpects her plea of hafte and fudden kindnefs,
and now begins to grow a little colder, till he had
better founded her intentions ; which by his Spies he
could not fo difcover, but that fhe feem'd as pure and
clear as Cryftal.

The King
will not
confent to
her going.

　　Yet *Edward* would not give confent fhe fhould be a
gadding; time paft away ; fhe labours hard, but fruitlefs, till at length fhe found fhe was abufed. *Guien*
muft be rather loft, than fhe fhould wander. Her
heart fo ftrongly fix'd upon this Journey, was torn as
much with anger as with forrow: Reafon at length o're-
came her Sexes weaknefs, and bids her rather cure,
than vent her Paflion. The opportunity thus fnatch'd
from her hopes, fhe feems well pleafed, and glad to ftay
at home ; no inward motion feem'd to appear, that
　　　　　　　　　　　　　　　　　　　　　　　　might

might beget fufpicion. *Spencer,* that was as cunning
as a Serpent, findes here a female Wit that went beyond him, one that with his own Weapons wounds
his Wifdome, and taught him not to truft a Womans
Lip-falve, when that he knew her breaft was fill'd with
rancour. When the nap of this Project was fallen off,
and *Spencer* with the King were feeking for fome other
bufh to ftop this gap, her judgment was fo fortunate
as to pretend a Journey of Devotion to St *Thomas* of
Canterbury; which by her jealous Overfeers (being a
Work of Piety) is wholly unfufpected. All things
·prepared, by a faithful Meffenger fhe gives her beloved
Servant *Mortimer* knowledge of the time, and her intention. Then, with the Prince her Son and Comfort,
that muft be made the Stale of this great action, fhe
fearlefs ventures on this holy Journey. The King
was well content that fhe fhould be abfent, and pray
to whom fhe would within the Kingdom; Her jealous
eyes fo watchful, had enforc'd him to take by ftealth,
what now he gets in freedom. *Spencer* is not difpleafed, but well contented, that wifht fhe would remain
an abfent Pilgrim. A fhort time bringing her to the
Shrine of her pretenfions, fhe makes as fhort a ftay,
but hafteth forward. *Mortimer* inform'd the Plot was
now in action, puts on his practice for a prefent tryal.
Some fay that with a Sleeping-drink he charm'd his
Keepers; I rather think it Drink that made them fleepy:
Whatever 'twas, by this he ftole his Freedom, and
flylie fcapes away unfeen, untaken. At the Sea-fide he
findes his Royal Miftrifs and the young Prince prepar'd
to go a Ship-board; the Earl of *Cane* and Bifhop of
Hereford ready to attend them; and he now comes, to
make the Confort perfect. All things fucceeding thus
fortunately, they loofe no time, but embarque, and
weigh their Anchor. *Winchelfey* had the honour of
their laft farewel, that did provide them fhipping.
Their Sails hoift up, the Heavens they finde propitious,
the

Pretending a Journey of Devotion,

She embarques for France with Mortimer.

the bluftering winds were quiet, and *Neptune* bears them without a rugged brow of angry billows; a pleafing fore-right Gale (as kept of purpofe) fills up their Sails, and brings them fafe to *Bulloigne*. Thus did our Pilgrims fcape the pride and malice of him which little dream'd of this Adventure: his Craft and Care, that taught him all thofe leffons of Cunning Greatnefs, here fell appa-rent fhort of all Difcretion, to be thus over-reach'd by one weak Woman. For her Efcape, it skill'd not, nor could hurt him: it was the rifing Son with caufe he fea-red; which who would have trufted with a Mother, juftly mov'd by their diforder? Where now were all his Spies, his fawning Agents that fed his ear with every little motion that did but crack within the Kingdom? Now it Thunder'd, they were afleep, as was their *Mini-on*-Mafter, elfe he would fure have feen, and foon pre-vented fo lame a Project, that pac'd afoot fo long a walk, fo foftly. But when the glorious power of Hea-ven is pleafed to punifh Man for his tranfgreffion, he takes away the fenfe and proper power by which he fhould forefee and ftop his danger.

The King fad at the News. This news flies fwiftly to the King, who entertains it with a fad heart, as juftly it deferved. The *Spencers*, with the Crue of their dependants, are nettl'd with a tale that ftarts their greatnefs; they think the Plot was furely laid, that took fo rightly; and in the makers Wit, condemn their Judgment, that led them by the hand to what they acted. *Mortimer*, whom *Spencer* deadly hated, was well ally'd, and ftrong in Friends and Kindred; he had a Caufe in hand would win affiftance, when that a Queen and an heir apparent back'd it. But now 'twas paft prevention; 'tis a vertue to make the beft of that we cannot fly from.

Edward, whofe yielding heart at firft mifgave him, grows fadly dull, and feems to read his Fortune; his melancholy thoughts have no impreffions but fuch as were engrav'd within his confcience. To take him off,

Spen-

Spencer contemns the danger, extenuating their beſt hopes, which were but fixed upon the French, a nation light and inconſtant, whom Money would take off, if Force ſhould fail him : he tells him he had cauſe to ſmile, not mourn, that was ſo freed of ſuch a Chamber-miſchief, that was more to be fear'd at home, than with her Brother. Laſtly, he prays him to be like himſelf, a Monarch, that well might bend, and yet not yield to Fortune ; 'twas now high time to order ſo his buſineſs, that there might be no farther fear of danger. *Baldock* the Chancellour ſets to a helping hand to revive his Spirits, which ſeemed ſo much dejected ; and briefly thus diſcours'd his better judgment.

Spencer encourageth him.

Sir, If you now ſhould droop, or ſhew a faintneſs, when your occaſions do expect your Valour, your ſubjects will believe you know more danger than they or ſee or fear ; which muſt be followed with a dull coldneſs over the whole Kingdom ; which what it may enforce, you may conſider. 'Tis eaſie to o'recome a weak reſiſtance, which yielding, fears the ſtroke before 'tis coming ; but nobler hearts are ever moſt triumphant, when they are round beſet with greateſt perils. Alas, what can the Queen a wandring Woman compaſs, that hath nor Arms, nor Means, nor Men, nor Money ? Think you her Brother will ſo back her paſſion, as to expoſe himſelf to ſuch a hazard ? France knows our Arms too well, too much , to tempt them, or come within our diſtance in our dwellings : admit he ſhould , what can he do to England , which hath a wooden wall will wet his courage ? Lewis, that had made him a ſure Party within the Kingdom long before he landed, when civil tumults had embroil'd our Forces, found here ſo ſharp and hotly curſt a welcome, as left your Predeceſſor ſoon his firſt poſſeſſion : he came in his own right, and yet forſook it ; can you then fear they'll venture for another, or hazard War that look for no advantage ? Put caſe they do, have you your Forces ready, you need not fear the French or any other : but you must then by your own sprightful carriage give life and courage to the *Valiant Souldier*; that fights your *Quarrel*, and his proper *Honour*; like to a careful *Steward*, still provided to give the new-come *Guest* a handsome *Welcome*. And, if I erre not; 'tis not much improper you let the Kingdom know the *Queens* departure, how far it swerves from duty, love, or reason. *Dangers* that be far off, may be prevented, with time, advice, and with a better leasure; yet 'tis discretion to catch the foretop of a growing evil : look to your *Ports* : your *Navie* well provided, no forraign *Force* can wrong your *Peace* or *Quiet*. For those within-door that may breed suspition; the ways are easie to secure their moving. Yet all this is too little, if you stagger, or with a drowzie coldness seem disheartned : 'tis life and action gives your *People* metal. For Gods sake then (great *Sir*) leave off this *Passion*, which wrongs your *Greatness*, and doth maze your servants; that see no cause but meerly your *Opinion*.

This Speech thus ended, the King forceth himself against his disposition, and cloaths his cheeks with smiles, his brow with gladness : with a more freedom he discourseth plainly the present state of his entangled business : a Declaration is sent out to all the Kingdom, that taints the Honour of the Queen, but more his Judgement.

The Queen is tainted.

The Ports are all stopt up, that none should follow : a Medicine much too late ; a help improper, to shut the Stable-door, the Steed being stoln : but 'tis the

The Ports are stopt,

nature of a bought Experience, to come a day too late, the Market ended. The Navie is sent out to guard the Frontier, and Watch and Ward is kept throughout the

the Navie sent out, and Watch and Ward every where.

Kingdom. These and many other grave Instructions are recommended to the *Spencers* wisdom, whom it concern'd as deeply as their welfare : they think not fit to trust the Care to others, but do become themselves the Supervisors ; which for a time of force enforc'd their absence ; in which short intermiss, the King relapseth to

his

his former errour, which gave him many sad and deep impreſſions : he thinks the breach of Wedlock a foul treſpaſs ; but to contemn her he ſo much had wronged, deſerv'd as much as they could lay upon him : But he was guilty in a higher nature ; he had upheld his Paraſites to brave her with too too fond a baſe preſumptuous daring : he fear'd his cruel actions, ſtain'd with bloud, would chalenge a quick and ſad requital, equal vengeance : he ſaw the Subjects full of grief and paſſion, apt and deſirous to embrace Rebellion ; and few or none declar'd themſelves to aid him, unleſs 'twere ſuch as ſtirr'd by meer compulſion, or private intereſt of their own ſafety. Such dull conceits did ſo ingroſs his fancie, that he almoſt deſpair'd of his own fortune. His Minions, now return'd from their employment, had much ado to level theſe deep reckonings ; which lay ſo heavie on his guilty Conſcience : yet at the length he gain'd his wonted temper, and acteth o'er afreſh his former Errours.

The cuſtomary habit of tranſgreſſion is like a Corn that doth infeſt his owner ; though it be par'd and cut, yet it reneweth, unleſs the Core be rooted out that feeds his tumour. The guilty Conſcience feels ſome inward motions, which flaſhing lightly, ſhave the hair of Miſchief ; the ſcalp being naked, yet the roots remaining, they ſoon grow up again, and hide their baldneſs : the operations of the ſonl of true Repentance, grubs up the very depth of ſuch vile Monſters, and leaves alone the ſcars of their abuſes.

The French King having notice of his Siſter's arrival, entertains it with a wondrous plauſible and ſeeming ſhew of gladneſs. After ſhe had well refreſh'd her ſelf and her little Son, (as yet a ſtranger to the riding of ſo long a journey upon a wooden horſe) with an Honorable attendance, befitting more her Eſtate, Birth and Dignity, than the preſent miſerable condition ſhe was in, ſhe is waited on to *Paris* : all the great ones and
bravery

The Queen entertain'd in France with ſeeming gladneſs.

Bravery of that Kingdom are fent to give her welcome, and to bring her to the King's prefence. When fhe beheld the Sanctuary of her hopes, her deareft Refuge, fhe falls upon her knee, and with a fweetly-becoming modeftie, fhe thus begins her Story. Her Royal Brother unwilling to fuffer fuch an Idolatry from her, that had a Father, Brother, Husband, fo great and glorious, takes her up in his arms, when thus fhe fpeaks her forrow.

The Queens
Addrefs.

Behold in me (dear Sir) your moft unhappie Sifter, the true picture of a dejected Greatnefs, that bears the grief of a defpifed Wedlock, which makes me flie to you for help and fuccour. I have, with a fufferance beyond the belief of my Sex, outrun a world of tryals: time leffens not, but addes to my afflictions; my burthen is grown greater than my patience: yet 'tis not I alone unjuftly fuffer; my tears fpeak thofe of a diftreffed Kingdom, which, long time glorious, now is almoft ruin'd. My blufhing cheek may give a filent knowledge, I too much love and honour the caufe of my afflictions, to exprefs it. Yet this in modeftie I may difcover; my Royal Husband is too much abufed; his will, his ear, his heart is too too open to thofe which make his errours their advantage: the hope of his return is loft; he ftill muft wander, while fuch bewitching Syrens are his leaders. But why do I include them as a number? 'tis onely one; the reft are but his creatures. How many of his brave and nobler Subjects have fold their lives to purchafe him his Freedom? All expectation fails; domeftick Quarrels have ta'en away their lives, that ftrove to help it: unlefs you pleafe your Arms fhall difinchant him, he ftill muft be abufed, his Kingdom grieved. I had not elfe thus ftoln to crave your favour. Made to your hand, you have a way is glorious, to let the world behold and know your vertue; Fortune prefents you with a juft occafion to crown your Glory with an equal Goodnefs: would you difpute it, can there be a motive more weighty, than to fuccour thefe poor Ruines which elfe muft lofe their portions, being Birth-right?

*right ? See here, and view but with a just compassion,
two Royal Plants depreſs'd, and like to wither, both Branches of the Flower-de-luce, the Root you ſprang from ;
which, but in you, have neither hope nor comfort. Would
your impartial wiſdom but conſider how good a work it is
to help diſtreſſes, a wronged Siſter cannot be forſaken, and
an Heir of ſuch a Crown be left unpitied. In ſuch an act
of Goodneſs and of Juſtice, both heaven and earth will
witneſs your true Valour, and your poor Handmaid joy in
ſuch a Brother. Let it not breed ſuſpicion, that I ſeek you
with ſuch a weak, forſaken, poor attendance : I was enforc'd to ſteal away at randome, and durſt not by my number be diſtruſted, by thoſe with Argus eyes obſerv'd my
actions. Though I am here, and thoſe behinde that love
me, beſides the Juſtice of my Cauſe, the ſtrongeſt motive,
I bring the hearts of a diſtreſſed Kingdom, that, if you ſet
me right, will fight my Quarrel : their Truth needs no ſuf-
pect ; you have for Warrant their Queen and Miſtris, with
their King that muſt be. Then, gracious Sir, extend your
Royal vertue. I challenge by that purer Bloud, aſſiſtance,
whereof my Birth-right gives me equal portion : let not ſucceeding Ages in your Story read ſuch a taint, that you forſook a Siſter, a Siſter juſtly griev'd, that ſought your Succour.*

Her willing tongue would fain have moved farther ;
but here the fountain of her eyes poured forth their
treaſure; a ſhowre of Chryſtal tears enforc'd her ſilence ;
which kinde of Rhetorick won a Noble pitie : the Paſſions of the minde being ſweetly mov'd, the heart
grows great, and ſeems to ſympathize their agitations ;
which produceth a ready willingneſs, that calls to action the foot, the hand, the eye, the tongue, the body, till
that the Engines ſlack that cauſe this vigour ; and then
they all revert to their firſt temper. The Queens diſcourſe and tears ſo far prevail'd, the King and all his
Peers are deeply moved ; their longing hearts beat

ſtrong-

The King
and his
Peers mo-
ved at her
diſcourſe.

strongly for expreffion, which might affure her, they
embrac'd her quarrel, and with their Lives would venture foon a tryal : Her Brother bids her caft her cares
to his Protection, which would make *Edward* know
and feel his errours ; his greater Subjects offer her their
Service, and vow to be Companions of her fortune.
The general voice of *France* proclaim'd a fury ftrain'd
to the height, to punifh her Oppreffors. This overture
for a while is fo hotly purfued, that fhe (poor Queen)
with an abufed confidence believ'd things as they feemed in fhew, true, perfect, real. 'Tis not alone her
errour, but a difeafe all flefh and blood embraceth ;
with eafe we credit what we wifh and hope for : yet
where fo great a Confequence waits on the action, there
is juft caufe to fear and doubt the fequel. Though
that our aims be juft, difcreet, and hopeful, yet if they
be confined to certain hazard, or do reflect upon the
private danger ; of that fame fecond hand that is engaged, reafon in juftice ftrengthens the fufpicion. To
right the Queen, and to reftore her Heir ; to eafe the
Subject, punifh the Oppreffor ; all thefe are works thus
far feem good and eafie : but thefe, not Will, but Power and Strength muft compafs, againft a potent King in
his own Kingdom ; which if it fell out well, return'd
with honour ; if ill, endanger'd *France* with an Invafion, which might perhaps prove fatal and unhappie.
Wife men are mov'd in Paffion, not in Judgment, which
fifts the depth and core of fuch great actions, weighing
the danger and advantage, with the hazard and dependance ; which if they turn the Scale, or make them e-
ven, takes off the edge of their propenfe affections,
which Caufe affwag'd the heat of this employment.

Spencer eyes
the *French*,   *Spencer*, whofe watchful eye was fixt on *Paris*, by his
Perfpectives fees the glorious welcome that waits upon
the Queen and her attendants ; he hears no other News,
but what provifions were made in *France* to ferve for
but fears
them not. War in *England* : he is not frighted, or a whit diftem-
                                                        pered

pered ; he knew the *French* were giddy, light, inconftant , apter for Civil Broyls than Forraign Triumphs ;
beginning more than Men , but in conclufion weaker
and more uncertain far than Women : he taxeth yet his
own improvidence , that gave the angry Queen fo fair
advantage; 'twas not the Power of *France* he feared,
nor all their threatnings, but the inteftine danger,
which feemed fearful : He knew the Subjects hearts
were quite eftranged ; which did expecting long for
fome Combuftion : feverity of Laws had kept them under ; 'twas not in duty, but by meer compulfion, which
backt by Forraign aid ; and fuch brave Leaders, would
break their Chains upon the leaft Alarum.

To take off *France* , he ftraight felects his Agents,
fuch as well knew the ways of thefe employments, and
lades them o'er with Gold, and found Inftructions ; bidding them freely bribe, and promife mountains, till they
had undermin'd and crofs'd the Queens proceedings : he
bids them charily obferve the quality of time, and place,
and perfon, proportioning their Rates with fuch difcretion, that thofe which moft could hurt were deepeft laden. Thefe Pinaces of State thus fraighted , arrive at
Paris , where the heat was almoft cool'd before their
coming ; yet they go on to make the bufinefs furer :
they fet upon the Pillars of the State, and feel their Pulfes ; who wrought like Wax againft the glorious Sun-
fhine of brighter Angels , which came fhowring downwards, and ftruck them dumb and deaf for oppofition :
Gold in an inftant chang'd the Council's temper , and
conquer'd without blowes their valiant anger. The
Queens diftreffed tears are now forgotten ; they gave
impreffions, thefe a real feeling : words are but wind, but
here's a folid fubftance ; that pierc'd not the ear , but
hearts of her affiftants.

The Plot full-ripe, to make it yet more perfect, they
fet upon the King, and fhew the danger. To force by
Sea a paffage into *England*, was a defigne as truely weak

as

He bribes them.

as hopeleſs ; where wants a Navie, and the full proviſion might give a ſure Retreat, or certain Landing. To
cope at home with ſuch a potent Kingdom, requir'd an
Army full of ſtrength, and mighty; which muſt be ſtill
ſupply'd with Men and Money ; which not ready here
in ſuch abundance , a Womans paſſion was too weak a
motive to levie Arms alone on that occaſion, which
brings no other gains but meerly Honour. The Engliſh
Nation were not ſo affected unto their Miſtris Quarrel,
as to venture legal revenge ; or elſe inteſtine rapine ;
which they muſt hazard , if they looſe ; or vanquiſh.
Laſtly , a bare relation of a female paſſion enforc'd the
Cauſe ; which whether true or falſe, was yet in queſtion ;
the Plaintiff had been heard, but no Defendant. Theſe
were the Reaſons which are daily tender'd to take the
French King off from his intentions ; which lov'd to
talk of War , but not to act it. A ſmall perſwaſion
quickly fills his ſtomack , that could not well digeſt a
War with *England.* Young Kings that want Experience, have not Judgment to touch the marrow of
their proper buſineſs, and ſound the depths of Councels : For Adviſers may be abuſed, and bought and
ſold to miſchief, while Servants raiſe their gain from
their diſhonour. This being ſo frequent, 'tis a Royal
Virtue, that hears, and ſees, but gives no reſolution in
things of weight, till he have reconciled his own with
judgment to the Councils reaſons : if that it be above
his reach that is in queſtion, let him not ſo rely upon the great ones, that their words prove a Law, which
have their workings, that aim more at their ends, than
his advancement. As Kings have Councellors of State
to eaſe their Burden, ſo ſhould they have a ſecond help
to guard their Honour ; a leſſer body of ſelected good
ones, whoſe wiſdomes privately inform him rightly of
what in goodneſs is moſt fit his judgment. State-
actions fill the Purſe, but foul the Conſcience ; and
Policy may bloom the Profit, blights the Honour,
which

which Kings fhould keep as tender as their Eyefight.

Though thus the fquares that fed her hopes were altered, the Queen is ftill led on with promis'd Succours, which at the upfhot meet with new excufes. She feeing thefe delays, and vain protractions, begins to doubt and fear there was fome juggling ; yet bears it ftrongly with a noble Patience, fhewing no Difcontent or leaft Sufpicion; hoping at worft that here in fafety fhe and her Son might anchor out their troubles. The Pofts that daily fly 'twixt *France* and *England*, had liberally inform'd the ftate of French Occurrents. *Spencer* inform'd the gap was ftopt on that fide, provides to quiet all at home if he could work it : he fets upon the difcontented Barons; that hated him, and envied more his Fortunes : he courts their favour, and imparts Promotions that might betray them, more with fhew than profit : he makes the Gentry proud, by giving Titles that feed ambitious mindes, but not content them ; and takes off from the People light Oppreffions , but keeps afoot the greateft Grievance, that kept them down from hope to fhake his Greatnefs. All fides do entertain it with a feeming gladnefs , though well they knew it was enforced kindnefs.

While each part thus diffembles their intentions, the Navie was call'd home; a Charge was ufelefs, where was no fear might caufe a forraign danger : the Ports were open'd, and the Watch furceafed that day and night attended on the Frontier. This hafte, as 'twas too fudden, wants affurance : the rifing Son was abfent, and ftill lookt for , while the declining dipt his cheeks in darknefs. To eafe this care, the Queen is ftrongly tempted by fuch as feem'd her friends, but were his Agents, to reconcile her felf unto her Husband, whom henceforth fhe might rule as fhe thought fitting. When this fell fhort,fhe is at leaft intreated to fend back her young Son, the Kingdoms comfort; which took it ill he fhould be made a Stranger, or in the power of a forraign Na-

D d

tion.

tion. Thefe fweet enchantments move no whit her yielding; that too well knew the Serpent that begat them; her Son fent back, they had the prey they lookt for, and fhe muft lack the prop muft keep her up-right.

This Project failing, they fall upon a new one. The King frames a Letter to his Holinefs, full of humility and fair obedience, yet craving help, and bitterly complaining that *Ifabel* his Wife had fled his Kingdom, pretending a m Voyage of Devotion, and had ftoln away his Son, his only comfort, attended by a Crue of trayterous Rebels, that ftrove to break the Peace of Chriftian Princes; amongft which one being 'tane in actual Treafon, had efcap'd his Prifon by a lewd Inchantment, whom he had caufe to fear abus'd his Wedlock. Laftly, the *French* King, his Alley and Brother, received and kept them, being often fummon'd to defift and leave them. The Pack of this complaint fo well contrived, was not oppofed by the *French* King's Council, who could be well content, that by commandment, their importuning Guefts were fairly quitted; Neceffity would colour actions of unkindnefs, if Houfhold-Laws were broke, or thofe of Nature. This Letter runs from hence to *Paris*, from thence to *Rome*, by that fame practick Agent, that in this Interlude had won the Garland; he bears a Picklock with him, that muft open the gates that were faft fhut to guard the Conclave: his firft Arrival finds a fair reception: Where Money makes the Mart, the Market's eafie. Thefe goodly glofes guilded o're with fhadows, muft win belief where there was none to anfwer: Had they been juft and true, the fact was odious, and might in Juftice challenge reformation; it was enough that here it is believed fo, the Fact was fully proved, the Reafon fmother'd. The Cardinals, that freely felt the *Englifh* Bounty, perfwade the Pope it was both juft and pious, fo great a Mifdemeanour fhould be queftion'd,

King *Edward* complains to the Pope.

ftion'd, that gave the Chriftian word fo lewd Example. On this flies out a prefent Admonition to the *French* King, that ftraight he free his Kingdome of this his Sifter-Queen and her Adherents, on pain of difobedience, Interdiction.

While this Device was moulding, out of *England* the Queen receives a large, but fecret Summons, that all her friends were ready to attend her with all things fitting on her firft arrival : more than the plagues of *Egypt* did opprefs them, which they nor could nor would endure longer: they bid her haften her return ; though her provifion were not enough, their Swords fhould fight her Quarrel. She with a joyful heart receives this offer, which like a precious Balm, clos'd up the wounds of her fad thoughts, made dull with her fufpicion. More to advance this weighty work declining ; fhe tells the King the tenour of this tender. His clouded brow, the character of Paffion, difcover'd foon the fignes of alteration, which yet feem'd more of Pitie than of Anger : he had but then read his Italian Summons ; which he plucks forth, and cafts his drooping Sifter , bidding her view, and wifely there confider; what danger he was in by her protection. The amazed Queen, when fhe beheld the Sentence , in ftead of help, would rob her of her refuge, fhe falls upon her knee imploring pitie, if not to give her Aid, to right her Honour, which was eclipfed with fo foul a Slander. A fhowre of mellow tears, as milde as *April*'s, thrill down her lovely cheeks, made red with anger : dearly fhe begs at leaft but fo much refpite until his Holinefs might be informed, her innocence was fuch fought no favour, but that the Law fhould give upon full hearing. She doth implore him that he would compare her adverfaries malice with his cunning, who not contented with her deep oppreffion, fought to betray at once her Hope and Honour, wrought with fuch art, and fuch a clofe conveyance, that here her Judgement had outrun her Tryal.

He

The Pope admonifhes the *French* King to quit the Queen.

She is enticed to return into *England.*

She tells the *French* King.

He fhews her the Popes Sentence.

He nothing forry for fo fair a warrant that took him off from charge and future hazard, and yet withal would cover fuch Unkindnefs, feems to lament the caufe, and his condition, that of neceffity muft yeeld obedience: he could not for her fake at one blow hazard the danger of himfelf and his whole Kingdom. Not to forfake her wholly, he perfwades her to entertain a

Perfwades her to Peace.

Peace; the King her Husband fhould yeeld to her Conditions: he'll effect it, that had a power to force it in his denyal; which he would venture, if the World gainfaid it. *Let him* (quoth he) *then ufe you ill, or not receive you, I'll make him know I can and will revenge it: fmall time is left you to confider or difpute it; advife with fpeed, and let me know your anfwer.*

She relates it to the Bifhop, *Cane*, and *Mortimer*.

The amazed Queen abandoned and forfaken, relates at full this far unlookt-for paffage unto the Bifhop, *Cane*, and *Mortimer*: their valiant hearts make good their Miftris forrows, and tell her they would fet her right with-

Who advife her not to return.

out the French-men; bidding her not confent to her returning, though it were foder'd up with fhowers of kindnefs: fhe well enough did know her Husbands humour, which would obferve no Vow, no Oath, no Promife: if *Spencer* once more feiz'd her in his clutches, fhe fhould be furely mew'd, and kept from Gadding. Mor-

Mortimer ftorms.

timer contains not in this ftrain his Paffion, but breaks into the bitternefs of Anger, taxing the *French* as bafe, unkinde, perfidious, that knew not what belong'd to

The Queen moderates.

love, or valour. The Queen, that knew the danger, mildly calms him, letting him truely underftand his weaknefs, that in fuch provocation might beget furprifal, when they muft be fent back without prevention. Though that her heart were fir'd, and fwoln with anger, fhe temporizeth fo, 'twas undifcovered: a whifpering murmur, mutter'd from the Courtiers, fays, that fhe fhould be fent with fpeed for *England*: fhe feigns to make provifion for her Journey, yet unrefolved which way to fcape, or whither; yet with this preparation fhe

be-

beguil'd the *French* that had cozen'd her ; for they had bargain'd to fee her fafe at home, and re-deliver'd. Being thus irrefolute, of means, of friends, of fuccour unprovided ; the Mafter failing, fhe attempts the Servants, who fing their Mafters tune by rote *verbatim* ; *they cannot give her fingle help or comfort.* Declining mifery that once is finking, findes it felf fhunn'd like fome infectious Fever, and goes alone in fhades and filent darknefs. Fortune's bright Sun-fhine walks with more profeffors, than her refplendence hath or beams or ftreamers ; but if her glory fink, or be eclipfed, they fhun her fall, as children do a Serpent : and yet fuch tryals guide not wretched Man's election. Affection, (that forfakes in choice the Judgement) is led alone by form, and not by fubftance ; which doth betray with eafe where it is trufted : if Vertue guide the choofer, the beginning is mutual goodnefs, which ftill ends in glory. The very height and depth of all Affliction cannot corrupt the worth of fuch a Friendfhip, that loves the Man more than it loves his Fortunes. The raging Storms and Winds may blow and batter, yet ftill this goodly Rock makes good his Station. The correfpondencie of firm Affections is purely innocent, fincerely grounded : if Private ends or Worldly aims o'er-weigh them, they then are but a meer Commerce and Traffick, which hold no longer than the Bargain is driving. Where Truth apparently doth warrant Love and Friendfhip, it lives and dies, but never changeth Colour. But to proceed : the Queen in this Diftraction findes, paft her hope, an unexpected Comfort ; this Heaven can do, when flefh and bloud's at weakeft. *Robert* of *Arthois*, a man both wife and valiant, that loved Goodnefs for her own fake, not for fafhion, at her firft coming tender'd her his Service : he was a well-refolved fteady States-man, not led by Complement, or feign'd profeffions : he had been abfent during all this paffage ; returning, hears and pities her Condition, blaming her Nations falfhood, and her

Robert of Artois.

misfortune, which he resolves to help out with his best Counsel : he seeks and findes the Queen, whom, sadly musing, he interrupts, and thus revives her spirits.

His Speech.

Great Queen, It is the more excellent part of Wisdome, with an equal Vertue to entertain the different kindes of Fortune ; this Peregrination of ours is a meer composition of Troubles, which seem greater or less, as is the quality of that heart that bears them : I must confess, you have too great a portion, the Justice of your Grief doth truely speak it ; but Tears and Sorrow are not means to right them. Just Heaven doth graciously behold and pity those that do with an active Hope implore it, and work as well as pray, the deeds of Goodness : your tender Sex, and former great Condition, have been a stranger to these bitter tryals ; a little time will make them more familiar, and then you will confess your Passions errour. They soonest perish yield to their Afflictions, and see no journeys end that tire with burden. For your own Vertues sake, resume your spirits ; your Sorrows are not such as you believe them. Behold in me, your true and faithful Servant, a resolution fixt to run your fortune ; you may no longer hazard your abode or being in this unworthy and unthank-ful Climate, paved o're and closely made to your destruction. Wherefore if my advice may sway your judgment, let speed and care prevent so sure and great a danger. Near to this place the Empire hath his Confines, where many Princes are may yield you Succour ; at worst, you there may finde a sure Protection, which in your Native Soil is more than doubtful. I will not yet presume to teach your judgment, that can much better sway your own Condition : Only I lay before you truly my Conceptions, which have no other aim than for your Safety. Your Wisdome may direct your best advantage, which I will second with my Life and Fortunes.

Which infinitely joys the Queen.

Infinitely was the Queen joy'd with his Relation, which weighing the quality of the man that spake it,
seem'd

feem'd juftly worth embracing : She findes it was fincere, not light or verbal, which makes it felf a partner
of her Sorrows ; fhe doubles many Thanks, and gentle
Proffers of true requital, which her Son performed
when he himfelf was forced to leave his Country.
Straight fhe provides to follow his directions, and with
a wary and fecret carriage, fettles her felf for her intended Journey ; yet ftill gives out fhe meant to go for
England, whither fhe fends a Poft to treat Conditions,
with Letters fmoothly writ in all fubmiffion ; and courting *Spencer* with a world of kindnefs ; fhe lets him know
that fhe relyed folely upon his Love to be the Mediator.
Unto her Royal Brother fhe difcourfeth, that now fhe
underftood the Peace was finifht, which made her firft
a ftranger to her Husband, who now would haften home
to make it perfect. And to the Council, which well fhe
knew were bribed to fend her back perforce, if fhe deny'd it, fhe more and more extols and praifeth *Spencer*,
as if 'twere he alone had wrought her Welfare. The
Englifh thus abus'd, the *French* deluded, both are fecure ;
fhe was providing homewards, which made the one remifs, the other carelefs ; elfe fhe, foreftall'd, had found
her Project harder. In this her courfe fhe fees but fmall
appearance, and few fuch Hopes as might induce Affurance ; yet fhe refolves to hazard all, and wander, rather than to return thus unprovided. Could fhe in reafon look for any Affiftance from Strangers, when her
Brother had denyed it ? or could fhe think the *Germans*
would be faithful, when her own Birthright had for gain
betray'd her ? Alas, fhe could not ; yet enforc'd, muft
venture that in her Hopes, could finde no other Refuge.
Neceffity, the Law of laws, makes Cowards valiant, and
him content that hath no Choice to guide him ; which
from the Barren'ft ground expects fome Harveft, that
elfe in danger would defpair and perifh. All things
prepar'd, and her Attendants ready, fhe takes a folemn
Leave, and thanks her Brother, affuring him fhe nothing
more

more defired, than that fhe might but live to quite his
Kindnefs.   His Anfwer, like his Gifts, was fhort and little.   And thus fhe leaves the Court, in fhew contented :
with a fad heart, a watry eye, a paffion highly inflam'd,
fhe journeys forward till fhe came nearer where the
Bounders parted.   The limits of ingrateful *France* fhe
then forfaking, gives them this parting Blow, to eafe her
Sorrow.

Her Farewel to France.

Farewel (quoth fhe) *farewel, thou glorious Climate,
where I firft faw the World, and firft did hate it ; thou
gaveft me Birth, and yet denyeft me Being ; and Royal
Kinred, but no Friends were real. Would I had never
fought thy Help or Succour, I might have ftill believ'd thee
kinde, not cruel : but thou to me art like a gracelefs mother,
that fuckles not, but bafely fells her children. Alas ! what
have I done, or how offended, thou fhouldft deny my life her
native Harbour ? Was't not enough for thee in my Diftref-
fes to yeeld no Comfort, but thou muft Expel me, and, which
was worfe, Betray me to my Ruine ? The pooreft foul that
claims in thee a dwelling, is far more happie than thy Royal
Iffue : but time will come thou wilt repent this Errour, if
thou remember this my juft Prediction ; my Off-fpring will
revenge a Mothers Quarrel, a Mothers Quarrel juft and fit
for Vengeance. Then fhalt thou feek and fue, yet finde more
favour from him thy Foe, than I could win, a Sifter.*

With this fhe weeping ends, and paceth forward,
the Wheel of Fortune turning : Grief grown greater,
few real Friends attend it, falfe forfake it : Infidelity,
the Plague of Greatnefs, is commonly at full, when
Hope doth leffen ; and ftrives to make the Tide of
Sorrow greater.   *Stapleton,* Bifhop of *Exeter,* who till

The Bifhop of Exeter forfakes the Queen.

now had faithfully follow'd the Queens party, and
made himfelf a fharer of her action, with an unnoble
prefident doth now forfake her, feeing the *French*
hopes vanifh'd, and thofe remaining hopelefs ; exami-
ning

ning the grounds of her adventure, almoſt as ſhort in hope as in aſſurance, he ſlily ſteals away to his old Maſter, which wins him Grace, but loſt his Life and Honour. Some think him from the firſt not found or real, but a meer ſtalking-horſe for *Spencer's* Cunning: but this hath no congruity with Reaſon. The Queens departure unknown and unſuſpected, in which he was a prime and private Actor, had he at firſt been falſe, had been prevented, at leaſt the Prince's; which had marr'd the project. Neither can I believe ſo mean or baſely of that ſame Reverend Honour of his Calling, that it would be a Conduit-pipe to feed the ſtomack of ſuch a tainted, foul, polluted Ciſtern. By this Treachery the reſolutions of the Queen are fully diſcover'd; the Landskip of her Travels ſoon ſurvey'd, begets a more ontempt than fear of danger. The coldneſs of the French King being underſtood, their flat denial yet contents not *Spencer*, who did expect his bargain for his Money: Had he had but the Prince, they had dealt fairly, while he was being in their proper power. But they, to juſtifie themſelves, profeſs it freely the Queen had gone beyond them with their Cunning; They thought ſhe had been homeward bound, as ſhe divulged. Thus Womens Wit ſometimes can cozen Stateſmen. Now are the *German* Natures ſifted, and their Motions, who fight but ill for words, and worſe for nothing. Their Conſtitutions dull and ſlow, were fitter to guard a Fort, than to invade a Kingdom. The Queen was bare of Money, void of Credit; which might beget them Valour, her aſſiſtance. Theſe were conceptions pleas'd our Minions fancy.

Time, that at length outſtrips the longeſt journey, hath brought our *Engliſh* Pilgrims into *Henault*. The Earl, a man was truely good and noble, reſolv'd ſo Royal Gueſts deſerv'd as brave a Welcome, eſteeming it a Vertue fit his greatneſs, to be the Patron

Is bravely welcomed by the Earl.

F f   of

of Majeſtick Ruines : He had a Brother youthful, ſtrong, and valiant, one that lov'd Arms, and made them his profeſſion ; this man obſerv'd the Queen, and ſees her ſorrow, which deeply ſunk, and mov'd a ſwift Compaſſion : when he beheld a Miſery ſo great and glorious, a ſtructure of ſuch worth, ſo fair and lovely, forſaken, unfrequented, and unfurniſht, by the curſt hand of an unworthy Landlord, he vows within himſelf to help repair it : He tells her, he pitied her Misfortune ; his heart as well as eye did bear him witneſs : He promis'd her his Service and Aſſiſtance, which he would both engage in this her quarrel ; and ſeems right glad of ſuch a fair occaſion to ſhew his Valour in ſo brave a Quarrel.

So fair a Morning made the Evening hopeful : By thoſe ſweet looks of her diſtreſſed Beauty, and the beſt language of ſo rich a Pleader, ſhe doth confirm his well-diſpoſed Affection ; whoſe willing offer ſeem'd more than Courtſhip. The gallant *Henaulder* engag'd, makes preparation to ſet upon this glorious Work, this great Employment. Pity, that ſtrains the Nerves of vertuous Paſſions, moves faſter far, when that which gives it motion doth reliſh Beauty, Juſtice, Goodneſs. The Tongue that harſhly pleads his own compaſſion, is for the moſt part entertain'd with like reſpondence ; when humble Sweetneſs, cloath'd in truth and plainneſs, invites the ear to hear, the heart to pity. Who by a crooked fortune is forced to try and to implore the help of Strangers, muſt file his words to ſuch a winning Smoothneſs, that they betray not him that hears or ſpeaks them ; yet muſt they not be varniſht o're with Falſhood, or painted with the terms of Art or Rhetorick ; this bait may catch ſome Gudgeons, but hardly him that hath a ſolid Judgment. 'Tis more improper where we ſue for favour, to ruſſle boyſterouſly, or grumbling murmur ſome unſavoury Prayers ; which ſeems to threaten rather a kinde of force, than hope

of

Margin notes:
His Brother pities the Queen,

and promiſes his Service.

He makes preparation.

of pity: So begging Souldiers fright a Country-Farmer.

The Earl being a man well broken in the affairs of State, having a knowledge of this his Brothers resolution, thinks it tasted more of Heat than sound Discretion; he condemns his haste, and blames his promise; and sending for him, with a grave, yet mild discourse, doth thus present the danger:

To undertake a War, is far more weighty, than hand to hand to fight a single Combat; the one needs many strengths; the other skill and valour. Who thinks with his own arm to gain a Conquest, may sell his Life, and yet not purchase Honour. I pity, as you do, this Royal Lady, and would assist her too, if I were able; but to attempt where is no hope to vanquish, makes Foes of Friends, and Friends far more unhappy. France has refus'd, a strong and warlike Nation; that King, a Brother, wisely waves the quarrel; he knows the English Strength, and so digests it, that he'll not undertake a War so hopeless. Think you your self more prudent, strong, or able, than is the Power and Strength of France *united? Or can you dream the* English *may be conquered by a few forward Youths that long for action? Do not mistake the work of your Adventure, which is too sad and great for greater Princes. I do commend your forward Valour, noble Pity; it shewes a vertuous Zeal and Will to Goodness: but measure well the act ere you begin it; your Valour else must have a lame Repentance. Where is the Sinew of the War that must maintain it? Nor she nor you have Arms, or Means, or Money; and sure Words will not conquer such a Kingdom. Yet if you will be fixt, on God's Name venture, I'll help you what I can: I'll be no Party. True Valour dwells not with an overdaring, but lives with those that fight by just discretion, where there is Hope at least, if not Advantage. Could you but credit the beginning, that in reason the world might think*
                                                                                        it

*it had a touch of Judgment, I must confess I should ap-
prove your Valour ; but you can only countenance your first
motion with confidence beyond the Moon or Planets : Then
leave betimes, before you be engaged, which after must
much more impair your Honour. We'll both assist her with
our Purse and Forces, yet do it so, the quarrel seem not
ours.*

Sir *John* with a quiet and attentive patience hears
out his Brother, knowing his admonitions sprung from
an honest Heart and grave Experience, yet thinks
rob'd by Age of youthful Vigour ; from which belief
he draws this sudden Answer.

His Answer.

*Sir, If all the world forsake this Noble Lady, my single
arm alone shall fight her quarrel ; I have engag'd my Faith,
and will preserve it, or leave my Bones within the Bed of
Honour. No After-age shall taint me with such baseness,
I gave a Queen my Vows, and after broke them. Such
presidents as these we seldom meet with, nor should they
be so slenderly regarded. The Mother and her Son, the
Heir apparent of such a Kingdom, plead in Justice Pity ;
Nor shall She basely be by me forsaken. Reasons of State
I know, not your own Nature, do take you off from such a
glorious Action, which your own Vertue tells you is full of
Goodness. Then sit you still, cry ayme : I'll do the business. Inglorious* France *may shame in his refusal ; nor
will I follow such a strain of baseness. Although no
Sister, 'tis a Queen that seeks it ; a Queen that justly merits Love and Pity. I have some Followers, Means, and
some Friends and State to stick too ; I'll pawn them all
ere she shall be forsaken. I know I can in safety bring her
thither, and she hath there her Friends will bid her welcome. That King hath lost his Subjects hearts, grown
sore with grievance ; his Minions hatred will be our
advantage : Admit the worst, her expectations fail her,
we then can make retreat without dishonour. But*

Edward

Edward then may chance revenge the quarrel; we have
those pawns will make our own Conditions; the King in
the remainder being ours, they'll buy our Peace, and not
incense our Anger. I'll not deny, 'tis good to weigh the
hazard; but he that fears each danger, shall do nothing,
since every humane Action hath Suspicion. I am resolv'd
your Love shall still command me; yet give me leave to be
mine own elector. I canot blaunch this act which I am
tyed to, without the taint of shame and foul dishonour,
which I will rather dye than once consent to, although
your self and all the world perswade me.

These words spoken so full home, with such a brave
resolution, stopt all reply, and farther contradiction.
The Queen, who had already a French and an Italian
trick, was jealous lest she here should taste a Flemish
one. The Earl's Speech had given her a doubtful belief, that he had been temper'd withal, seeing his first
temper so much cooled: She knew well enough, if
Money could prevail, it would be tender'd freely;
and she must then be bought and sold to mischief.
Many of her Domestick Spies were here attending, as
she well knew and saw, to work her ruine. Spencer
'tis true had sent his Agents hither with like Instructions,
and their Bills of lading; but here they finde their pains
and labour fruitless. The Earl was himself, not led by
Counsel; and had a heart of steel against corruption,
though he was loath to back alone this quarrel; which
did proceed from Want, not Will to help her: yet he abhorr'd the very thought of selling his Fame and Honour
by so foul Injustice. Yet those that had the charge were
not so hopeless, but that a little time might hap to work it:
As all Courts have, his had a kinde of people, and these
were great ones too, that boldly warrant and undertake
to undermine their Master; which dayly fed them more
and more with Money, while they give only words in-
stead of payment. The Briber trades but on poor ad-

G g　　　　　　　vantage,

The Queen
declines to
grant her
request to
the Earl,
her jea-
lousy.

The Queen
jealous of
Treachery.

Spencer's A-
gents fru-
strated.

vantage, that buys but Hope, and that at beft uncertain; which often fails, although 'tis dearly purchas'd: And reafon good, fince this may be a Maxime; Corrupted mindes, that to do the actions of Injuftice will prejudice the Soul and Confcience, by the contracting of a wicked enterprife for gain or lucre, will never refufe, in hope of a greater advantage, to fell themfelves to a fecond mifchief.

The Queens doubts increafing, fhe importunes the haftning her journey:

But without need.

But now, the Queens doubts increafing, and her longing grown to the height of her expectation; fhe is enforced with more importunity to haften on the advancement of her Journey: fhe makes her winning looks (the handmaids of her Hopes) exprefs their beft ability, more to enflame the heart of her Protector. But alas! thefe motives need not; ambition of Glory, the natural operations of Pitie, and the honeft care of his engagement, had made him fo truely hers, and careful of this defigne, that he leaves no means or opportunity unattempted, that might fet it forward. Already had he gotten together Three hundred well-refolved Gallants, that vow to live and dye in this fair Quarrel. Here was the body of this preparation, the pillar that this Enterprize muft ftick to. Confidence is certainly, in the actions of this nature, a fingular Vertue, and can work Wonders; elfe we cannot but believe this little Army fcarce ftrong enough to conquer fuch a Kingdom. The Queens hopes muft in reafon have been very defperate, if her Domeftick expectation had not been greater than her forreign Levy: But more could not be had, without fome doubt, more hazard, and a longer protraction; and thefe are believed fufficient to try their fortune, if not to mafter it. They ftay not therefore to attend the gaining of a multitude, which might at their arrival rather beget fufpicion, than win affiftance. If the intelligence kept touch, they were fure of Men enough, and they had Leaders.

Spencer's purloyning Brokers feeing the flood coming, which

which yet would, as they thought, at beſt prove but a
Neap-tide, ſince they fail'd in the deepeſt Myſtery of
their employment (for here was room for no corruption) reſolve yet not to make their labour altogether
fruitleſs, but to give their great Maſter a true touch of
their willingneſs and ability; the remainder of that
Money which fell ſhort in the Maſter-piece, they employ to gain a true and full underſtanding of the
height and quality of this Army, and principally to
what part it was directed. Gold, that makes all things
eaſie, fails not in this his forcible Operation; which
brings unto them the information of the Men, Arms,
and number, with the quality of the Navy that was to
waft them, and the very Haven intended for their place
of landing. Though, the Circumſtances duely conſider'd,
the bulk of this Enterprize was in it ſelf contemptible
enough; yet to improve their own diligence, they
extenuate and leſſen it in their advertiſement; they
ſend away a forerunning Poſt, to anticipate the doubt,
and foreſtal the danger. But now all proviſions are
ready, and attend the moving of theſe hopeful Adventurers. The Queen with a lively look, the Pre-
ſager of her future fortune, takes a ſolemn leave of
her kinde Hoſt, with many hearty thanks, which muſt
ſtand for payment till ſhe had recover'd the ability to
free the reckoning; which after ſhe, as truely, performed, by matching the King her Son to a Daughter of
the Houſe of *Heinault.*

 At *Dordrecht,* the Prince and She with their Retinue
are led a ſhipboard, whence they depart and ſteer
their Courſe for *Dongport*-haven, which was the place
reſolv'd on for their Landing; that part being held the
fitteſt and the readieſt to give them ſuccour. The Heaven, that favour'd their deſigne, was more propitious,
and from their preſent Fear procures their Safety.
Spencer being largely inform'd of their intentions, had
made a ſound proviſion, to give them a hotter welcome

than

The Queen
embarques
at Dort.

than they could withstand or look for, had their directions held as they had meant them. Scarce had they run the Mornings-Watch, the Skies grew cloudy, a sullen darkness spread all o're the Welkin; the blustering Winds break loose with hollow roaring, and angry *Neptune* makes his Level Mountains: The watry Element had no Green-sickness, but curled banks of snow that sparkle fury. These Callenders at once assail the Vessel, whose Lading was the Hope and Glory of a Kingdom; the wooden House doth like a Mew triumphing, bestride the angry Billow; and as a Horse well-mannag'd, doth beat his Corvet bravely, without the hazard of his careful Rider.

She is frighted at Sea. The Queen, that knew no Flouds, no Tempests, but those which sprung from Sighs and Tears of Passion, grows deeply frighted, and amaz'd with danger: The little Prince, that ne're had felt such motions as made him deadly sick without disorder, takes it unkindly; and with sick tears laments the hansel of his first profession to be a Souldier. All are confus'd; the Mariners dejected, do speak their tears in language seem'd to conjure. Three days together tost and tumbled, they float it out in hope without assurance; in all which time the poor distressed Vessel durst neither wear a Band, or bear a Bonnet. The violence at length being somewhat swaged, and the bright Sun appearing, smiling sweetly, they finde themselves in view of Land, but where they knew not, nor thought it fit by landing to discover. While thus irresolute they rest debating, a second doubt enforc'd their resolution; their Victual was too short to feed their number till they could tack about for some new Harbour; a fault without excuse in such employments; this made them venture forth at *Harwich* to try their fortune:

She lands at *Harwich*. Unshipping of their Men, their Arms, their Luggage, was long in action, and with much disorder; three days are spent in this; while they are forced to make

the

the naked Sands their strength and bulwark. This made great *Spencer's* errour most apparent; the least resistance here, or shew, or larum, had sent them back to Sea, or else surpriz'd them; a little strength at Sea had stopt their passage, or made them lawful prize by such a purchase: But After-wits can help precedent Errours, if they may be undone, and then new acted. Yet to excuse this oversight, in shew so wretchless, 'twas his Intelligence, not Judgment fail'd him: knowing the weakness, he esteem'd his vantage in suffering them to land secure and certain: He would not blaunch the Deer, the Toyl so near, which he was confident would give possession of those he had so long pursued and sought for. To raise a Guard to wait upon each quarter, if it were Wisdome, might be no Discretion, as his affairs then stood; such motions promis'd rather a Guard to bid them welcome, than resist them: as it would cause a fear, so 'twas a Summons to such as were resolv'd to back their Party: He made that place alone secure, where he expected, and they themselves resolv'd to make their landing; the rest he leaves at random, and to Fortune, rather than make things worse by more Commotion.

But now this weather-beaten Troop march'd boldly forward, finding as yet few friends, but no resistance: Whoso had seen their Body, might have deemed they had been come to rob some Neighbour-Village, rather than bent to bid the King to such a Breakfast. St. *Ha-mondes*, an Abbey of black Monks, had the honour to give their long-lost Mistriss the first Welcome: Here She receives a fair and free refreshing, and yet but a faint hope of present succour, without the which she knew her case was desperate. The bruit of this strange Novelty was here divulged; which like a Thunder-shower, or some Land-water that had drown'd the Marshes, and o'reflown the Level, doth make the Cattle run to seek for succour: But when they knew the bent of her in-

H h   tentions

Marching forward. She is refresh'd at St. Hamonds Abbey.

tentions not fixt to rifle, but reform the Kingdom, they come like Pigeons by whole flocks to her affiftance. Soon flew the News unto the grieved Barons, whofe itching ears attentive, long'd to meet it : It doubled as it flew ; and ere it toucht them, three hundred *Henaults* were ten thoufand Souldiers. They lofe no time, for fear of fome prevention. *Henry* of *Lancafter*, whofe Brothers Death and proper grievance inflam'd his heart with Grief, his hand for Vengeance, with a ftrong troop of Friends and ftout Attendants, was the firft great one that encreas'd her Party; while many other brave and noble Spirits do fecond him themfelves, and all their Forces. By thefe Supplies the Queen and her great Strangers are quickly cured, and freed from their firft Quartane that fhak'd their hopes with fo much agitation.

Lancafter firft joyns her.

The flumbring King had flept out all the Prologue of this fad Tragedy, which he fufpects would end in blood and mifchief: As in his pleafures, in this weighty bufinefs he had rely'd fecure on *Spencer's* Wifdome ; but now the hollow murmur of his danger thunder'd fo loud, that he enforc'd, awakes, and fees nought but the face of a defpairing Sorrow : each day brings news of new revolt, each hour a Larum, that threatned guilty Souls with Blood and Vengeance : His ftartled Council frighted, fainting, hopelefs, fall to furvey the ftrength of their purfuers ; but while they are a regiftring their Forces, they are inform'd the Storm grows ftrong and greater, and like a Ball of Snow increas'd by motion. Their proper Weaknefs, and the Ill-affection of thofe which fhould defend their Soveraigns quarrel, makes action doubtful, and the end as hopelefs ; fo that no certain way remain'd to ftop the current. Now is the Errour tax'd, and Judgment blamed; that neither barr'd the Gates, nor ftopt the Entry, fince in the Houfe itfelf was no affurance. Now is the Cruelty that judg'd the Barons dearly repented, which was

The King is defpairingly forrowful: his Council ftartled.

come

come for vengeance. Now is the Tyranny of all that
Grievance, which had abus'd the King, and robb'd the
Kingdom, condemn'd by his own Actors, as a motive
in Justice fit to be reform'd and punish'd. Lastly, the
purchase gain'd by such corruption as sold Promotions,
Places, Justice, Honour, yields no assistance, but doth
prove a burden, which bruis'd the hearts and thoughts
of them that bare it. Affliction, fittest Physick, sole
Commandress for all diseased Minds, polluted Bodies,
when she doth sharply touch the sense of our transgressions, begets a Sorrow, and a sad Repentance; making
us know our selves and our own weakness, which were
meer strangers to our own Conditions: This she effects
in all; though full Repentance be a work proper to a
true Contrition, which by amendment makes her
Power more perfect. A Minde that's prepossest, by
Custome hardned, with a resolved Will, that acts Injustice, observes the first part of her Precepts; sadly
sorry, yet 'tis not for his actions, but those errours
laid him open to so curst a tryal: The point of Satisfaction or Amendment it thinks too deep a ransome,
hard a sentence, which easeth not, but addes to his
misfortune. If here might end the end of mans Creation, this had some colour for such crafty Wisdome;
but where Eternity of Bliss or Torment doth wait upon
the Soul, that leaves the Body a prey to Death, and
to a base Corruption, it is an act of madness to betray
it with humane Policy, without Religion. Actions of
goodness must be truely acted; not sacrificing part, but
all the Offering, observing every point that is requir'd
to make up a Repentance full and perfect. This Lesson is too hard for those great Babies that suck the
milk of Greatness, not Religion. The Fundamental
part being fixt to get unjustly, believes a restitution
more improper, which makes their cares and former
labours fruitless, and in an instant blights an age of
gleanings: These be the Meditations of a Statesman,
grown

grown plump and fat from other mens Oppreſſions; they live in doubtful pleaſures, dye in terrour; what follows after, they do feel for ever.

Our Councellors, though they were deeply toucht with cauſe, had yet no leaſure but to deliberate their proper ſafety, which findes a poor protection, dull, and hopeleſs. Their Enemies rejoyce; their Friends turn craven, and all forſake the pit before the battle. Neceſſity, that treads upon their heels, admits no reſpite; they muſt reſolve to fight, or flye, or ſuffer: This makes them chuſe that courſe which ſeem'd moſt hopeful, to temporize, which might beget advantage; the fury of this ſtorm in time would leſſen; the giddy motions of the Vulgar ſeldome laſted, which throng to all that tends to Innovation: A Kings diſtreſs once truely known, would win him ſuccour; ſince thoſe which break his peace not ſeek his ruine. With theſe vain hopes he ſeeks to guard the City, and make the *Tower* ſtrong of all Proviſion; knowing that he which hath but *London* ſure, though all the reſt be loſt, may yet recover.

The King ſuſpects the City of *London*.

But *Edward* will not hear to keep the City; their multitude he fear'd would firſt betray him: He knew they were a crew of weaker Spirits, for fear would ſell their fathers, or for profit; they never ſift the Juſtice, or the quarrel, but ſtill adhere and ſtick to him that's ſtrongeſt: had he ſtill kept this Hold, and took the *Tower*, but with the ſtrength he had, and might have levied, he then had bridled up the wavering City, and kept his Adverſaries at a bay too long and doubtful for their affairs, which were but yet uncertain. The guard of this place he commends to *Stapleton* Biſhop of *Exeter*: This Charge did not properly ſuit with his profeſſion, unleſs 'twere thought his tongue could charm Obedience: but he already had been falſe, betray'd his Miſtriſs, and with more reaſon might be now ſuſpected. It ſeems they had no choice, and ſtrong

preſum-

presumptions the City would not long remain obedient : if so, the fact, was worse and more unworthy, to leave so good, a friend in such a hazard. The King, with *Arundel* and both the *Spencers*, with small attendance get them hence to *Bristow* : His Army was much less in his own Kingdom, than those the Queen had rais'd by forreign pity. This Town was strong and able, well provided, and had a Haven, whence in occasion they might venture further : But, yet the King might have the same suspicion, which made him leave and quit the strength of *London*. *Arundel* and *Winchester* do undertake the City, *Edward* and *Bristow* would make good the Castle; here was the refuge they resolve to stick to; which in the Citizens assurance, seem'd defensive.

Betakes himself to *Bristow.*

The Queen understanding the Royal Chamber was forsaken, and left to the custody of the Bishop her old Servant, that had given her the slip in her Travels; quickly apprehends the advantage; addressing a fair, but mandatory Letter from her self and her Son to *Chickwell*, then Lord Mayor, to charge him so to reserve and keep the City to their use, as he expected favour, or would answer the contrary at his peril. Upon the receipt of this Letter, he assembles the Common-Council; and by a cunning-couch'd Oration, the Recorder makes known the Contents; which is no sooner understood, but the general Cry, that observ'd the Tide turning, proclaim it reason to embrace the Queens Party; who was so strongly provided to reform the Disorders of the Kingdom. *Stapleton* having gotten the knowledge of this passage, sends to the Mayor for the keys of the Gates, for the Kings assurance, and his proper safety; who being incens'd with the affront of this inconsiderate Bishop, apprehends him, and delivers him to the fury of the enraged multitude; who neither respecting the Gravity of his Years, or the Dignity of his Profession, strike off his Head, without either Arraignment, Tryal, or Condemnation: This brain-sick and heady act had too

The Queen sends a mandatory Letter to the Mayor of *London*, to keep the City for her and the Prince.

Bishop *Stapleton* beheaded by the Multitude.

I i   far

far engag'd them to reconcile them ; they muſt now
either adhere ſolely to the Queen, or to taſte a bitter
Penance. The King had an ill Memory in point of
deſert ; but the actions of ſo unjuſt a Diſorder he kept
regiſtred in braſs ; until he gain'd the opportunity of
Revenge ; then he never fail'd it. It was a mad part,
on ſo poor an occaſion, to act ſo bloody a Tragedy,
which took away all hope of Reconciliation, if the
Wheel had turned : However the ſquares had went,
they were upon terms good enough, ſo long as they
contain'd themſelves in any temperate condition : But
this was a way which incens'd the one part, and not
aſſur'd the other. But the actions of this ſame heady
monſter Multitude never examine the Juſtice, or the
dependance, but are led by Paſſion and Opinion ;
which in fury leaves no Diſorder unacted, and no Villany unattempted. But certainly this was a meer cunning practice of the Mayor, who being underhand
made ſure to the adverſe Party ; reſolv'd to make it of
a double uſe ; the one, to help on the opinion of his
devotion to the Queen, in the puniſhment of him that
betraid her ; the other, by this action to make the
Citizens deſperate of favour, and ſo more reſolute ;
who elſe, being mutable as Weather-cocks, might alter
on the leaſt occaſion. Let the conſideration be what
it will ; the Fact was inhumane and barbarous, that
ſpilt, without Deſert or Juſtice, the Blood of ſuch a
Reverend Prelate ; who yet had ſo much happineſs,
as to leave to his Honour in the Univerſity of *Oxford*,
a remarkable Memorial of his Charity and Goodneſs,
But now to ſeek out the reward of this vertuous Service, four of the principal and moſt eminent Burghers
are ſelected to make known their proceedings and devotion ; who are graciouſly received, entertain'd, and
highly thanked, for their lawleſs bloody Fact ; which
was ſtiled an excellent piece of Juſtice. Though the
deed had been countenanced ; in that it ran with the

ſway

sway of the time, and the Queens humour; yet certainly no great cause of commendation appears; which is so more properly due to the Hangman, which performeth the grave Ceremonies of his Office by Warrant, and the actual part on none but such as the Law hath made ready for his Fingers.

Now is the Queen settling her remove for *Bristow*, where the Prey remain'd her Haggard-fancy long'd for: She was unwilling to give them so much advantage, though she believ'd it almost impossible, as to hazard the raising of an Army; or so to enable their Provisions and Defences, that it might adjourn the hope of making her Victory perfect. She saw she had a great and Royal Army, well provided; but how long it would hold so, she knew not; the principal strength and number consisting of the giddy Commons; who like Land-floods, rise and fall in an instant: they had never yet seen the face of an Enemy, nor did rightly understand what it was to bear Arms against the King, whom they must here behold a party. These considerations hasten her on with more expedition. All the way as she went, she is entertain'd with joyful Acclamations: Her Army still grows greater, like a beginning Cloud that doth fore-run a Shower. When she was come before this goodly City, and saw his strength, and the Maiden-Bravery of their opposition, which gave her by a hot Salley, led by the valiant *Arundel*, a testimony of her Welcome, she then thinks that in the Art of War there was somewhat more than meer Imagination; and justly fear'd left the Royal Misery would beget a swift Compassion; which was more to be doubted of him in his own Kingdom, since she herself had found it in a forreign Country. But smiling Fortune, now become her Servant, scarce gives her time to think she might be hinder'd. The Townsmen, that knew no Wars but at their Musters, seeing themselves begirt, the Market hinder'd; which was

their

The Queen sets out for *Bristol*.

Whence a hot Salley upon her.

their chiefest and best Revenue, begin among themselves to examine the business; They saw no likelihood of any to relieve them, and daily in danger of some sad surprizal. They saw their Lives, Wives, Children and state at stake for the defence of those that had oppress'd them, and wrong'd the Kingdome by their foul Injustice: they measur'd the event of an unruly Conquest, where many look for Booty, all for Pillage. This did so cramp their valiant hearts, that the Convulsion seeks a present Treaty.

The Queen seeing a Pusillanimity beyond her hopes, and a taint unlook'd for, makes the use, and hits them on the blind side; and answers plainly, She will have no Imparleance, no discoursing; if they desir'd their own Peace, and her assured Favour, they then must entertain and follow her Conditions; which if they but delay'd, the next day following they should abide their Chance, she would her Fortune.

This doom (as it sounds harshly) was deem'd too heavy; but no intreaty could prevail; she would not alter. They yet desire to know what she requir'd; and that she grants, and thus unfoldeth : *Your Lives and Goods* (quoth she) *shall rest untouched, nor shall you taste your selves the least Affliction, so you deliver up with speed your Captains, and in the time prefixt resign the City.* A choice so short, so sharp, so peremptory, being related in the staggering City, breeds straight a supposition, not without reason, she had some certain practis'd Plot within them, or else some way assured for to force the City. They could have been content she had their Captains, since it would set them free from fear and danger; but to be Actors in so foul a Treason, or sacrifice their Guests that came for succour, this they conceit too false and poor a baseness. No more Imparleance is allow'd, or will be heard, no second motion; the breach in their faint hearts is so well known, that nothing is allow'd but present Answer : This smart proceeding melts their leaden Valour,

which

which at the firſt had made ſo brave a flouriſh, and brings *Arundel*, *Winchefter*, and the Town to her poſſeſſion.

It is yielded.

When mans own proper portion is in queſtion, and all he hath at ſtake, be it but doubtful, his eye doth more reflect on his own danger, than on the Laws of Juſtice, Friendſhip, Honour. Charity, 'tis true, begins at home; but ſhe's a Vertue hath no ſociety with Fraud or Falſhood; neither is the breach of Faith, or touch of Treaſon, allow'd within the verge of her rich Precepts. I do confeſs, Neceſſity may drive him to ſuch a bitter choice, that one muſt periſh; but this ſhould be, when things are ſo near hopeleſs, that there be more than words to give it juſtice. A wiſe and noble minde adviſeth ſoundly upon the act, before it is engaged; but being ſo, it rather ſleeps with Honour, than lives to be the map of his thus tainted Conſcience. The intereſt of Friends, of Gueſts, of poor oppreſſed, (though diverſly they touch the Patrons credit) yet all agree in this one point of Vertue, Not to betray, where they have vow'd aſſiſtance. Had theſe faint Citizens not given aſſurance, had they not vow'd to keep their Faiths untainted, the other had not truſted nor incloſed themſelves within ſo weak and falſe a Safeguard. But they were moſt to blame, that would ſo venture their Lives within the power of ſuch a Berry, where they might know were none but ſuckling Rabbets, that would ſuſpect each Mouſe to be a Ferret. Had they but had a guard, ſecur'd their perſons, they might have awed them, or themſelves have ſcaped.

Part of the prey thus gotten, no time is loſt to call them to a reckoning. Sir *Thomas Wage*, Marſhal of the Army, draws up a ſhort Information of many large offences, which are ſolemnly read to the attentive Army, with a Comment of all the harſh aggravations might make them more odious. The confuſed clamour of the Multitude, ſerves for Judge, Jury, and Verdict;

which

which brings them to a sharp Sentence to be forthwith
hang'd, and their Bodies to remain upon the Gallows:
Revenge brooks no delay, no leisure Malice. Old

Old *Spencer*
Executed.

Spencer feels instantly the rigour of this Judgment:
The Green before the Castle is made the place of Execution. Nature that gave him Life, had almost left him;
her Vigour was near spent, her Beauty wither'd; he
could not long have liv'd, if they had spar'd him.
Ninety cold Winters he had past in freedom, and findes
untimely Death to end his Story: He parts without
complaint or long discoursing; he speaks these few
words only, free from passion: *God grant the Queen may
finde a milder Sentence, when in the other world she makes
her Audit.* The King, and his unhappy Son, the sad

The King
and young
Spencer a-
maz'd.

Spectators of this Heart-bleeding Tragedy so full of
horrour, are with his dying farewel so amazed, that
scarcely they had speech, or breath, or motion; so bitter a Preludium made them censure their own conditions were as nearly fatal. The King, a Sovereign, Father,
and a Husband, did hope these Titles would be yet
sufficient to guard his Life, if not preserve his Greatness; but these prov'd all too weak: Where Crowns
are gain'd by Blood and Treason, they are so secured.
Spencer had not a grain of hope for mercy: the Barons
Deaths prejudg'd his coming fortune. The Queen
used not to jest where she was angry; his Fathers end
assur'd her inclination, and bade him rather venture any
hazard, than that which must rely on female pity.
With a world of Melancholy thoughts he casts the
danger, yet could not finde a way that might prevent
it. The Castle in it self was strong, but weakly furnisht. Time now he sees could promise no assistance;
their Adversaries were full bent to work their ruine,
either by publick Force, or private Famine; so that in
their abode was sure destruction. The King in this declar'd himself a Noble Master; he priz'd his Servants
Life as his own Safety, which won them both to try
their utmost hazard.   The

The Queen impatient to surprize this Fortress, doth batter, undermine, and still assail it; but these were all in vain, and proved fruitless; the Rampiers were too strong, too well defended : She threatens and intreats, but to small purpose; here were no Citizens that might betray it: Alas, there needed none, as it succeeded; the proper Owners wrought their own confusion; they leave their strength, and closely try their fortune, which made them board a Bark rode in the Harbour, in hope to get away undescryed : This was the Plot, or none, must work their freedome. But all things thrive alike with him that's falling. The Gale averse, they softly tide her onwards ; the Wind will not consent to give them passage, but rudely hurls them back to their first Harbour. Thrice had they past St. *Vincents* Rock, famous for *Bristow* Diamonds; but in that Reach are hurryed back with fury: The Elements of Earth, of Air, of Water, conspir'd all at once to make them hopeless.

The Queen batters the Castle.

The King and Spencer betake to a Bark, but are beaten back by Weather.

Sir *Henry Beaumonde* quartered next the Haven, being inform'd that this gadding Pinnace had often attempted passage without reason, the wind contrarious, and the weather doubtful, suspects that her designe was great and hasty ; on this he seiz'd her, and surveys her lading, which prov'd a prize beyond his expectation: within her hollow bulk, a Cell of darkness, he findes this pair obscur'd, not undiscover'd. The King hath gracious words, and all due reverence ; but *Spencer* is contemned, and used with rigour. This ends the War, and gave the work perfection. Fortune, that triumphs in the Fall of Princes, like a Stepmother, rests not where she frowneth, till she have wholly ruin'd and o'rethrown their Power, that do precede or else oppose her Darlings.

The Bark seized.

The Queen having thus attained to the full of her desire, resolves to use it to the best advantage: Ambition seis'd her strongly, yet resigneth to her incensed

Passion

Paſſion the precedence ; her own good nature (though
ſhe might adventure) ſhe would not truſt ſo far, to ſee
her Husband ; nor did ſhe think it fit thoſe valiant
ſtrangers begun the work, ſhould view or ſee the
Captive ; ſuch ſights ſometimes beget as ſtrange impreſſions ; inſtantly he is convey'd to *Berklay*-Caſtle, there to
remain reſtrain'd, but well attended. *Spencer* is hardly
kept, but often viſited ; 'twas not with pity, which be-
fits a Priſoner, but with inſulting joy, and baſe deriſion.
Their eyes with ſight, and tongues with rayling glut-
ted, the act muſt follow that may ſtop the rancour,
which gives him to the Marſhal lockt in Irons : He here
receives the ſelf-ſame entertainment his aged Father
found ; alone the difference, he had a longer time, and
ſharper Sentence: All things thus order'd, the Queen
removes for *London*, meaning to make *Hereford* her
way, and the laſt Journey of her condemned Priſoner,
that attends her each place ſhe paſſeth by. A world of
people do ſtrain their wider throats to bid her welcome,
with yelping cries that ecchoed with confuſion. While
She thus paſſeth on with a kinde of inſulting Tyranny, far ſhort of the belief of her former Vertue
and Goodneſs ; ſhe makes this poor unhappy man attend her Progreſs, not as the antient *Romans* did their
vanquiſh'd Priſoners, for oſtentation, to increaſe their
Triumph ; but merely for Revenge, Deſpite, and private Rancour ; mounted upon a poor, lean, ugly Jade,
as baſely furniſht ; cloath'd in a painted Taberd, which
was then a Garment worn by condemned Thieves alone ;
and tatter'd raſcally, he is led through each Town behinde the Carriage, with Reeds and Pipes that ſound
the ſummons to call the wondering Crue together might
abuſe him ; all the bitter'ſt actions of diſgrace were
thrown upon him. Certainly this man was infinitely
vicious, and deſerv'd as much as could be laid upon
him, for thoſe many great and inſolent Oppreſſions,
acted with Injuſtice, Cruely, and Blood ; yet it had
been

The King
ſent to *Ber-
kly* Caſtle.

Spencer in-
ſulted over.

been much more to the Queens Honour, if fhe had given
him a quicker Death , and a more honourable Tryal,
free from thefe opprobrious and barbarous Difgraces,
which favour'd more of a favage, tyrannical difpofition,
than a judgment fit to command, or fway the Sword
of Juftice.

Though not by Birth, yet by Creation he was a Peer
of the Kingdom , and by the Dignity of his place one
of the moft eminent ; which might (if not to him in his
particular, yet in the Rights due to Nobility and Greatnefs) have found fome more honourable a diftinction,
than to be made more infamous and contemptible than
the bafeft Rogue , or moft notorious Cutpurfe. It is
affuredly (give it what title you will) an argument of a
Villanous Difpofition , and a Devilifh Nature , to tyrannize and abufe thofe wretched ruines which are under the Mercy of the Law , whofe Severity is bitter
enough without aggravation. A Noble Minde doth
out of native Goodnefs fhew a kinde of Sweetnefs in
the difpofition, which, if not the Man, doth pity his
Misfortune ; but never doth increafe his forrow by
bafer ufage than becomes his Juftice. In Chriftian Piety, which is the Day-ftar that fhould direct and guide
all humane Actions, the heart fhould be as free from all
that's cruel, as being too remifs in point of Juftice.
The Life of Man is all that can be taken ; 'tis that muft
expiate his worft Offences ; the Law muft guide the
way ; Juftice, not Fury, muft be his Judge ; fo far
there is no Errour. But when a flux of Torment follows Judgment, which may be done in Speech as well
as Action , it gives too many Deaths to one Offender ,
and ftains the Actors with a foul difhonour. To fee
fuch a Monfter fo monftroufly ufed, no queftion pleafed the giddy Multitude, who fcarcely know the civil
grounds of Reafon: the recollected Judgment that beheld it, cenfur'd it was at beft too great and deep a
blemifh to fuit a Queen, a Woman, and a Victor.

The Queens Cruelty.

L l　　　　　　Whether

Whether her Impofition, or his patient Suffering were greater, or became firft weary, he now is brought to give them both an ending, upon a Gallows highly built of purpofe; he now receives the end of all his Torments; the Cruelty was fuch, unfit to be recorded. Whether it were the greatnefs of his heart, or it were broken, he leaves the world with fuch a conftant parting, as feem'd as free from fear, as fruitlefs plaining.

Spencer hanged.

Four days are fcarcely ended, ere *Arundel* doth tafte the felf-fame fortune. Until the laft Combuftion, I finde no mention in the Story of this Noble Gentleman, neither could I ever read any juft caufe why his Life was thus taken from him, unlefs it were a Capital Offence not to forfake his Mafter: It was then a very hard cafe, if it muft be adjudged Treafon to labour to defend his King and Soveraign, to whom he had fworn Faith and Obedience, fuffering for preferving that Truth and Oath, which they had all treacheroufly broken, that were his Judges. If it were deemed a fault deep enough to be taken in company with thofe that were corrupt and wicked, I fee yet no reafon why he alone fhould fuffer, and thofe their other Creatures were permitted many of them unqueftion'd, fome preferr'd, and none executed. But we may not properly expect Reafon in Womens actions: It was enough the incenfed Queen would have it fo, againft which was no difputing.

Arundel the like.

Her bufinefs thus difpatcht, fhe comes to *London*, where fhe hath all the Royal Entertainment due to her Greatnefs. The Citizens do run and crowd to fee her, that if the Wheel fhould turn, would be as forward to make the felf-fame fpeed to fee her ruine. Affoon as here fhe had fettled her affairs, and made things ready, fhe calls a Parliament, and fends forth Summons for the appearance, which as foon enfued; herein fhe makes her Hufband feal the Warrant, who God knows fcarcely knew what fhe was doing, but lived a Reclufe,

The Queen comes to London.

She calls a Parliament.

well

well and furely guarded. When this grave Affembly was come together, the Errours and the Abufes of the Kingdom are laid full open; which touch'd the King with a more infolent liberty than might well become the tongues of thofe which muft yet be his Subjects. Many ways of Reformation for forms fake are difcuffed, but the intended courfe was fully before refolved; yet it was fit there fhould be a handfome Introduction. The iffue at length falls upon the point of Neceffity, fhewing, that *Edward,* by the imbecillity of his judgment, and the corruption of his nature, was unfit longer to continue the Government, which was fo difeafed and fick, that it required a King more careful and active: as if the conferring it upon a green Youth, little more than an Infant, had been Warranty enough for thefe Allegations; but they ferv'd turn well enough, where all were agreed; and there was not fo much as a juft fear of oppofition: It ne're was toucht or expreft by what Law, Divine or Humane, the Subject might Depofe, not an Elective King, but one that Lineally and Juftly had inherited, and fo long enjoy'd it: this was too deep a Myftery, and altogether improper for their refolution. A fhort time at length brings them all to one Minde, which in a true conftruction was no more than a mere Politick Treafon, not more dangerous in the Act than in the Example. The three Eftates *unâ voce* conclude the Father muft be Depofed, and his unripe Son muft be Invefted in the Royal Dignity. Not a Lord, Bifhop, Knight, Judge, or Burgefs, but that day left his Memory behinde him; they could not elfe fo generally have forgot the Oaths of their Allegiance, fo folemnly fworn to their old Mafter, whom they had juft caufe to reftrain from his Errours, but no ground or colour to deprive him of his Kingdom; who that day found neither Kinfman, Friend, Servant, or Subject to defend his Intereft. It is probable he could not be fo generally forfaken, and not unlikely but that he

had

They conclude to depofe the King.

had some in this Assembly well-affected, which seeing the violence and strength of the Current; knew their contestation might endanger themselves, and not advantage him in his possession. But this justifies them not, neither in their Oaths, Love, or Duty, which should have been sincere and eminent: He that had here really express'd himself, had left to Posterity an honourable Memorial of his Faith, Worth, and Valour. Never will the remembrance of that stout and reverend Bishop dye, who in the Case of *Richard* the Second exprest himself so honestly and bravely. Civil respects, though they deeply touch in particular, warrant not the breach of publick engagements; neither is it properly Wisdome, but Craft, infringeth the Laws of Duty or Honesty: If that may be admitted, what Perjury may not finde an excuse, what Rebellion not a justifiable answer? But it is clear, there may not be a wilful violation of Oaths, though it tend deeply to our own loss and prejudice.

The Resolution being now fully concluded, that must uncrown this unhappy King, divers of both Houses are sent unto him to make the Declaration; who being come into his presence, *Trussel* the Speaker of the lower House, in the Name of the whole Kingdom, makes a Resignation of all Homage and Fealty, and then doth read the Sentence. *Edward,* that had been aforehand informed, the better to prepare him, had arm'd himself with as much Patience, as his Necessity could give him; with an attentive ear hears all full out; which done, he turns away without answering a word. He knew it was in vain to spend time in Discourse or Contestation, which must be the ready way to endanger his Life; and in his consenting with a dangerous example to his Successours, he had both their Power and his own Guilt made evident to Posterity; which might have made the practice more frequent and familiar. He had still a kinde of Hope that his Adversaries would

The Speaker makes a resignation of Homage, & reads the Sentence.

The King answers not a word.

would run themselves out of breath, when there would be both room and time to alter his condition. Thus this unfortunate King, after he had with a perpetual a-gitation governed this Kingdome eighteen years, odde months and days, lost it partly by his own Disorder and Improvidence, but principally by the treacherous Infi-delity of his Wife, Servants, and Subjects. And it is most memorable, an Army of three hundred Strangers entred his Dominion, and took from him the Rule and Governance, without so much as blow given, or the loss of any one man, more than such as perished by the hand of Justice.

Though in a sinking Greatness all things conspire to work a fatal ruine, yet in our Story this is the first pre-sident of this nature, or where a King fell with so little Honour, and so great an Infidelity, that found neither Sword or Tongue to plead his quarrel. But what could be expected, when for his own private Vanities and Passion, he had been a continual lover and abetter of unjust actions, and had consented to the Op-pression of the whole Kingdom, and the untimely Death of so many Noble Subjects? It is certainly no less ho-nourable than just, that the Majesty of a King have that same full and free use of his Affections, without Envy or Hatred, which every private man hath in his œconomick Government: Yet as his Calling is the greatest, such must his Care be, to square them out by those same sacred Rules of Equity and Justice; if they once transcend, or exceed, falling upon an extremity of Dotage or Indulgence, it then occasions those Er-rours that are the certain Predictions of an ensuing Trouble, which many times proves fatal and dangerous. Let the Favourite taste the King's Bounty, not devour it; let him enjoy his ear, but not ingross it; let him participate his love, but not enchant it. In the eye of the Commonwealth if he must be a Moat, let him not be a Monster. And lastly, if he must practise on the Subject, let it be with moderation, and not with rapine. If in either of these there be an excess, which makes the King a Monarchy to his Will, and the Kingdom a prey to his Passion, and the world take notice it be done by the Royal Indulgence, it begets not more hatred than multiplicity of errour; which draw with them dangerous Convulsions, if not a desperate ruine to that State where it hath his allowance and practice. As there ought to be a limitation in the Affection of the one, so ought there to be a like Curiosity in the quality of the other: Persons of meaner condition and birth exalted above proportion, as it taxeth the Kings Judgment, impaireth both his Safety and Honour. Neither is it proper, that the principal Strengths and Dignities should be committed to the care and fidelity of one man onely; such unworthy and unequal distribution wins a discontent from the more capable in ability and blood, and carries with it a kinde of necessary impulsion still to continue his greatness; else having the keys of the Kingdom in his hand, he may at all times open the gates to a domestick Danger, or a forreign Mischief. The number of Servants is the Masters honour; their truth and faculties his glory and safety; which being severally employ'd and countenanced, make it at one and the self-same time perspicuous in many; and being indifferently heard, do, both in advice and action, give a more secure, discreet, and safe form of proceeding. Kings in their deliberations should be served with a Council of State, and a Council of particular Interest and Honour; the one to survey the Policy, the other the Goodness of all matters in question; both composed out of Integrity, not Corruption: these delivering truely their Opinions and Judgments, it is more easie for him to reconcile and elect: But when one man alone supplies both these places in private and publick, all the rest follow the voice of the Drone, though it be against their own Conscience and Judgment.

ment. The Royal Glory fhould be pure, and yet
tranfparent, fuffering not the leaft eclipfe or fhadow;
which appears vifibly defective, when it is wholly led
by a fingle advice never fo grave and weighty: let the
projection, if it be entertained, have the tefte of a
Council; but let the act and glory be folely the Kings,
which adds to the belief of his ability, and more affures
his greatnefs. If the heart of Majefty be given over
to the fenfuality of Pleafure, or betray'd by his proper
Weaknefs, or the cunning of him he trufteth; yet let
him not neglect the neceffary affairs of a Kingdom, or
pafs them over by Bills of Exchange to the providence of another: In fuch an act he lofeth the Prerogative of an abfolute King, and is but fo at fecond-
hand and by direction. It is the Practique, not the
Theorique of State, that wins and affures the Subject; If the ability of that be confined or doubtful, it
eftrangeth the will of Obedience, and gives a belief
of liberty to the actions of Diforder, and Injuftice.
Such an Errour is not more prejudicial in the Imbecillity, than in the Example. Royal Vanities finde a
ready imitation, fo that it becomes a hazard that a
carelefs King makes a diffolute Kingdom. Mans nature
is propenfive to the worfer part; which it embraceth
with more facility and willingnefs, when it wins the
advantage of the time, and is led by fo eminent a
prefident. From this confideration, natural Weaknefs,
or temporary Imperfection, fhould be always masked,
and never appear in publick, fince the Court, State,
and Kingdom, practife generally by his Example. As
in Affection, fo in Paffion, there are many things e-
qually confiderable. I muft confefs, and do believe,
that King worthy of an Angelical Title, that could
mafter thefe rebellious Monfters, which rob him of his
Peace and Happinefs: But this in a true perfection, is
to Flefh and Blood moft impoffible; yet both in Divinity and Moral Wifdome, t is the moft excellent Ma-
fter-

ster-piece of this our peregrination, so to dispose them, that they wait upon the Operations of the Soul rather as obedient Servants, than loose and uncontrouled Vagabonds. Where the Royal Passions are rebellious and masterless, having so unlimited a Power, his Will becomes the Law ; his hand the executioner of actions unjust and disorderly, which end sometimes in Blood, commonly in Oppression, and evermore in a confused perturbation of the Kingdome. The Warranty of the Law wrought to his temper, not that it is so, but that he must have it so, justifies him not, though he make a Legal Proceeding the justification of his Tyranny ; since the Innocency of the Subject seldome findes protection, where the fury of a King resolves his ruine. The rigour of humane Constitutions are to the Delinquent weighty enough ; let them not be wrested or inverted ; which makes the King equally guilty, and the actor of his own Passions, rather than those of Justice or Integrity. He should on earth order his proceedings in imitation after the Divine Nature, which evermore inclines more to Mercy than Justice. Lives cannot, being taken away, be redeemed ; there ought then to be a tender consideration how they be taken, lest the Injustice of the act, challenge a Vengeance of the same nature. As the quality of the act, so is the condition of the agent considerable in point of Judicature ; wherein there may be sometimes those dependencies, that it may be more honourable and advantageous to pardon, or delay execution , than to advance and hasten it : howsoever, it is the more excellent and innocent way, to fall short of the better hand, and to suffer the Severity of the Law rather seem defective, than an apparent taint in the suffering disposition and goodness. The actions of Repentance are registred in the table of our Transgressions, where none to the guilty Conscience appears more horrid and fearful, than those which by an inconsiderate haste or corruption of the Will have been acted in

Blood

Blood and Paffion. So great a height as the Majefty of a King, fhould be cloathed with as fweet a temper, neither too precipitate, or too flow; neither too violent, or too remifs; but like the beating of a healthy Pulfe, with a fteady and well-advifed motion, which preferves a juft Obedience and Fear in thofe which are vicious, and begets a Love and Admiration in all, efpecially fuch as fo gracioufly tafte his Goodnefs.

I have dwelt too long in this digreffion; yet I muft (though it a little delay the concluding part of this Hiftory) fpeak fomewhat that is no lefs proper for him that fhall have the happinefs to enjoy fo fair and large a room in the Royal affections. There muft be in him a correfpondent worth, as well of Wifdome and Obedience, as of Sincerity and Truth; which makes no other ufe of this fo great a bleffing; but to his Soveraigns Honour, and his own credit; and not to advantage himfelf, by the oppreffion of others, or improving the particular by the ruine of a Kingdome. If the Mafters actions be never fo pure and innocent; yet if out of affection he become the Patron of the Servants mifdemeanours and infolencies, by protecting or not punifhing, he makes himfelf guilty; and fhares both in the grievance and hatred of the poor diftreffed Subject. The general cry feeing the ftream polluted, afcribe it to the Fountain-head, where is the Spring that may reform and cleanfe it. By this one particular errour of Protection, he that will read the Hiftory of our own, or thofe of Forreign Nations, fhall finde a number of memorable Examples, which have produced Depofition of Kings, Ruine of Kingdoms, the Effufion of Chriftian Blood, and the general Diftemper of that part of the world, all grounded on this occafion. Let him then that out of his Mafters Love, more than his own Defert, hath made himfelf a fortune, be precifely careful, that by his diforder he endanger not the ftair and prop of his Preferment; which he fhall make firm and

per-

permanent, in making Humility and Goodnefs the Adamant to draw the love both of his equals and inferiours: Such a winning Sweetnefs affures their hearts, which in the leaft contempt or infolence are apt and ready to receive the impreffions of Envy and Hatred; which if they once take root, end not in Speculation, but Actions either publickly violent, or privately malicious; both tending to his ruine and confufion. If he ftray from this Principle, ftriving to make an imperious height beget fear, and the opinion of that fear the rock whereon he builds his Greatnefs; let him then know, that the firft is the Companion of Truft and Safety, the other a Slave, that will break loofe with opportunity and advantage. Neither hath it any touch of Difcretion, or Society with Wifdome, or Moral Policy, to glorifie his new-acquired Greatnefs with unneceffary amplifications, either in multiplicity of Attendants, vanity of Apparel, fuperfluity of Diet, fumptuoufnefs of Structures, or any other ridiculous eminency, that may demonftrate his Pride or Ambition: Wife men deride it, Fools applaud it, his Equals envy it, and his Inferiours hate it. All jumping at length in one conclufion, that his Fortune is above his Merit, and his Pride much greater than his Worth and Judgment. But this prefuming Impudence ends not here: Kings themfelves may fuffer for a time, but in the end they will rather change their Affections, than to be dazled and outfhin'd in their own Sphere and Element.

The Queen and *Mortimer* in this his Minority take upon them the whole Sway and Government of the Kingdome. The Act wherein they exprefs'd themfelves and their new Authority firft, was the Commitment of *Baldock*, the *quondam* Lord Chancellor,

The young King crowned.

Now is this young King Crowned with a great deal of Triumphant Honour, but with a more expectation of what would become of this giddy world, which feem'd to run upon wheels, by reafon of fo fudden and fo great a revolution.

The Queen and Mortimer bear fway.

cellor, who hath the Great Seal taken from him, and was sent to *Newgate*. It may be wonder'd why he was so long spared; they had use of his Place, though not of his Person; and had no Power, if they had thrust him out, to have brought in another, or to have executed it by Commission, unless they would admit it as an act of the old King, until the new were Crowned. This Cage was fit for such a Coysterel; but yet his place being so eminent, it was believed somewhat unworthy; yet succeeding time made it not much out of square, when *Trisilian* Lord Chief Justice was hang'd, for interpreting the Law against Law and his own Conscience, for the Kings advantage. Now the recollected spirits begin to parallel time present with that precedent, and to meditate upon that act which had disrobed and put down an anointed King, that had so long sway'd the Scepter, to whom they had so solemnly sworn Faith and Obedience: They finde the State little altered, onely things are thought more handsomly carried, and the Actors were somewhat more warrantable; yet the Multitude, according to the vanity of their changeable hearts, begin already to be crop-sick, wishing for their old Master, and ready to attempt any new Innovation: such is the mutability of the inconstant Vulgar, desirous of new things, but never contented; despising the time being, extolling that of their Forefathers, and ready to act any mischief to try by alteration the succedent; like *Æsops* Frogs, if they might have their own fancy, each Week should give them a new King, though it were to their own destruction. This occasions many unpleasing Petitions and Suits tender'd to the new King and his Protectors, for the releasement of *Edward's* Imprisonment, or at least for more freedom, or a more noble usage. But these touch too near the quick, to beget a sudden answer. As things stood, they neither grant nor deny, either of them carrying with it so dangerous a hazard: If he were free, they must shake

hands

They commit *Baldock* to *Newgate*.

Trisilian Lord Chief-Justice hanged.

hands with their greatnefs; and a flat denial would have endanger'd a fudden tumult. They give good words, and promife more than ever they meant to perform, yielding many reafons why they could not yet give a definitive refolution; this for the prefent fatisfies.

The black Monks are more importunate, and take not this delay for an anfwer; but being ftill adjourn'd over with protraction, they labour to bring that about by Confpiracy, which they could not do by Intreaty: in their publick Exhortations they inveigh againft the feverity of the King's ufage, and invite their Auditory to fet to a helping hand to the procurement of his Freedom; they extenuate his Faults, and transfer them to them that had the guidance of his affairs, and not to his own natural Difpofition; they tax the impropriety of the time, when the Kingdom was under the Government of a Child and a Woman; and fpare no point that might advance compaffion for the one, or procure a diflike of the other. Neither are they content with

a verbal incitation, but fall to matter of fact, that others might move by their example: They make one of their number, named *Donhead*, their Captain; a good, ftout, bold, and factious Fellow; one that was daring enough, but knew better what belong'd to Church-Ornaments, than the handfome carriage of a Confpiracy, that was to be managed by Armes, and not by the liberty of the Tongue; whofe liberality

claps him by the heels, where he not long after dyes, before he had fo much as mufter'd his Covent.

This gathering Cloud thus difpers'd without a fhower, the Queen and *Mortimer*, to take off the people from harping farther upon this ftring, fend forth divers plaufible Proclamations, intimating a ftrict charge for the reformation of divers petty Grievances; and withal are divulged fundry probabilities of Forreign dangers from *France* and *Scotland :* which were prefently

fently underftood to be but mere fictions, in refpect at
the fame inftant fhe frees herfelf of her forreign Aid,
which in fuch an occafion might have as well ferved to
defend the Kingdome ; as to invade it. They made,
it is true ; an earneft fuit to be gone, having well
feather'd their nefts ; but if the fear had been fuch as
was bruited, I think the Queen both might and would
have retain'd them. It may be their addiction to Arms
was weary of fo long a Vacation; or they were defirous to fhew themfelves at home with honour, whence
they had parted with fo poor an expectation; and per-
adventure fhe was unwilling they fhould be witnefs of
that unnatural Tragedy; which fhe faw then broyling
in *Mortimer's* breaft ; though not refolved on ; which
muft have wounded her reputation in that Climate,
where fhe had won fo great a belief of her Wifdome,
Vertue, and Goodnefs. Liberally and nobly fhe requites every man, according to his Merit and Condition ; but to Sir *John* of *Heynault*, whofe Heroick Spirit
gave the firft life to this action; and to the Oracle of
her recovery, and all thofe of the better fort, fhe prefents many rich Jewels; and Annuities of yearly Revenue, according to the quality of the time in being.
They hold themfelves Royally requited ; and taking a
folemn leave, are honourably accompanied to *Dover*,
where they take their Farwel of the Kingdom, with a
much merrier eye than when they firft beheld it.

Whofo fhall wifely confider the defperate attempt of
this little handful of Adventurers; and their fortunate
iffue, may juftly efteem it one of the moft memorable
Paffages of our time, fince it was merely guided by pity
and compaffion ; without pay, without provifion, to
attempt an act not more dangerous than hopelefs; yet
they gave it perfection, without fo much as the lofs of
any one man ; and returned home glorious in honour,
rich in purchafe; not gained by pillage, robbery, or unjuft rapine (the hope and revenue of a War;) but by

Sir *John* of
Heynault
and the reft
rewarded.

They de-
part the
Kingdom.

O o

the

the juſt reward due to their Valour and Vertue. The
cauſe of ſo fair a progreſſion, and ſo ſucceſsful an end,
may have divers probabilities likely enough to ground
our judgment; As the ſincerity of the Intention, the
goodneſs of the Work, and many other, which may
be alledged: but the moſt eſſential may be drawn from
this; they were (though but a ſmall one) yet an entire
body, compoſed of ſuch as knew what appertain'd to
Arms and Breeding; Men that were vertuouſly in-
clin'd, and aw'd with the true ſenſe of Religion (in the
Wars of late years become a mere ſtranger) where no
Victory is eſteem'd diſhonourable, no Purchaſe unlaw-
full. Certainly our Wars and our Plantations nearly
reſemble, being both uſed as a Broom to ſweep the
Kingdome, rather than an enterprize to adorn it; which
makes the event ſo unfortunate in War; which alone
falls properly within the compaſs of this Treatie, it
being the greateſt and moſt weighty work; that either
gives honour or ſafety to a Kingdom: They ſhould be
begun with Juſtice, and managed as well with Wiſdome as Valour; their beginning ſhould be with a
choice care, which makes the ending fortunate. The
number of bodies is not the Strength, their fury not the
Bulwork; it is the Piety and true Valour of an Army,
which gives them Heart and Victory; which how it can
be expected out of Ruffians and Goal-birds, that are
the ſcum of the Commonwealth, I leave to your conſideration. I commend his Curioſity, that would
not buy a piece of Plate ſtoln from Orphans, though
he might have had it at an under-value, lawfully e-
nough; but more his reaſon, which would not commix
it with his own, for fear left it might occaſion a puniſhment upon his which were innocent, and not toucht
with a Guilt that might in Juſtice challenge Vengeance.
But in the Military Practice it is believed, ſo a man
have ſhape and limbs, 'tis no matter though he have
murder'd his own Father, or committed Inceſt with his

Mother; it is his metal , not his conditions, gives him
admittance : Hence spring Treachery, that forsakes his
Colours; Treason, that betrays the Captain ; and at the
best , those actions of Bloud and Murder, that cry rather for Vengeance, than promise Victory. A General,
it is true, that hath his Army made to his hand, cannot
distinguish their conditions ; the first act is the errour of
those entrusted ; yet if he in the knowledge continue,
and not punish the practice of so barbarous actions,
though it be against an enemy, it must wound his Honour, and endanger his Safety ; liable to the accompt
of those transgressions, which are acted by those that
are under his charge without a just punishment. It is
an Observation remarkable , that a Press coming into
the Country, there is a great deal of shift made in every Town and Village to lay hold of all the most notorious debauch'd Rascals, to fill up the number ; these
clear the Coast, and are believed fit Champions to fight
for their Sovereigns Honour, and the Kingdoms Safety ;
and the rather, because in want of Pay (the ruine of an
Army) they are best able to live by their Trade. But
what follows? They are either led to the Slaughter, or
by the Divine Justice prove the ruine of the Enterprise ;
or returning, practise private Villanies with more confidence ; or publick Mutinies, under pretence of want of
Wages.

But I will leave them to a reformation, and proceed
to the Tragedy of this unfortunate King, who is now
taken from the Earl of *Lancaster*, and delivered over by
Indenture to Sir *Morrice Berkley* and Sir *John Matravas*.
They lead him back to the Cage of his first Imprisonment ; carrying him closely, and with a reserved Secrecy, lest his Friends in the knowledge of his Remove
might attempt his Freedome. And to make his Discovery more difficult, they disfigure him, by cutting
off his Hair, and shaving of his Beard. *Edward*, that
had been formerly honourably used, and tenderly served,

The King taken from the Earl of *Lancaster*, & delivered to Sir *Morrice Berkley* and Sir *John Matravas*.

They remove him in disguise.

ved, is bitterly grieved with this Indignity; and one
day among the rest, when they came to shave him,
which was attempted without fire, and a cold liquor,
his eyes pour forth a stream of Tears in sense of his
Misfortune, which to the inquisitive Actors gives this
answer, *He would have some warm water, in spight of all
their malice.* Another time, in the presence of two or
three of those that were as well set to be Spies over
him, as to guard him, in a deep Melancholy Passion
he thus discours'd his Sorrow. *Is mine offence* (quoth

*he) so great and grievous, that it deserves nor pity nor
assistance? Is Christian Charity, all Goodness lost; and
nothing left in Subject, Child, or Servant, that tastes of
Duty? Is Wedlock-love forgotten so fully; all at once
forsake me? Admit my errours fit for reformation; I will
not justifie my self, or censure others. Is't not enough that
it hath taken from me my Crown, the Glory of my former
being, but it must leave me void of native comfort? I yet
remain a Father, and a Husband; a Soveraign and a Master lost, cannot deprive me of that which is mine own, till
Death dissolve me: Where then is filial Love? Where
that Affection that waits upon the Laws of God and Nature? My wretched Cares have not so much transform'd
me, that I am turn'd to Basilisk, or Monster. What can
they fear, that they refuse to see me? unless they doubt
mine eyes can dart destruction. I have no other Weapons
that may fright them; and these (God wot) have only
tears to drown them. Can they believe or once suspect a
danger in visit of a poor distressed Captive? Their hardned
hearts I know are not so noble, or apt to take a gentler
milde impression, by seeing these poor ruines thus forsaken;
What then occasions this so great a strangeness, or makes
them jealous of so poor a venture? Are they not yet content in the possession of all that once was mine, now theirs?
But by what title, their Arms can better tell, than can
their Conscience. My misled harmless Children are not
guilty; my Wife betrays them, and false Mortimer; who*
                                                        else

*else I know would run to see their Father. Justly I pay
the price of former folly, that let him scape to work mine
own confusion: Had he had his desert, the price of Treason, he had not liv'd to work me this dishonour. But
time will come my wrongs will be revenged, when he shall
fall with his own weight unpitied. Thou wretched state
of Greatness, painted Glory, that falling find'st thine own
the most perfidious; must thou still live, and yet not worthy
of one poor look? It is a meer Injustice: Would they would
take my Life, 'tis that they aim at. I will esteem it as an
act of pity, that, as I live, but hate mine own Condition.*

Here with a deep sigh of scalding Passions, his tears
break loose afresh, to cool their fury. All sadly silent
while he rests perplexed, a stander-by makes this uncivil answer, whom *Mortimer* had placed to increase his
sorrow. *Most gracious Sir, the Queen your Wife, and
Children, are justly jealous of your cruel nature; they know
too well your heat and former fury, to come too near so great
and sure a danger; besides, they are assur'd that your intentions are bent to work them hurt, or some foul mischief,
if they adventure to approach your presence.* The King is uncivilly upbraided.

The Queen my Wife (quoth he) *hath she that Title,
while I that made her so am less than nothing? Alas poor
wretched woman, can her invention, apt for mischief,
fashion no one excuse but this so void of reason? Is there
a possibility in her Suspition? Can I, being so resolved,
act a Murder, or can their false hearts dream me so ill-
minded? I am, thou seest, a poor forsaken Prisoner, as
far from such a Power, as Will to act it; they too well
know it, to suspect my nature. But let them wonder on,
and scorn my sorrow; I must endure, and they will taste
their errour. But fellow, thou that tak'st such sawcy
boldness to character and speak thy Sovereigns errours,
which thou shouldst cover, not presume to question; Know,
Edward's heart is as free from thine aspersions, as thou or
they from Truth or Moral Goodness.* When he had ended
these words, he retires himself to his Chamber, sad and His Answer.

melan-

melancholy; thinking his Cafe was hard and defperate, when fuch a paultry Groom durft fo affront him.

The Queen and *Mortimer* revelling in the height of their Ambition, had yet a wary eye to the main, which they knew principally confifted in the fure keeping of their Prifoner. They fee their plaufible income was but dully continued, there being a whifpering murmur not fo clofely mutter'd, but that it came to their ears, which fhew'd an abfolute diflike of the manner of their proceedings. Though they had all the marks and effen-tial parts of Sovereignty, the name alone excepted, yet they had unquiet and troubled thoughts: What they wifh'd they had obtain'd, yet there was ftill fomething wanting to give it perfection. Such is the vanity of our imagination, which fafhions out a period to our de-fires, that being obtain'd, are yet as loofe and reftlefs. Ambition hath no end, but ftill goes upward, never content or fully fatisfied. If man had all that Earth could give; and were fole Monarch of the world, he yet would farther; and as the Giants did make War with Heaven, rather than lofe thofe Symptomes of his Nature. Fear to preferve what is unjuftly gotten, doth give the new-made great one agitation, which fome-thing limits his immenfe affections, that do believe he muft ftill mount up higher, and elfe would fwallow all within his compafs. This made this pair ftop here a-while, to ftrengthen and more affure what was al-ready gotten : They know the people giddy, falfe, in-conftant; a feather wagg'd would blow them to com-motion. They fee the Lords, that were their prime Supporters, feeming content, in heart not fatisfied ; the bough was lopt that fhadow'd ore their greatnefs ; an-other was fprung up as large and fearful; which though more noble, yet no lefs afpiring. The drooping tongue of the dejected Kingdom doth grumble out his ex-pectations cozen'd.

The Grievance ftill continues great and heavy, not chang'd

Side notes:

The Queen and *Morti-mer* unquiet ftill.

chang'd in fubftance, but alone in habit; a juft compaffion aggravates the clamour, to fee their former
King fo hardly ufed, fhort of his Honour, Merit, Birth,
and Calling. Thefe paffages related, tingled the ears
of our great *Mortimer*; he knew that all was now at
ftake, which unprevented muft hurl them back again
with worfe conditions. No longer can he mince his
own Conceptions, but plainly tells the Queen the caufe
muft perifh, *Edward* muft dye; this is the only refuge
muft make all fure, and cleanfe this fad fufpicion; fo
long as he remain'd, their fear continues, as would the
hope of them attempt their ruine. The Warranty of
Arms had a fair colour; that fhould be levied to attempt his refcue, which had a Royal ftamp to raife and
make them current. If fuch a Project fhould be once
in action, it would be then too late to feek to crofs it.
All men are apt to pity fo great a King oppreffed; and
not fo much look on what he had been, as what he is,
and being reftor'd he might be.

   The Queen, whofe heart was yet believed innocent
of fuch foul Murther, is, or at leaft feems, highly difcontented; She acknowledges his prefent Sufferings greater
than his Offences, or might become the King, her Lord
and Husband; and holds this act of too too foul Injuftice, which ftiles her Son a Homicide, and her a
Monfter: The crimfon Guilt of fuch a crying action
could not efcape the cruel hand of Vengeance: If it
might be concealed from humane Knowledge, the All-
knowing Power of Heaven would lay it open. She
thinks it more than an act of Bloud, to kill a Husband,
and a King, that fometimes loved her: She thinks her
Son not of fo ill a nature, as to flip o're his Fathers
Death untouch'd, unpunifh'd, when that he was grown
up in power to fift it. Thefe motives made her thus
return her Anfwer.

   Let us refolve (dear Friend) to run all hazards, rather
than this that is fo foul and cruel; let us not ftain our
                           Souls

Marginal notes:

Mortimer's ears tingle.

He tells the Queen, the King muft die.

She feems difconten- ted.

She returns her Anfwer.

Souls with Royal Bloud and Murder, which seldome scapes unseen, but never unpunish'd, especially for such a fear as is but casual: while we are innocent, at worst our danger is but privation of this glorious shadow, which Death can take, when we believe it surest; but if we taint the inward part with such a tincture, our proper Guilt will bring continual terrour, a fear that never dyes, but lives still dying. If Edward do get loose, what need we fear him, that pull'd him down when he was great, at highest? Why should we then resolve his Death or Murder? this Help may serve when we are desperate of other Remedies, which yet appears not. To act so great a sin without compulsion, addes to the deed, and makes it far more odious; nor can it plead excuse if after question'd, that hath no cause but merely Supposition. Say that he were a dead man, gone and hopeless, neither our fears or dangers are more lessen'd; we are still subject to the self same hazard, and have to boot our proper Guilt to cause it. Those that do hate or envy us, can fashion other pretexts, as fair as this, to shake us; which we shall better crush, while we are guiltless. Then think upon some other course as sure, more harmless; ne're can my heart consent to kill my Husband.

Mortimer being nettled with this Reply, so far wide of the aim which in his bloudy thoughts he had so constantly resolved on, thought he would return the Queen as bitter a Pill, as she had given him to bite on; which makes him thus reply in anger.

Madam, who hath the time to friend, and doth neglect it, is justly falling scorn'd, and sinks unpitied. Have you for this endur'd so bitter tryals, to be at length a foe to your own safety? Did you outrun your Troubles, suffering meanly, but to return unto your first condition? If it be so, I must approve your Reasons, and say your grounds were like your project, hopeful; You see your glorious Morning now turn'd cloudy; the Kingdom doth repine to see our Greatness, yet have no hope but in the King deposed; who

                                                              taken

taken away, what fear can justly move us ? Your youthful
Son we'll rule till he grows older, and in that time esta-
blish such a Greatness, as he shall hardly touch or dare to
question. To cast a world of doubts is vain and senseless,
where we enforc'd must either act or perish; and to be nice
in that hath no election, doth waste out time, and not prevent the errour : If you stick fast in this your tender pity,
I must in justice then accuse my fortune, that gave my heart
to such a female Weakness. Is there a disproportion in
this action, to keep the Crown with bloud, that was so
gotten ? Is there a more restraint to keep than get by Treason ? If so, I yield, and will sit still and ruine. Had Edward known or fear'd, he had prevented, nor you nor I had
had the Power to hurt him : But he neglected time, and now
repents it ; and so must we, if we embrace his errour. Fear
is far less in sense than apparition, and makes the shadow
greater than the subject, which makes a faintness as the
Fancy leads it, where is small reason to be so affected. You
urge it cannot be concealed or hidden. I not deny but it
may be discovered; such deeds may yet be so contrived and
acted, that they prevent all proof, if not suspicion. But
why do I spend time in this perswasion ? let him get free,
whom we so much have wronged, let him examine our proceedings, sift our actions, perhaps he will forget, forgive,
be reconciled : and spare your tears, lest that your mighty
Brother should chance grow angry: if you lose your Greatness,
you may if you be pleased abide the tryal. Mortimer's
resolv'd, since you refuse his judgment, you neither prize
his safety, nor his service ; and therefore he will seek some
other refuge before it be too late, and too far hopeless.

   With this he flings away in discontentment, as if he   *Mortimer flings away.*
meant with speed to quit the Kingdom. The amazed
Queen pursues and overtakes him, who seem'd unwil-
ling to prolong the treaty: *Stay, gentle* Mortimer,   *The Queens expostulati-on.*
(quoth she) *I am a Woman, fitter to hear and take ad-*
vice, than give it ; think not I prize thee in so mean a
fashion, as to despise thy Safety or thy Council. Must Ed-

ward *dye, and is there no prevention ? Oh wretched state of Greatness, frail Condition , that is preserv'd by Bloud, secur'd by Murder ! I dare not say I yield, or yet deny it; Shame stops the one, the other Fear forbiddeth : only I beg I be not made partaker, or privy to the time, the means, the manner.* With this she weeps, and fain would have recanted, but she saw in that course a double danger.

Mortimer, that had now what he lookt for, assures her he would undergo the act and hazard; which would not have moved, if not inforced by those strong motives of their certain danger. He requests alone the King might seal a Warrant, that he may change anew his former Keepers. Sir *Morice Barcklaye*, as it seems, had been aloof, off, treated with, but was not pliable, or apt to fasten; he was both careful of his Charge, and Masters Safety ; this takes him suddenly from his custody. Sir *Thomas Towurlie* supplies his place, with his old partner ; they having received their new Warrant, and their Royal Prisoner, carry him by sudden and hasty Journeys to *Cork*-Castle, the place that in all the world he most hated. Some say that he was foretold by a certain Magician, who as it seems was his Craftsmaster, that this place was to him both fatal and ominous. 'Twas ill in him to seek by such ill and unlawful means the knowledge of that, which being known did but augment his sorrow. Whatsoever the cause was, his arrival here makes him deeply heavy, sad and melancholy: his Keepers, to repel this humour, and to take him off from all fear and suspicion, feed him with new hopes and pleasant discourse, improving his former entertainment both in his Diet and Attendance ; while his misgiving spirit suspects the issue : Though he would fain have fashion'd his belief to give them credit, yet he had such a dull cloud about his heart, it could receive no comfort.

The fatal Night in which he suffer'd shipwrack, he eats a hearty Supper, but stays not to disgest it ; immediately

diately he goes to Bed, with forrow heavy; affoon he takes his Reſt, and ſleeps ſecurely, not dreaming of his end ſo near approaching. Midnight the Patron of this horrid Murder being newly come, this Crew of perjur'd Traitors ſteal ſoftly to his Chamber, finding him in a ſweet and quiet Sleep, taking away his Life in that advantage.

He is murdered.

The Hiſtorians of theſe Times, differ both in the time, place, and manner of his Death; yet all agree, that he was foully and inhumanly murther'd, yet ſo, that there was no viſible or apparent ſigne which way 'twas acted. A ſmall tract of time diſcovers the Actors, and ſhews evidently that it was done by an extremity of Violence: they long eſcape not: though *Mortimer*'s greatneſs for the preſent time keep them both from queſtion and puiſhment, yet by the Divine Juſtice they all meet with a miſerable and unpitied Death; and the Maſter-work-man himſelf in a few years after ſuffered an ignominious Execution.

The Queen, who was guilty but in circumſtance, and but an acceſſory to the Intention, not the Fact, taſted with a bitter time of Repentance, what it was but to be quoted in the Margent of ſuch a Story; the ſeveral relations ſo variouſly expreſt of their Confeſſions, that were the Actors and Conſenters to this deed, differ ſo mainly, that it may be better paſt over in ſilence, than ſo much as touch'd; eſpecially ſince if it were in that cruel manner, as is by the major part agreed on, it was one of the moſt inhumane and barbarous acts that ever fell within the expreſſion of all our *Engliſh* Stories; fitter rather to be paſs'd over in ſilence, than to be diſcours'd, ſince it both diſhonoureth our Nation, and is in the Example ſo dangerous. It ſeems *Mortimer* was yet a Novice to *Spencer*'s Art, of that ſame *Italian* trick of Poyſoning, which queſtionleſs had wrought this work as ſurely, with a leſs noiſe, and fewer agents: It had been happy if ſuch a Villany had never gain'd knowledge

ledge or imitation in the World : since it came to be
entertain'd as a necessary servant of State , no man that
runs in opposition, or stands in the way of Greatness,
is almost secure in his own house, or among his Friends
or Servants. I would to God we had not fresh in
our Memory so many bleeding Examples, or that this
Diabolical Practice might stop his career with the Mischief it hath already done : But so long as the close conveyance is deemed a Politick Vertue, and the Instruments by Power and Favour are protected, what can be
expected, but that in short time it must fall under the
compass of a Trade or Mystery, as fit for private Mur-
therers as Statesmen?

But leaving the professors of this execrable practice
to their deserts, and that guilt which still torments them;
Thus fell that unfortunate King *Edward* the Second,
who by the course of Age and Nature might have out-
run many years, had not his own Disorder, the Infidelity of his Subjects, and the Treachery of those that
had deprived him of his Kingdome, sent him to an untimely Death and Ruine. Many Reasons are given,
probable enough, to instance the necessity of his Fall,
which questionless may be the secondary means; but
his Doom was register'd by the inscrutable Providence
of Heaven, which with the self-same Sentence punish'd
both him and *Richard* the Second his great Grandchild,
who was coequally guilty of the same Errours, that
both betrayed them and the Peace of their Kingdome.
Henry the Sixth, though he tasted of the same Cup of
Deposition, yet there was more reason to induce it :
Henry the Fourth his Grandfather was an Usurper, and
had unjustly got the Crown by pulling down the House
of *York*, and exalting that of *Lancaster*, which in Justice brings it back again to the right Inheritour ; yet
were not those times innocent of those enormities which
occasion'd their confusion. It is most true, that *Henry*
himself was a sweet harmless condition'd Man, religious,

and

and full of Moral Goodnefs; but he was fitter for a
Cloifter than a Crown, being tranfported with a Divine Rapture of Contemplation, that took him off from
the care of all Worldly Affairs; while *Margaret* his
Wife, Daughter of *Reynard* that ftil'd himfelf King of
Naples and *Jerufalem*, acted her part with a like imitation; though fhe had not a *Gavefton*, a *Spencer*, or a
Duke of *Ireland*, yet fhe had a *Suffolk*, and a *Somer-
fet*, that could teach the fame way to the Deftruction
and Depofition of her Husband.

These three fympathized in their Royal Inheritance,
in their Depofitions, Deaths, and Fortunes; and thefe
alone, fince the Conqueft of the *Normans*, unlefs we
rank into the number *Edward* the Fifth, which muft be
with an impropriety, fince he was by *Richard* his Tyrannical Uncle murdered before he was Crowned:
If we example him with them, we may it is true conclude his cafe moft miferable, that loft the Crown before he enjoy'd it, or had the perfection of years to
make known his Inclination. The event that followed
the others, efpecially the two precedent, may be fitly
a Caution and Admonition to Pofterity, and teach
them what it is to hazard a Kingdome, and their own
Lives, by the continuing of a wilful Errour. Certainly
we have had other Kings fully as vicious, that have
out-liv'd their Vices, not dying by a violent hand, but
by the ordinary and eafie courfe of Nature; they were
more cautelous and flexible, and were content in the
more moderate ufe of their own Vices.

The Condition of this our *Edward*, the fubject of
this Story, was not in it felf more hurtful, than dangerous to the Peace and Tranquillity of the whole Kingdome. If by Heat of Youth, Height of Fortune, or
the Corruptions of Nature, the Royal Affections flie
loofely and at random; yet if it extend no farther than
the fatisfaction of the private Appetite, it may obfcure
the glory, but not fupplant the ftrength and fafety of a

Scepter.

Scepter. But when it is not only vicious in it self, but doth patronize it in others, not blushing or shrinking in the justification, it is a fore-running and presaging Evidence, that threatens danger, if not destruction. It is much in a King, that hath so great a Charge deliver'd over to his care and custody, to be himself dissolute, licentious, and ill-affected; but when he falls into a second errour, making more delinquents Kings, where one is too much, he brings all into disorder, and makes his Kingdome rather a Stage of Oppression, than the Theater of Justice, which opens the ready way to an ensuing Misery. The heart of the Subject as it is obliged, so it is continued by the Majesty and Goodness of the King: if either prove prostitute, it unties the links of Affection; those lost, the breach of Duty succeeds; which hunts after nothing but Change and Innovation. The bridle of the Laws is too weak a restriction, especially when it is infring'd by him, that is most bound to protect it. Neither can the King in Justice blame or punish the breach, when he himself goes the way of subversion of those Precepts, which should preserve his Peace and Obedience. It is so singular and so weighty a Consideration, that a Burthen should never be imposed upon the Subject by extent of the Prerogative; that may beget a just Grievance, besides the grief in payment; the novelty of the act, incites to a tumultuous opposition. Where there is neither Law to warrant, nor fit president to induce the Injustice of the demand, such actions begin in Complaint; which unredressed fall into an extremity, which draws with it a desperate hazard. If the tye of Duty and Allegeance preserve the Obedience to the Crown inviolate, let him beware that is the Prime Instrument, or Seducer; for he must be persecuted with implacable hatred, which ends not until he be made a Sacrifice to expiate and quench the fury, or the endangering of his Master by his unjust Protection. It is no less proper for the Majesty jefty and Goodnefs of a King, in cafe of a general Complaint, to leave thofe great Cedars to the trial of the Law, and their own purgation; this makes known the integrity and equality of his Juftice, which fhould not be extended to the grubbing up of Brambles and Shrubs, while monftrous Enormities of a greater height and danger fcape unlopped. The accumulation of his Favour, though it be a property of his own Power, yet ought it in fome meafure to be fatisfactory, as well in the prefent worth of him elected, as in his future progreffion; elfe in the continuance he windes himfelf into the danger of participating his hatred, as well as protection of his Errour. The eye of the Subject waits curioufly upon their Sovereigns actions, which if they feem to degenerate from his Wifdome and Greatnefs, and preferring a private Inconvenience before the redrefs of a publick Grievance, it by degrees varies the integrity of the heart, and begets a liberty of Speech; which fall often on the actions of Revolt and Tumult. Neither is it proper (if there muft be a Dotage in the Royal Affections) that the object of their weaknefs fhould fway and manage the Affairs of State; fuch an Intermixture begets Confufion, and Diforder, accompanied with Envy, Hatred, and a world of Errours: If the King be never fo innocent, yet in this courfe he cannot avoid the actions of Injuftice. Experience tells the right ufe of a Favourite. A good Caufe in the integrity of time warrants it felf, and needs no fupporter: But Imperfection, Fraud, Difhonefty, and Weaknefs in true Worth, fly to his protection, that by his ftrength they may prevail, which in Equity and Juftice are meerly corrupt and counterfeit: Money, Friends, or Favour engageth him, and he his Mafter; hence proceed all manner of Oppreffion and Diforder. Let the Spring-head be never fo pure and unpolluted, yet fuch a Diver makes it foul and muddy. A fmooth Tongue finding a favourable hearing, fets a fair glofs

upon

upon the blackeſt Overture; Love and a ſeeming Goodneſs leads, where all ſeems currant; which hatches
daily broods of grief and miſchief: Thus doth the
Kingdom ſuffer, ſo miſguided. Had this unhappy ſubject of this Story not been thus abuſed, had he been
worſer far, he had ſubſiſted; but when for his inglorious Minions, *Gaveſton* and *Spencer*, who ſucceſſively
enjoy'd him, he made the Kingdome a prey to their
Inſolence, he found both Heaven and Earth conſpir'd
his ruine. So great a Fall theſe latter times produce
not; a King in a potent Kingdome of his own, depoſed
by a handful of Strangers, who principally occaſioned
it, without ſo much as any Kinſman, Friend, or Subject
that either with his Tongue or Sword declar'd himſelf
in his Quarrel. But you may object, He fell by Infidelity and Treaſon, as have many other that went before and followed him. 'Tis true; but yet withal obſerve, here was no ſecond Pretendents, but thoſe of
his own, a Wife, and a Son, which were the greateſt
Traytors: had he not indeed been a Traytor to himſelf, they could not all have wronged him. But my
weary Pen doth now deſire a reſpite; wherefore leaving
the perfection of this, to thoſe better Abilities that
are worthy to give it a more full expreſſion; I reſt,
until ſome more fortunate Subject invite a new Relation.

THE

AN
Alphabetical TABLE.

S ſ   And

The TABLE.

The TABLE.

S ſ 2   Scots

The TABLE.

FINIS.

Cottoni Posthuma: Divers Choice Pieces, wherein are discussed several Important Questions, concerning the Right and Power of the Lords and Commons in Parliament. By the Renowned Antiquary Sir Robert Cotton Baronet. London: Printed by M. C. for C. Harper, and are to be Sold in Fleet-street, the Exchange, and Westminster.

The true Portraiture of King Edward the
Second King of England & Lord of Ireland
Duke of Aquitaine etc: He Raigned 19. yeares &
Seven Months: Buried at Glocester:

F. sculpsit.

THE
HISTORY

Of the moſt unfortunate Prince

King EDWARD II.

WITH

Choice *Political* Obſervations on Him
and his unhappy Favourites,
GAVESTON & SPENCER:

CONTAINING

Several *RARE PASSAGES* of thoſe Times,
Not found in other *Hiſtorians.*

---

*Found among the Papers of, and (ſuppoſe.! to be)
Writ by the Right Honourable*

HENRY Viſcount FAULKLAND,

Sometime Lord Deputy of Ireland.

LONDON:

Printed by *A. G.* and *J. P.* and are ſold by *John
Playford,* at his Shop near the *Temple-Church,* 1680.

Books *sold by* John Playford, *at his Shop near the* Temple-Church.

MUsic's *Recreation* on the *Viol Lyra-way*, containing a Collection of New Lessons, with Instructions for Beginners. Price 2 *s.*

Apollo's Banquet for the *Treble-Violin*, containing new Theater-Tunes, Ayres, Corants, Sarabands, Jigs, and Horn-pipes; to which is added, the Tunes of the new *French* Dances: Also Rules and Directions for Practitioners on the *Treble-Violin.* Price 1 *s.* 6 *d.*

The *Treasury of Music*, containing three Books of *Select Ayres* and *Dialogues* to sing to the *Theorbo-Lute*, or *Bass-Viol*; Composed by Mr. *Henry Laws*, and others. All bound in one Volum in Folio. Price 10 *s.*

Choice *Ayres*, *Songs*, and *Dialogues*, being most of the newest Songs sung at Court, and at public Theaters. Composed by several Gentlemen of His Majesties Music, in Folio, newly reprinted with large Additions. Price 3 *s.*

The *Musical Companion*, containing Catches, Ayres, and Songs, for two, three, or four Voices, bound up in Quarto. Price 3 *s.* 6 *d.*

The *Introduction to the Skill of Music*, both Vocal and Instrumental, by *J. Playford*, in Octavo. Price bound 2 *s.*

THE

PREFACE.

HENRY CARY, *Viscount* Faulkland, (*among whose Papers the following History was found*) *was born at* Aldnam *in* Hertford-shire; *his extraordinary Parts, being a most accomplish'd Gentleman, and a complete Courtier, got him such an Esteem with King* James, (*who for his great Learning and Sagacity is stiled* The English Solomon) *that he thought him a Person fitly qualified to be Lord Deputy of* Ireland, (*the Government of which place required at that time a Man of more than ordinary Abilities*) *which Trust he very well discharged. Being recalled into* England, *he lived honourably here, 'till by an unfortunate accident he broke his Leg in* Theobald's Park ; *of which soon after he died. He was a Person of great Gallantry, the Ornament and Support of his Countrey, which he served with no less*

Faith-

The Preface.

Faithfulness and Prudence abroad, *than Honour and Justice at* home, *being an excellent Statesman. During his stay at the University* of Oxford, *his Chamber was the Rendevouz of all the eminent Wits, Divines, Philosophers, Lawyers, Historians, and Politicians of that time; from whose Conversation he became Eminent in all those Qualifications.*

The Subject of the following History (supposed to be written by the above-mentioned Nobleman) is the unhappy *Lives, and untimely Deaths, of that Unfortunate* English *King* Edward *the Second, and his two Favourites* Gavelton *and* Spencer; *for his immoderate love to whom, (says Dr.* Heylin) *he was* hated *by the Nobles, and* contemned *by the Commons. This King (saith Sir.* Richard Baker) *was a comely Person, and of great strength, but much given to drink, which render'd him unapt to keep any thing secret. His greatest fault was, he loved but one, for if his Love had been divided, it could not have been so violent; and though Love* moderated *be the best of Affections, yet the* Extremity *of it is the* worst *of Passions.* Two Virtues were eminent in him, above all his Predecessors, Continence *and* Abstinence; *so* continent, *that he left* no *base* Issue
behind

The Preface.

behind him ; so abſtinent , *that he took no*
baſe Courſes *for raiſing Money.*

Our Author cloſes his Hiſtory without decla-
ring the Particulars of the Murder of this
Prince , wherefore I ſhall give you an account
thereof , as I find it ſet down by the aforeſaid
Sir Richard Baker.

Many ways were attempted to take away
his Life. Firſt , they vexed him in his Diet,
allowing him nothing that he could well endure
to eat , but this ſucceeded not : Then they
lodged him in a Chamber over Carrion and
dead Carcaſes , enough to have poiſoned him ;
and indeed he told a Workman at his Window,
he never endured ſo great a miſery in all his
Life ; but neither did this ſucceed. Then they
attempted it by Poyſons , but whether by the
ſtrength of his Conſtitution , or by the Divine
Providence, neither did this ſucceed. At laſt
the peſtilent Achitophel, *the Biſhop of* Hereford, *deviſed a Letter to his Keepers, Sir* Thomas Gourney, *and Sir* John Mattrevers,
blaming them for giving him too much liberty,
and for not doing the Service which was ex-
pected from them ; and in the end of his
Letter wrote this Line, Edvardum occidere
nolite timere bonum eſt ; *craftily contriving*
it

The Preface.

it in this doubtful sence, that both the Keepers might find sufficient warrant, and himself excuse. The Keepers guessing at his meaning, took it in the worst sence, and accordingly put it in Execution. They took him in his Bed, and casting heavy Bolsters upon him, and pressing him down, stifled him; and not content with that, they heated an Iron red hot, and through a Pipe thrust it up into his Fundament, that no marks of Violence might be seen; but though none were seen, yet some were heard; for when the Fact was in doing, he was heard to roar and cry all the Castle over. This was the lamentable End of King Edward of Carnarvan, Son of King Edward the First.

What became of the Actors and Abettors of this deep Tragedy, Sir Winston Churchill tells us in these words, with which I shall conclude.

Poor Prince, how unkindly was he treated, upon no other account but that of his own overgreat kindness! Other Princes are blamed for not being ruled by their Counsellors, he for being so: Who whilst he lived, they would have him thought to be a Sot, but being dead, they could have found in their hearts to have made him a Saint. How far he wrong'd his people
doth

The Preface.

doth not appear, there being very few or no
Taxations laid upon them all his time; but
how rude and unjust they were towards him, is
but too manifest. But their violence was se-
verely paid by Divine Vengeance, not only upon
the whole Kingdom, when every Vein in the
Body Politic was afterwards opened, to the endangering the letting out of the Life-blood of
the Monarchy in the Age following; but upon
every particular Person consenting to, or concern'd in his Death. For as the Throne of his
Son that was thus set in Blood (though without
his own guilt) continued to be imbru'd all his
Reign, which lasted above fifty Years, with
frequent Executions, Battels, or Slaughters;
the Sword of Justice, or his own, being hardly
ever sheath'd all his time: So 'tis said, that
the Queen her self dyed mad, upon the apprehension of her own, in Mortimer's disgrace, who
was executed at Tiburn, and hung there two
days to be a spectacle of Scorn. The King's
Brother Edmond had this punishment of his
Disloyalty, to be condemn'd to lose his Head
for his Loyalty, it being suggested (and happy
it had been for him if it had been prov'd) that
he endeavoured the Restoration of his Brother;
his Death being imbitter'd by the mockery of
Fortune, whilst by keeping him upon the Scaf-
fold five hours together, before any body could
be

The Preface.

be found that would Execute him, he was deluded with a vain hope of being saved. The Fiend Tarlton, Bishop of Hereford, who invented the cursed Oracle that justified the Murderers, dyed with the very same Torture, as if the hot Iron that sear'd his Conscience had been thrust into his Bowels. Of the two Murderers, one was taken and butcher'd at Sea, the other dyed in Exile, perhaps more miserable. And for the Noblility in general, that were Actors in the Tragedy, they had this Curse upon them, that most of their Race were cut off by those Civil Discords of their divided Families, to which this strange Violation gave the first beginning, not long after.

THE

The LIFE of

EDVVARD II.

KING OF

ENGLAND.

EDWARD the Second, born at *Carnarvan*, was immediately after the death of *Edward* the First his Father, crowned King of *England*. If we may credit the Historians of those times, this Prince was of an Aspect fair and lovely, carrying in his outward appearance many promising predictions of a singular expectation. But the judgment, not the eye must have preheminence in the censure of Human passages, the visible Calender is not the true character of inward perfection, evidently proved in the Life, Reign, and untimely Death of this unfortunate Monarch.

His

His Story Eclipſeth this glorious Morning, making the noontide of his Soveraignty full of Tyrannical oppreſſions, and the Evening more memorable by his Death and Ruine. Time, the diſcoverer of truth, makes evident his impoſture, and ſhews him to the World, in Converſation light, in Will violent, in Condition wayward, and in Paſſion irreconcileable.

Edward his Father, a King no leſs Wiſe than Fortunate, by his diſcreet Providence, and the Glory of his Arms, had laid him the ſure Foundation of a happy Monarchy. He makes it his laſt care ſo to inable and inſtruct him, that he might be powerful enough to keep it ſo. From this Conſideration he leads him to the *Scotiſh* Wars, and brings him home an exact and able Scholar in the Art Military. He ſhews him the benefit of Time and Occaſion, and makes him underſtand the right uſe and advantage. He inſtructs him with the precious Rules of Diſcipline, that he might truly know how to obey, before he came to command a Kingdom. Laſtly, he opens the cloſet of his Heart, and preſents him with the politic Myſteries of State, and teacheth him how to uſe them by his own Example, letting him know, that all theſe helps are little enough to ſupport the weight of a Crown, if there were not a correſpondent worth in him that wears it.

Theſe Principles make the way open, but the prudent Father had a remaining task of a much harder temper. He beheld many ſad remonſtrations of a deprave and vicious Inclination, theſe muſt be purified, or his other cautions were uſeleſs, and to little purpoſe. A corruption in Nature,

that

that by practice hath won it self the habit of being ill, requires a more than ordinary care to give it reformation. Tenderness of Fatherly Love abuseth his belief, and makes him ascribe the imperfections of the Son, to the heat of Youth, want of Experience, and the wickedness of those that had betray'd his unripe Knowledge, and easie Nature, with so base impressions. He imagins, Age, and the sad burthen of a Kingdom, would in the sence of Honour, work him to thoughts more innocent and noble; yet he neglects not the best means to prepare and assure it. He extends the height of Entreaty, and useth the befitting severity of his paternal Power, making his Son know he must be fit for a Scepter, before he enjoy it. He takes from him those tainted humours of his Leprosie, and enjoyns him by all the ties of Duty and Obedience, no more to admit the Society of so base and unworthy Companions. *Gaveston*, the *Ganimede* of his affections, a Man, as base in birth as conditions, he sentenceth to perpetual Exile.

The melancholy Apparitions of this loth to depart, gives the aged Father an assurance, that this *Syren* had too dear a Room in the wanton Cabinet of his Son's heart. He strives to enlighten his mind, and to make him quit the memory of that dotage, which he foresaw in time would be his destruction. But death overtakes him before he could give it perfection, the time is come, that he must, by the Law of Nature, resign both his Life and Kingdom.

He summons his Son, and bequeaths him this dying Legacy, commanding him, as he will in another day answer his disobedience, never to repeal his fentence. To his Kindred and Peers, that with fad Tears, and watry Eyes, were the companions of his Death-bed; he fhortly dif-courfeth the bafe conditions of this Parafite, and lets them underftand, both their own, and the Kingdom's danger, if they withftood not his re-turn; if it were occafioned. They knew his in-junctions were juft, and promife to obferve them, he is not fatisfied till they bind it with an Oath, and vow religioufly to perform it. This fends him out of the World with more confidence, than in the true knowledge of his Son's wilful difpofition he had caufe to ground on.

The Father's Funeral Rights performed, *Edward* in the pride of his years undertakes the Crown, and guidance of this glorious Kingdom. He glories in the advantage, knowing himfelf to be an abfo-lute King, and at liberty; yet thinks it not enough, till the *belief* of the Kingdom did equally affure it. He efteems no Act more proper to confirm it, than running in a direct ftrain of oppofition againft his Predeceffor's will and pleafure. The ftrong motives of his violent affection fuggefts reafons, that the Majefty of a King may not be confined from his deareft pleafure. When he was a Son, and a Subject, he had witneffed his obedience, being now a King and a Soveraign, he expects a correfpondence of the fame nature. Where there was fo ready an inclination in the Will, Reafon found ftrength enough to warrant it, which made him make *Gavefton*'s return the firft Act of his Sove-raignty. No proteftation of his Lords, nor per-fuafion of his Council, can work a diverfion, or win fo much as a befitting refpect. The Barons
that

that were unable to withftand, are contented to
obey, attending the iffue of this fo dangerous a
refolution. Where the News was fo pleafing, the
Journey is as fudden, *Gavefton* lofeth not a minute,
till he felt the embraces of his Royal Lord and
Mafter.

Edward having thus regained his beloved *Damon*,
is fo tranfported with his prefence, that he forgets
the will and ordinary refpect due to the greateft
Lords and Pillers of his Kingdom; and hence proceeds their firft difcontent and murmur. Many
ways are invented to diffolve this enchantment,
but none more fit and worthy then to engage him
in the facred knot of Wedlock. The Intereft of a
Wife, was believed the only remedy to engrofs or
divert thofe unfeddly affections, which they beheld
fo loofely and unworthily proftituted. *Ifabel*,
the Daughter of the *French* King, the goodlieft
and beautifulleft Lady of her time, is moved, and
the tender on w fides as plaufibly accepted.

This fends *Edward*, fcarce a King of nine
Months ftanding, into *France*, and brings him
back, feas'd of a Jewel, which not being rightly
valued, occafioned his enfuing Ruin. The excellency of fo fweet and vertuous a companion could
not fo furprize her Bridegroom, but *Gavefton* ftill
kept poffeffion of the faireft room in his affections.
He makes it more notorious by creating him Earl
of *Cornwal*, and the Gift of the goodly Caftle
and Lordfhip of *Wallingford.*

Gavefton applies himfelf wholly to the humour
of the King, and makes each word that falls from
his mouth an Oracle; their affections go hand in
hand, and the apparent injuftice of the one never

found contradiction in the other. The Subjects
Voice was so fortunate, that it was always concurrent where the King maintained the party: If
the discourse were Arms, *Gaveston* extoll'd it as
an Heroic Vertue; if Peace, he maintained it
not more useful than necessary; unlawful pleasure
he stiled a noble Recreation; and unjust Actions,
the proper and becoming Fruits of an absolute
Monarchy. These Gloses so betray the willing
ear that heard them, that no Honour is thought
good and great enough for the Reporter. The
greatest Commands and Offices are in the person or
disposure of *Gaveston*. The command of War,
and all Provisions Foreign and Domestic, are committed solely to his care and custody. All Treaties
for Peace or War had their success or ruin by his
direction and pleasure. The King Signed no Dispatch private or public, but by his consent or ap-
pointment. So that all men believed their Soveraign
to be but a meer Royal shadow, without a real
substance. Neither was it enough to advance him
beyond his desert, or the rules of a modest proportion; But his Power must be made more extant in
the Commitment to the Tower of the Bishop of
Chester, whom he quarrels as the occasion of his
first banishment.

These insolencies, carried with so great a height
and contempt, are accompanied with all the remon-
strances of a justly grieved Kingdom. The ancient
Nobility that disdain'd such an Equal, justly exclaim
against the Iniquity of the time, that made him
their Superiour. The grave Senators, that understood their own worths, are discontent to see themselves rejected, while Upstarts, by Money or Favour,
possess

poſſeſs the higher places. The Soldier that with
his Blood had purchas'd his Experience, laments
his own diſhonour, ſeeing unworthy Striplings
advanced, while he like the ruins of a goodly
Building is left to the wide World without uſe or
reparation. The Commons in a more intemperate
faſhion make known their griefs, and ſad oppreſſions.

Gaveſton, that both ſaw and knew the general
diſcontent, ſought not to redreſs it, but with an
ill adviſed confidence ſtrives to out-dare the worſt
of his approaching danger. *Lincoln*, *Warwick*,
and *Pembrook*, whoſe noble hearts diſdained the
o'regrown height of this untimely Muſherompt,
let the King know their fidelity, and his apparent
Error. He muſt free himſelf, and right them,
or elſe they will ſeek it in another Faſhion.

Edward knew their Complaints were juſt, yet
was moſt unwilling to hear or relieve them; till
ſeeing their ſtrong reſolution, and himſelf wholly
unprovided to withſtand the danger, he makes
his affections ſtoop to the preſent neceſſity, and
conſents to a ſecond baniſhment of his ſo dearly
beloved Favourite. *Gaveſton*, in the height and
pride of his ambition, is enforced to leave his
Protector, and to make *Ireland* the place of his
Abiding. With a ſad heart he takes his leave,
departing yet with a more deſire of revenge, than
ſorrow for his abſence.

All things thus reconciled, the Kingdom began
to receive a new life; mens hopes were ſuitable
to their deſires, and all things ſeem to promiſe a
ſwift and fair Reformation. But the bewitching
Charms of this wily Serpent made it ſoon evident,

that alone his death muſt prevent his miſchief. The perſonal correſpondency taken away, the affections of the reſtleſs King becomes far more violent. In the ſhort *interim* of his abſence, many reciprocal and ſweet meſſages interchangeably paſs betwixt them: *Edward* receives none, but he returns with a Golden Intereſt. He is not more ſenſible of his loſs, than the Affront and Injury, which perſuades him, it were too great indignity for him to ſuffer at the hand of a Subject: Though with his own hazard he once more calls him home, pacifying the incenſed Lords with an aſſurance of reconciliation and amendment. Thoſe ſtrict Admonitions ſo fully expreſt, were not powerful enough to reclaim the Fondneſs of the one, and Inſolency of the other.

The King regaining thus his beloved Minion, dotes on him in a far greater meaſure; and he to make the Muſic perfect, is of a far more violent temper. He affronts and condemns his Adverſaries, the ancient Nobility, ſurreptitiouſly waſting and imbezelling the Revenues of the Crown. He enflames the King's heart, ſo apt to receive it with all the motives of revenge, unquietneſs, and diſorder. The Jewels of the Crown, and that rich Table and Treſſels of Gold, are purloin'd and pawn'd to ſupply this wanton Riot. He had ſo true a knowledge of his Maſter's weakneſs, that he made him ſolely his. His Creatures were alone prefer'd, his Agents were the guides, and no man hath the King's ear, hand, or purſe, but ſuch as were by *Gaveſton* prefer'd or recommended.

Edward in his voluptuous ſenſuality ſupplies the place, but he had the ſole execution of that Royal
Pre-

Prerogative, that was alone proper to the Crown. The Nobility, whofe Lyon-hearts ftrugled betwixt the fence of their juft grief and allegiance, at length refolve, the King as to himfelf, muft be fo to them and the Kingdom, or they may no more endure it. With grave and weighty Reafons, they make the King know both the error and the vanity of his Affections; letting him truly under-ftand, that they had a dear Intereft, both in him and the Kingdom, which they would no longer fuffer to be fo abufed and mifguided.

Edward, being himfelf thus hardly preft, and that no entreaty or diffimulation could prevail, he muft now fet right the diforders of the King-dom, or have his work done to his hand, with lefs honour and more danger. Once more he fub-fcribes to their will, which he fees he cannot with-ftand or alter. *Gavefton* is again banifh'd, and makes *Flanders*, the next Neighbour, the place of his reception. Infinite was the joy of the Kingdom, who now expected a fecure Freedom from that dangerous Convulfion that threatned fo apparent an inteftine ruin.

This their imaginary Happinefs was made more real and perfect, in the knowledge that *Windfor* had bleft them with an Heir Apparent. The Royal Father is pleafed with the News, but had not (whe-her his divining Spirit, or *Gavefton*'s abfence were the caufe) thofe true expreffions of joy that in juftice became fo great a Bleffing. The abfence of his Minion could not lighten his heavy Soul, but all other comforts feemed vain and counterfeit. his diftracted brains take new and defperate refolu-tions; he revokes the fentence of his grief, and vows to juſtifie it againſt the utmoſt ſtrength of Contradiction.

He that dares do thoſe things that are diſhoneſt and unjuſt, is not aſham'd to juſtifie and maintain them : This Error gave this unfortunate King more Enemies than he had Friends to defend them. Kings that once falſifie their Faiths, more by their proper Will than a neceſſary Impulſion, grow infamous to foreign Nations, and fearful or ſuſpected to their own peculiar Subjects. He that is guilty of doing ill, and juſtifies the action, makes it evident, he hath won unto himſelf a habit of doing ſo, and a daring impudence to maintain it by the protection, of which he believes all things in a politic wiſdom lawful. This poſition may for a time flatter the Profeſſor, but it perpetually ends with Infamy, which ſtands with Reaſon and Juſtice ; for as vertue is the Road-way to perfection, ſo is the corruption of a falſe heart, the true path to a certain and an unpittied ruin.

The enraged Barons are not more ſenſible of their own diſparagement, than the inconſtancy and injuſtice of their Soveraign. They think this affront done to them and the whole Kingdom, of too high a nature to be diſpens'd with, yet with a temperate reſolution they a while attend the iſſue. The Actions of injuſtice ſeldom leſſen ; they believe progreſſion to be in all things an excellent Moral vertue. He that hath a will to do ill, and doth it, ſeldom looks back until he be at the top of the Stairs. This makes the ill affected return of this our Favourite, more infamous and hated. With an imperious ſtorm he lets the Lords know, he meditates nothing but revenge, and
waits

Waits a fit advantage to entertain it. They believe time ill loft in fo weighty a caufe, and therefore draw themfelves and their Forces together, before the King could prevent, or his abufer fhun it. The Clouds prefaging fo great a ftorm, he ftudies the beft means he could to avoid it. The general diftaft of the Kingdom takes from him the hope of an able party. *Scarborough* Caftle his laft refuge he makes his Sanftuary, but it was too weak againft the number of his Enemies, and the juftice of their quarrel. He falls at length into the power of thofe, from whom he had no caufe to expeft protection or mercy. The Butterflies of the time, that were the friends of his Fortunes, not him, feeing the Seafon chang'd, betake themfelves to the warmer Climate. His Greatnefs had won him many Servants, but they were but Retainers, that like Rats forfook the Houfe when they beheld it falling. The Spring was laden with many glorious and goodly Bloffoms, but the Winter of his Age leaves him naked, without a Leaf to truft to.

In this uncomfortable cafe remains this glorious Cedar, in the hands of thofe whom in his greater height he had too much condemn'd and abufed. They refolve to make fhort and fure work, unwilling to receive a command to the contrary, which they muft not obey, though it fhould come from him to whom they had fworn Obedience. Forfaken, unpittied, fcorn'd, and hated, he falls under the the hands of Juftice. *Gaverfeed* is the place which gives the Epilogue to this fatal Tragedy, whence his Adverfaries return more fatisfied than affured.

Thus

Thus fell that glorious Minion of *Edward* the Second, who for a time appeared liked a blazing Comet, and fway'd the jurifdiction of the ftate of *England*, and her Confederates. He did not remember in the fmiles and embraces of his lovely Miftris, that fhe was blind, nor made himfelf fuch a refuge as might fecure him when fhe prov'd unconftant. Such a Providence had made his end as glorious, as his beginning fortunate, leaving neither to the juft cenfure of Time or Envy.

The King's vexations in the Knowledge, are as infinite as hopelefs, his Paffions tranfport him beyond the height of Sorrow. He vows a bitter revenge, which in his weaknefs he ftrives to execute with more fpeed than advifement. The graver Senators, that had moft Intereft in his favour, mildly difcourfe his lofs to the beft advantage. They lay before him his contempt and abufive carriage, his infolence, Honour beyond his Birth, and Wealth above his Merit, which muft to all Ages give a juft caufe to approve their Actions, and his Fortune. The leaft touch of his memory adds more to the King's affliction, who is fixt not to forget, or forgive, fo bold and heinous a Trefpafs.

The operations in the King were yet fo powerful, but the jealoufies of the Actors are as cautelous, fo fair a warning-piece bids them in time make good their own fecurity. *Lincoln*, the principal Pillar of this Faction, follows his Adverfary to the Grave, but with a much fairer Fortune. This Man was a goodly piece of true Nobility, being in Speech and converfation fweet and affable; in refolution grave and weighty; his aged temper active above

above belief; and his wifdom far more excellent in a folid inward knowledge, than in outward appearance.

When the harbinger of Death pluck'd him by the Sleeve, and he faw, and knew he muft leave the World, he calls unto him *Thomas* Earl of *Lancafter*, that had married his Daughter, giving him a ftrict Impofition on his Death-bed, that he fhould carefully maintain the welfare of the Kingdom, and make good his place among the Barons. This reverend old Statefman faw the King's ways, and knew him to be a moft implacable Enemy, and with a kind of fpeculative prediction, would often feem to lament the Mifery of the time, where either the King, Kingdom, or both muft fuffer. The Son, whofe noble Heart was before feafoned with the fame impreffions, affures it, which he in time as really performs, though it coft him the lofs of his Eftate, Life, and Honour.

Things are too far paft to admit a reconciliation; the King's Meditations are folely fix'd upon revenge; and the Lords, how they may prevent, or withftand it. The Kingdom hangs in a doubtful fufpence, and all Mens minds are varioufly carried with the expectation of what would be the iffue. Meditation and interceffion brings it at length to Parliamentary difcuffion, which being affembled at *London*, enacts many excellent Laws, and binds both the King and Lords by a folemn Oath to obferve them. Thus the violence of this Fire is a while fuppreffed; and raked up in the Embers, that it may (in opportunity and advantage) beget a great danger.

.A

A new occasion prefents it felf, that makes each part temporize for a while, and fmothers, the thoughts of the enfuing Rumour. *Robert le Bruce* re-enters *Scotland*, whence he had been by *Edward* the First expuls'd, inverting all the *Englijh* Infti-tutions, that had fo lately fetled the Peace and fubjection of the Kingdom. *Edward*, tender of his Honour, and careful to preferve that pur-chafe, that had proved fo dear a bargain, adjourns his private fpleen, and provides to fupprefs this unlook'd for Rebellion. He knew the juftice of his quarrel, and wakens from the Dream, that had given him fo large a caufe of forrow. He gives his intentions a fmall intermiffion, and a lefs refpite; with all fpeed he levies an Army, and leads it with his own Perfon. Whether it were the juftice of Heaven, or his own misfortune or improvidence, the *Scots* attend and encounter him, making *Eaftrivelyn* the fatal witnefs of his difafter. His Army loft and defeated, he returns home laden with his own fhame and forrow. His return is welcomed with a ftrange Impoftor, that pretends himfelf the Heir of *Edward* the Firft, and the King the Son of a Baker. A Tale fo weak in truth and probability wins neither be-lief or credit. *Voidras*, this imaginary King, is apprehended, and makes *Northampton* Gallows the firft Stair of his Preferment. His Execution is ac-companied with as ftrange a ftory, which fuggefts the inftigation of a Spirit, that in likenefs of a Cat, had for two years fpace advifed it.

The King, with a true feeling grief, lamenting his difhonourable Return from *Scotland*, where his noble Father had fo oft difplay'd his victorious

Arms,

Arms, doth vow with a fpeedy refcue to revenge
it. He communicates his refolution with the
whole body of his Council, who are in their advice equally concurrent in the Action. The former lofs exacts a more care, and a better provifion. *York*, as the fitteft place, is made the Senate
of this grave Affembly. Thither refort all the
Sages of the Kingdom, and make it their firft
deliberation to fecure *Berwick*, that is one of the
Keys of the Kingdom, and expofed to the greateft
hazard. This Charge is given to Sir *Peter Spalden*,
who was believed able enough, both in fidelity
and valour. A fhort time difcovers him truly
poffeft of neither. A fmall Sum of Money, with
an expectant Preferment promifed, betrays the
truft repofed, and gives the *Scots* the full poffeffion
of the Charge to him committed.

The Pope, wifely forefeeing into the mifery of
this diffention, out of his Chriftian and pious
care, fends over two Cardinals, to mediate a
Peace and Agreement. They being arrived
in *England*, find the King well difpofed, fo the
Conditions might be reafonable, and fuch as might
become his Intereft and Honour. They pafs from
hence into *Scotland*, and are by the way with a
barbarous Example furprized and robb'd. The
King is infinitely difcontented with fo inhuman an
Act, that threw a taint upon the whole Nation.
Great enquiry is prefently made, which finds out
the Actors, and fends Sir *Peter Middleton*, and
Sir *Walter Selby*, to a fhameful and untimely execution. Immediately at the heels of this follows
another Example, no lefs infamous, and full of
danger.

Sir

Sir *Gilbert Denvil*, and others, pretending themselves to be Outlaws, with a jolly Army, to the number of Two hundred, ramble up and down the Country, acting divers notorious Infolencies and Robberies. The Fame of an attempt fo new and unexpected, without a fpeedy prevention, feemed to intimate a greater danger. A Commiffion is immediately fent out, which apprehends the heads of this encreafing mifchief, and delivers them over to the hand of Juftice. They which confeft themfelves out of the protection of the Law, and glory in their being fo, fall under his rigour.

Thofe that duly examined the truth of this action, believed the pretence to be but a Mask, that hid a more perilous intention. The King, by his untemperate and undifcreet actions, had loft the hearts of his People, and there was a general face of difcontent throughout the whole Kingdom. The Ulcers feftered daily more and more, which feemed to prefage and threaten, without fome fpeedy prevention, a dangerous iffue. All Men difcover their ill affections, expecting but a Patron that durft declare himfelf, and adventure to hang the Bell about the Cat's Neck. If this diforderly attempt, which was but to taft the Peoples Inclinations, had fucceded, the King (as it was to be feared) had much fooner felt the general lofs, and revolt of his whole Kingdom. But this work was referved to future time, and the operation of thofe, who had the time to effect it with more power and pretence of Juftice. The crying Maladies of this Climat were fuch, that the Divine Power fent down at one and the felf-

fame

fame inſtant his three fatal Executioners, *Plague*, *Dearth*, and *Famine*, to call upon us for a repentant Reformation. No part of the Kingdom is free, but was grievouſly afflicted by the unmerciful Proſecution of one, or all theſe fatal angry Siſters. So great a Miſery was too much, but it is ſeconded with a ſudden Invaſion of the hungry *Scots*, who apprehending the advantage of the preſent Viſitation, and ill Eſtate of their Neighbours, like a Land-Flood, over-run the naked and unprovided Borders.

The Arch-Biſhop of *York*, a grave and wiſe Prelate in his Element, but as far from the Nature, as Name of a Soldier, reſolves to oppoſe this over-daring and inſolent Eruption. He levies in haſt an Army, in number hopeful; but it was compos'd of Men, fitter to pray for the ſucceſs of a Battel, than to fight it. With theſe, and an undaunted hoping Spirit, he affronts the *Scots*, and gives them Battel, making *Mitton* upon *Swale*, that honoured his Enemies with the Glory of a ſecond Triumph, the place of his Diſaſter. Many Religious Church-men, with the purchaſe of their Lives, begin their firſt Apprentiſhip in Arms; whoſe loſs chriſt'ned this overthrow *The White Battel*.

The intent of this grave Prelate was queſtionleſs worthy of a great and ſingular Commendation, but the Act was wholly inconſiderate, weak, and unadviſed. It was not proper for his Calling to undertake a Military Function, in which he had no experience; neither did it agree with his Wiſdom or Piety to be an Actor in Blood, though the occaſion were ſo great and weighty. Too much care

C   and

and confidence improperly exprefl, doth many times overthrow and ruin the Caufe it feeks to ftrengthen and advantage. There ought to be in all confiderations of this nature, a mature Deliberation before we come to Aftion, elfe we lofe the Glory of our Aims, and commit all to the uncertain hazard of Time and Fortune. The Cardinals are now returned out of *Scotland*, by whom the King truly underftands that the hopes of Peace are defperate. Their leave taken, and loffes fairly repaired, they return to *Rome*, acquainting his Holinefs with the fuccefs of their Employment. The Pope being truly informed, that the *Scots* were neither conformable to his Will, or the general Good, excommunicates both that ufurping King and Kingdom.

The King, nearly touch'd with the lofs of *Berwick*, enflamed with the Infolency of his barbarous Enemies, and grieved with fo great a lofs of his People, refolves no more to fuffer, but to tranfport the War into the very Bowels of *Scotland*. To this effeft, with fpeed he haftens out his Directions, and gives prefent Order for the levying of Men, Arms, and Money, to begin the War, and continue it. The Royal Command, and defire of Revenge, gives Wings to this Refolution. An Army is ready, and attends the King's Pleafure, before he conceits his Will truly underftood, or bruited. Nothing is wanting but his own Perfon, or a fit Commander to lead them; he 1 ofeth no time, but appears in the Head of his Army before his Enemies had the leaft knowledge of this Affembly. With a hopeful expeftation he leads them on, and makes *Berwick* the Rendezvous,

that

that fhould make his Number compleat and perfeƈt.
Before this Strength that had the warranty of Art
and Nature, he makes the firft Experiment of this
Expedition. The Town begirt, was not more
confident of their own ftrength, than affured of a
fpeedy fupply or refcue. This gave the King a
longer delay than he believed, and his Enemies
leafure to raife and enable their Provifions, They
faw it a work too full of Danger and Hazard, to
venture the breach of the Body of fo great an
Army, that in Worth and Number fo far exceeded.
The memory of former Paffages and Trials,
taught them how to underftand their prefent condition; this begets in them a Refolution more
folid and hopeful. They leave the Road-way, and
war rather by Difcretion than Valour, which
fucceeds fo fortunately, that they furprize all the
Englifh Provifions, and enforce the King to a fecond
Return, more Fortunate, yet much lefs Honourable. It is true, he retreated, and brought back
his Army in fafety, but he had quitted the Siege
which he had vowed to continue againft the United
Power of *Scotland*, and loft wholly all that Wealth
and Luggage he had carried with him.

This fill'd all Men's mouths with a complaining
Grief, and made Foreign Nations think the *Englifh*
had loft their former lufter, and renowned valour.
It was wondred, that an Enemy fo weak and contemptible, fhould three feveral times fucceffively,
bear away the Garland from thofe, that had fo
often, and knew the way fo well to win and
wear it.

But now begins a fecond Fire of a higher Nature, that made the Kingdom a Theater ftain'd

with

with the noblest Blood, that within her Confines
had or Life or Being. The King, discouraged
with his Foreign Fortune, lays aside the thoughts
of Arms, and recalls into his wanton Heart the
bewitching vanities of his Youth, that had formerly bred him such Distemper. He was Royally
attended, but it was by those that made their
Tongues, rather the Orators of a pleasing falshood,
than a true sincerity. € These were fit Instruments
for such an ear, that would not hear, unless the
Music answered in an even correspondency. The
Infidelity of the Servant is in a true Construction
the Misery of the Master, which is more or less
dangerous, as is the weight and measure of his
Employment. It is in the Election of a Crown a
principal Consideration, to chuse such Attendants,
whose Integrity may be the Inducement, as well as
the Ability, else the Imaginary help proves rather
a Danger than Assistance. Neither is it safe or honourable, for the Majesty of a King, to seem to de-
pend solely on the Wisdom, Care, or Fidelity of
one particular Servant. Multiplicity of able Men
is the Glory and Safety of a Crown, which falls
by degrees into confusion, when one Man alone
acts all parts, whence proceeds a World of Error
and Confusion.

The King was not ignorant, that such a course
would make such as were his but at second hand,
yet he resolves to make a new choice, of one to
supply the room of his lost beloved *Gaveston*.
Though his diseased Court was furnished with a
large variety, yet his Eye fixeth on *Hugh*, the
younger of the *Spencers*, who was always tracta-
ble and conformable to the King's Will and Pleasure.

fure. This Man was in fhew fmooth and humble, of an infinuating Spirit, one that knew his Mafter's ways, and was ever careful to obferve them. He had applied himfelf wholly to *Edward's* will, and fed his wanton pleafures with the ftrains of their own Affection. Heat of Spirit, and height of Blood confult more with Paffion than Reafon, and a fhort Deliberation may ferve, where the Subject was fo pleafing, and to each fide agreeable.

The King, to make his Refolutions eminent, with more haft than advifement, makes him his Lord Chamberlain, and lets the World know, it was his Love and Will that thus advanc'd him. Scarcely is this new great Officer warm in his unbefitting Authority, but he exactly follows his Predeceffor-precedent to the Life, making all things lawful that were agreable to his Mafter's Will, or his fantaftical Humour.

The Peers of the Kingdom, that faw the fudden and hafty Growth of this undeferving Canker, refolve to lop or root it up, before it fhould o'retop their Lufter. *Spencer*, that in the precedent Story of *Gavefton*, beheld the danger of his own condition, begins in time to provide and ftrengthen a Party. His aged Father, fitter for his Beads than Action, he makes a young Courtier, and wins the King to give him Power and Affiftance. He labours to remove from his Mafter's ear all fuch as might endanger him, and fupplies their places with fuch as were his Creatures. Thofe that were too high for fuch a furprifal, by Perfuafion, Money, or Alliance, he feeks to engage, and make the Parties of this his coming Faction. The Body of the Court thus affured, his Actions in

C 3   the

the State went in an even Correfpondency. Thofe
that held him at a diftance, valuing their Fidelity
and Honour before fo bafe an advantage, faw
themfelves difgracefully cafhier'd, and others in-
ftalled in their Rooms, that had neither Worth,
Birth, or Merit. The Factious Entertainers of his
proffered Amity, not only enjoy their own, but
are advanced higher, which made them but the
Inftruments to act and further the Corruptions of
his Will and wicked Nature.

This Foundation laid, they now feem to contemn all fear of danger, and in that affurance,
exprefs their Contempt and Scorn againft the Nobility, who they knew would never entertain their
Society or Friendfhip. While thus the Rule and
Manage of all the Royal Affairs in their Power,
was daily more and more abufed, the Incenfed
Barons meet at *Sherborough*, where the Earl of
Lancafter, the Prime Agent, lays before them
(in a fhort and grave Difcourfe) the Iniquity and
Danger that feemed eminently to threaten both
them and the whole Kingdom, if fuch a Refolution
were not taken, as might affure a fpeedy Prevention. The Fore-knowledge of their Soveraign's
Behaviour, which would obferve no Rule or Proportion in his immodeft Affections, gave them fmall
hope to prevail by Perfuafion or Entreaty. They
too well underftood that *Spencer*'s Pride was too
great and haughty to go lefs without Compulfion,
and they muft fink a Key, or neither the Kingdom
or themfelves (againft fo Inveterate a Hatred)
could expect in reafon Safety or Affurance. *Hert-*
ford, *Mowbray*, and *Clifford*, fore a higher pitch,
and in plain terms affirm, That all other Refolu-
tions

tions were vain and hopeless, 'twas only Arms that
muſt right the Time and State ſo much diſorder'd.
Benningfield and *Mortimer* approve this Reſolution,
and as ſoon give it Life and Action. They enter
furiouſly on the Poſſeſſions of their Enemies,
ſpoyling and waſting like profeſs'd Enemies.

Such an Outrage flies with a nimble Wing to
the ears of the Owner, who as ſoon makes the
King the ſharer of his Intelligence, and encreaſeth
it to his own advantage. The King ſenſible of ſo
great an Affront; and as tender of the one, as cruel
to the other, publiſheth by Proclamation the ſen-
tence of his Royal Will and Pleaſure. The Actors
of this Miſdemeanor muſt appear and juſtifie themſelves, or preſently forſake the Kingdom.

The Lords that ſaw their Intereſts at Stake, as
they had begun, reſolve to maintain the Quarrel.
New Levies and Preparations are dayly made, to
make good the ſucceeding Iſſue. Yet the more to
juſtifie thoſe Arms, that in the beſt conſtruction
was deemed Rebellions, they ſend to the King a
fair and humble Meſſage. The Tenour whereof
lets him know, their Intentions were fair and honeſt, and the Arms thus levied, were rather to
defend, than offend his Perſon; only they in all
humility deſire, he would be graciouſly pleaſed to
remove and puniſh thoſe Vipers, which had too
near a Room in his Royal Heart, whereby they
had overthrown and undone the Peace and Tranquillity of the Kingdom.

The King that fears, is enforc'd to believe:
he knew their Informations were juſt, and he had
no Power to deny, or withſtand them. He aſſures
a Reformation; to make it more real, he adjourns

it to the ensuing Parliament, which is immediately summoned to appear at *London*. The jealous Lords, that too well knew the cunning and hatred of their malicious Adversaries, appear like themselves, bravely attended with a Crew of lusty Yeomen well Arm'd, which stiled this *The Parliament of White Bands*. The Major, seeing such a Confluence from all parts of the Kingdom; so ill enclined and well appointed, with a careful Providence reinforceth the City Guards, and planteth a strong Watch throughout all the strengths and parts of his Jurisdiction.

This great Assembly being now met, the complaining Barons find in both Houses a ready Belief, and as sudden a Censure. A solemn Declaration gives the King knowledge of their Sentence, which commands both the *Spencers*, Father and Son, into perpetual Exile. The King, as weak in his disability, as wilful in the least advantage, gives a sad and unwilling consent; which being known, gives the *Spencers* no time of Imparleance; their Judgment is immediately put in Execution, and they find more Servants than they desired to attend them to *Dover*, where they are immediately ship'd to go seek a new Fortune. The Elder, whose Snowy age, and more Innocence, deserved Pity, makes his Tears witness his true sorrow, and his Tongue unfold them. He taxeth his Son's Vanity and Ambition, and his own Weakness, that had so easily consented to his Ruin. He laments his misfortune, that in the Winter of his Age had cast him from his Inheritance, and had made him the Sea-mark and scorn of a whole Kingdom. He confesseth the folly, that led him (by indirect
means)

means) to the preservation of his high and ill acquired Greatness. He wisheth his carriage had been such, that in this so sad a change of Fortune, he might have found either Pity or Assistance. But it is the inseparable Companion of Greatness that is gotten in the By-way, and not by a just Desert or Vertue. It labours to support it self more by cunning and falshood, than by a sweet and winning temper, when it is of all other the most erroneous Maxim, that believes, Affections can be in a subordinate way gotten or assured. They are the proper Functions of the Soul, which move alone in their own course, without force, or the least impulsion. All other ways are but Temporary Provisions, that serve the present advantage; but he that by a just Desert wins the love and belief of his worth, hath laid a sure Foundation, making his Honour his own, and the Succession hereditary and permanent, to his everlasting Glory.

These imperious Servants thus removed, the Father, in obedience of his Doom, betakes himself to a Foreign Quietness. The Son, of a more turbulent and revengeful Spirit, keeps still a Seaboard in the skirts of the Kingdom, and falling short in Power, to requite the Authors of his disgrace, he expresseth his malice to the whole Nation. The Merchants free from all suspitions in their Voyages and Returns, are pillaged and rifled, and he the principal Actor.

Such a Domestic Piracy begets a general terror and exclamation, which fills the King's ears, and presseth (as it required) a speedy prevention or remedy. He knew the Action was foul, but it

was

was one of his own that had done it; and such a one that was too dearly valued, to be either perfecuted or punished. He studies first to satisfie his own Passion, before he right this injurious carriage against the Subject. This makes him reject the wholefom Admonitions of Friends, the Validity of his Laws, and those fearful Apparitions that present him with the danger of so foul an Enterprize, while with an Example new, and full of assured hazard, he repeals the sentence of their Exile. This Act gave him too large a time of Repentance, and may be a befitting instance to all ensuing posterity. The Actions of a Crown are Exemplary, and should be clean, pure, and innocent; the stains of their Errors dye not with them, but are regiftred in the story of their Lives, either with Honour or Infamy.

But to proceed in this Hiftorical Relation: The *Spencers* thus recalled, and reinvefted in their former Favour, they exprefs themfelves in another kind, and now by a strong hand strive to crush by degrees all those of the adverfe Faction. Sir *Bartholomew Baldfmer* was the first that tafted their fury and injuftice. His Caftle of *Leedes* in *Kent*, under a pretended and feigned Title, is furprized and taken from him, without a due Form, or any Legal Proceeding. Their return, and the abrogation of that Law that banifhed them, was provocation enough, there needed not this fecond Motive to enflame the hearts of the angry Barons. But when the unjuft Oppreffion of the Knight (their Ally and Confederate) was divulged, and came to their ears, they vow a bitter Revenge, and make fpeed to put it in Execution. They fee
the

the Fruits of their dalliance, and long abused confidence, and waken out of that slumber that had fed him with the *Chimera's* of so dull and cold a proceeding.

The King, who formerly had been so often surprized, in time arrives to provide a Remedy: he knew his Arms and not his Tongue must plead the injustice of his Actions, wherein if he again failed, he feared another manner of Proceeding. The *Spencers*, that evidently saw the eminency of their own dangers, make it their Master-piece to crush the Serpent in the head before it grew to perfection. They knew the height of their Offences were beyond the hope of mercy, and there was no way left of assurance, but that, which they must wade through in blood, and make good with the Sword their Lives, or else be sure to lose them. An Army is provided, and appears at *Shrewsbury* almost before it was bruited. The first exploit seiseth the two *Mortimers*, that had begun again their former Invasion of the *Spencers*. Their strength was great enough for such an Incursion, but much too weak to withstand or encounter this Royal Army. This first hansel so fortunate, gives life to their Adversaries, and Imprisons them in the Tower, before their Associates could be truly informed, or ready to relieve them.

There is now left no time to dispute: The Barons must with their Arms warrant their Proceedings, or they must miscarry in the Action. They had soon gathered a strength, with which they resolve to encounter the King at *Burton*. The knowledge of the great Power that came against them, and their own Weakness, wins them to a
retreat,

retreat, not more dangerous than difhonourable: But their Reafons were juft and weighty ; the Earl of *Lancafter* had fent Sir *Robert Holland* to raife his Tenants and Friends, which he hoped would in time reinforce his Army.

Valence Earl of *Pembrook*, that commands his Mafter's Forces, feeing the diforder of their going off, lays hold of the advantage, and chargeth them fo hotly, that they break and betake themfelves to their heels, with great loffes and confufion. *Holland* entrufted by the Earl of *Lancafter*, having accordingly performed the work he was employed in, marching up to the Refcue, is advertized of the State of their Affairs, which makes him feek his own Peace, and refign this fupply wholly up, to be difpofed of at the King's Will and Pleafure. The Supply fo unexpected is gracioufly received, and there is a fet refolution to employ it to the beft advantage.

The defpairing Lords, with their Adherents with much ado recover *Pomfret*, there a fecond Deliberation is taken, which held it the fafeft courfe to pafs on, and to poffefs the Caftle of *Donftanborough*, which was deemed a ftrength tenable enough until they could reinforce their Party, or work their own Conditions. This Refolution is prefently attempted with more haft than fortune. Sir *Andrew Harkely* meets and encounters them at *Burrowbrig*, where *Hertford*, *Clifford*, and others, died honourably, in maintaining a brave defence, while *Lancafter*, *Mowbray*, and many of their Adherents were taken, and with their Heads paid the ranfom of their Errors. The *Spencers*, like two furious Tigers that had feized their Prey,

give

give not their incenfed Mafter leave to deliberate
on the weight of fo fad a Work; the Lives of many
brave Subjects are taken away in an inftant, and
each part of the Kingdom is ftained with lofs of
that noble Blood, that had been much more glori-
oufly fpent in a Foreign War, than in thefe Domeftic and Civil Tumults.

Edward, that was apparently guilty of too
many other Vices, drowns their memory in this
fo cruel and bloody a Tyranny. The wreaking
Blood of fo many brave Gentlemen fo unfortu-
nately and untimely loft, doth cry for vengeance,
and hurry on the deftruction of the chief and principal Actors. Mercy fhould precede the feverity
of Juftice, if not to all, yet to fome, fince they
were not alike guilty. If *Lancafter* had been of
fo unnoble a Difpofition, the *Spencers* had neither
had time nor caufe to rejoyce in his Ruin. How
often had they by a full advantage had Power of
thefe their Enemies, yet made it evident, their
aims were not Blood but Reformation. And affuredly in this their laft Act, their Intents towards
the Crown were innocent in all other refpects,
than the defire of fupporting it with more Honour.
As things fell afterwards out, it had been to the
King a Happinefs if their Arms had prevailed, for
this Victory was the principal and fundamental
Caufe of his enfuing Ruin. Fear, and the expectation of danger, kept both him and his Favourites
in a better temper, fo long as there was fo ftrong
a Bridle. Certainly in the Regiment of a Kingdom, it is a wife and difcreet Confideration to
maintain and uphold a divided Faction, and to
countenance them fo, that the one may be ftill a

coun-

counterpoise to the other; by this means the King
shall be more truly served and informed.

The Subject that is too far exalted, and hath no
one to contradict or question him, considers not
the Justice, but the Means to preserve him, by
which the Judgment of the King is taxed, and he
is robb'd of the Hearts of his People. The greater
the height, the stronger is the working to maintain it, which seldom goes alone, but is accompanied for the most part with those State-Actions of
Impiety and Injustice, which draws with it so perpetual an envy and hatred; that it leads him head-
long to a fatal and dishonourable Conclusion.
Though the Fury of this enraged King had so fully
acted this bloody Tragedy, yet *Mortimer* is spared,
rather out of Forgetfulness than Pity, whose Life
had been more available than all these, that with
so great a speed had felt his Rigour. But he is
reserved for a second course, to teach the *Spencers*
that same *legem talionis*, and *Edward*, the plain
Song of his Error. The Kingdom seems now in
better Peace and setled; the principal Pillars of
the Common-wealth are taken away, and those
which remained are utterly disheartned in the danger of so fresh an Example.

This gains such a liberty to these triumphing
Sycophants, that they make the whole Kingdom,
as it were, the just Fruits of an absolute Conquest.
The King approves and maintains their Actions,
giving them the Regal Power for their Warranty.
All kind of insolent and unjust Oppressions are now
confidently practised, without contradiction or
question. No Exaction or unlawful Action is left
unattempted, while the grieved Kingdom languish-
                                                    eth

eth under the burden, yet durſt not ſtir to redreſs
it. The great Ones ſuffer baſely beyond their Birth
or Honour, yet look faintly one upon another,
not daring to revenge their Quarrel. The Commons murmuring complain, yet find not a Man
that will give them heart or leading.

The watchful *Spencers*, that ſaw and knew the
general hatred, and infamy of their own conditions, leſſen not their height, or fear the Sequel.
With a politic care they uſe their beſt means to
prevent it. The King's Humour naturally vicious,
they feed, with all the proper objects, that might
pleaſe or more betray his ſenſes. They ſtrive to
make him alike hateful to his Subjects, that in the
change of Fortune they might together run one
and the ſelf-ſame hazard.

There is yet another piece of State to this great
work as proper. *Edward* is but a Man, and a
Creature in nothing more conſtant than his Affections, yet theſe with age and time may alter, this
gap muſt be ſo ſtop'd, that they may be more aſſu-
red. *Hugh*, the younger of the *Spencers*, who
had a ſearching Brain, wiſe and active, believes
this work had two ſeveral dependences, the one
to keep him in continual Fear, the other in a perpetual Want. Theſe being marſhalled with Diſcretion, he knew would knit faſt his Maſter's Love,
and add to the opinion of his Wiſdom and Fidelity ; impoſing a kind of neceſſary Impulſion ſtill
to continue him. In his Breaſt alone was lock'd all
the paſſages and myſteries of State, whereby he
was moſt able to provide for the future inconveniences.

From this ground, with a kind of loose scorn, he continues the *French* Correspondence, and secretly contriveth a continuance of the *Scotish* Rebellion. He omits no Act of Contempt against the antient Nobility, that they might in the sence of their disgrace be, or at least dayly threaten some new Combustion. The confluence of so many threatning dangers work the wished effect, and keep the king in perpetual fear and agitation. The ill success of his Armies, and Expeditions in their Memory, help strongly to encrease it: Yet is not his faithful Servant neglective in the second and remaining part. He so orders his business within doors and without, that the Royal Treasure of the Crown is profusely wasted and spent without Accompt or Honour. The antient Plate and Jewels of the Crown are in the Lombard, and their Engagement drowned, before it had the warmth of a sure possession. The Subject is rack'd with strange Inventions, and new unheard of Propositions for Money, and many great Loans required, beyond all proportion or order. 'Lastly, the Royal Demeans are set at Sale, and all things that might make Money within the Kingdom.

To supply these inconveniences, which are now grown to a greater height than the Plotter of them intended; a new Parliament is called at *York,* where the elder *Spencer* is advanced to the Earldom of *Winchester*; and *Harkely,* another Chip of the same Block, is made Earl of *Carlisle. Baldocke,* a mean Man in Birth, Worth, and Ability, is made Lord Chancellor of *England.*

In this Parliament, which was by Fear and Favour made to his hand, he makes known the

great-

greatnefs of his Want and Occafions, the juftly aggrieved Commons entring into a deep confideration of the times, freely give the fixth Penny of all the Temporal Goods throughout the whole Kingdom.

When this Act came to the general knowledge, it utterly eftranged the Hearts of the Subjects, which plead an Impoffibility to perform it, in refpect of thofe many former Exactions. Yet after fome light conteftation it is levyed, no man daring to make fo much as a fhew of refiftance.

If we may credit all the Antient Hiftorians, who feem to agree in this Relation, there were feen at this time many Sights, fearful and prodigious. Amongft them no one was fo remarkable, as that which for fix hours fpace fhewed the glorious Sun cloathed all in perfect Blood, to the great Admiration and Amazement of all thofe that beheld it. Following times, that had recorded it in their Memories by the fequel, believed it the fatal Prediction of the enfuing Miferies. Thofe that more aptly cenfure the prefent view of a Wonder, conceited, the juft Heavens fhew'd their incenfed Anger, for the Noble Blood of the Earl of *Lancafter*, and his Adherents, fo cruelly fhed, without Compaffion or Mercy.

The *Scots* working on the condition of the times, fo much dejected and amazed, feize the advantage. They faw by the laft Parliamentary Proceedings, that the King was fo enabled, as the hope of any Attempt in *England*, was altogether hopelefs. Yet they refolve to be doing fomewhere within the King's Dominions, or at the leaft his Jurifdiction. This draws them to affemble themfelves, and to

D

Attempt

Attempt a furprifal of the Northern places of *Ireland.* As the Action was vain, fo the Succefs proved as unfortunate; they are defeated, flain, overthrown, and return not with the twentieth part of their number.

The King remembring thofe many Indignities he had fuffered, and refenting this their laft Attempt, with an implacable fcorn and anger, refolves to let them fpeedily know that he meant to call them to an after reckoning. Upon this he fends out his Summons, to call his Men of War together, and makes all Provifions be prepared, for this fo conftantly refolved a Journey. His former Misfortunes had inftructed him to undertake this Defign much more ftrongly and warily. And this fo grave a Confideration brought him together the remaining Glory and Strength of the greater part of his Kingdom. With thefe he marcheth forward, and invadeth the nearer parts of *Scotland*; but whether it were the Infidelity of thofe about him, the will and pleafure of Him that is the Guider and Director of Human Actions, or the unfortunate Deftiny of this unhappy King, he is enforc'd to return, without doing any Act that is truly worthy his Greatnefs or Memory.

The wily *Scots*, that durft not fet upon the Face of his Army, wait upon the Rear, and in a watch'd opportunity, furprife his Stuff and Treafure. This fends him home a third time a difcontented Man, and whether with a juft Guilt, or to transfer his own Fault upon others, the newly created Earl of *Carlile* is put to a fhameful Execution. The Grounds againft him were very probable, but not certain, and it was enough that he is believed,

like

like *Judas*, for Money to have fold his Mafter. The principal Motive that may lead us to think he was deeply faulty, was the Honour and Gravity of his Tryal, which gave him, on a full hearing, fo fincere and fharp a Sentence.

Scarcely is the King fettled, after his tedious Journey, when comes a ftranger News, That the *French* King had made a Hoftile Attempt upon the Frontier parts of *Guyen*, which was feconded with a Declaration, That he was no longer refolved to entertain the Friendfhip or Peace with *England*.

This Feat had been cunningly before-hand wrought by the fecret working of *Spencer*, yet he defired to have it ftill in Agitation, and not in Action. He wifht his Mafter thence might be poffeft with the fear of War, and not feel jt. The *French* were of another mind, they faw into the great Diforders and Mifguidance of *England*, and thought it a fit time, either by War or Policy, to unite fo goodly a Branch of their Kingdom. It is true, they had matcht a Daughter of *France* to the Crown of *England*, and had folemnly fwore a Peace, but thefe they thought might be with eafe difpenft with on fo weighty a Caufe, and fo fair an Advantage. *Edward* feeing into the danger, and taxing bitterly the Infidelity of the *French*, begins to furvey his own Condition, whereby he might accordingly fort his refolution, either to entertain the War, or to feek Peace upon fome Honourable, or at leaft reafonable Conditions.

He in this paffage finds himfelf more hated and feared, than beloved; he faw his Coffers empty, the *Scotifh* War and Surprifal had quite exhaufted

D 2   the

the Sinews of his laſt Parliamentary Contribution.' He feared the Inclination of the Subject would re- fuſe any further Supply, or in conſenting, make it conditional, which he was wholly unwilling to undergo or adventure.

Laſtly, The Misfortune that waited on him ever ſince he was abſolute, he feared had eſtranged and dejected ſo the Hearts of his Soldiers, that they would hardly be drawn forth, or act any thing with their accuſtomed Valour and Reſolution. In this Diſtraction, he ſeeks not by the Advice of a grave Council to qualifie or prevent it, this Me- dicine he conceits worſe than the Diſeaſe, but calls unto him *Spencer*, the Cabinet of his Heart, he alone is thought fit to communicate this deep Secret, and to give the Reſolution. His Father *Baldock*, and the reſt of that Faction, by his per- ſuaſion and entreaty, are admitted to make the Party greater, and the Diſcourſe more ſerious and likely. Before them is laid the Condition of the King, the Eſtate of the Kingdom, their own Danger, and the Intentions of their Foreign Ad- verſary. Many ſeveral ways are deviſed and ad- viſed, and in concluſion, no one is believed more ſound and proper, than that the Queen ſhould per- ſonally mediate the Atonement with her Royal Brother. This as it was cunningly laid, ſo had it a double uſe and reflection. The *Spencers* ſaw the Subject more inclinable to adore the riſing Sun, in which Act they thought the Queen's Me- diation and Preſence would be a dangerous Inſti- gator. They believed her abſence could not work ſuch and ſo great an aſſiſtance as might counter- vail the domeſtic danger. They knew the *French*

light

light and inconstant, and those which with a kind of natural fear, abhorr'd the *English* Wars, out of the limit of their own Kingdom. And in the worst construction they conceited Money, or a resignation of that part was holden by the King in *France*, would beget a Peace at their own will and pleasure. Yet these Considerations were attended with some doubts, which delayed and put off the execution.

The Queen, who had long hated the Infolency of the *Spencers*, and pitying the languishing Estate of the Kingdom, resolves in her mind all the possible ways to reform them. Love and Jealousie, two powerful Motives, spurr'd her on to undertake it. She saw the King a stranger to her Bed, and revelling in the embraces of his wanton Minions, without so much as a glance or look on her deserving Beauty. This contempt had begot in her Impressions of a like, though not so wanton and licentious a Nature. She wanting a fit Subject for her Affections to work on (her Wedlock being thus estranged) had fixed her wandring Eye upon the goodly shape and beauty of gallant *Mortimer*. He was not behind hand in the reception and comely entertainment of so rich and desired a Purchase. But his last Act had lodg'd him in the *Tower*, which was a Cage too strait to crown their desires with their full perfection, yet is there a sweet correspondency continued, Letters and many loving Messages bring their Hearts together, though their Bodies were divided.

By these is *Mortimer* informed of the Resolution for the intended Journey of his Royal Mistress, whom he vows to attend, or lose his Life

In the adventure. The Queen understanding the Intentions of her Servant, strives to advance her dispatch, and hastens it with all her best indeavours. But where was so great an Inconstancy, there could be no expectation, that this Proposition should be more assur'd or permanent. New delays and doubts interpose, insomuch, that the hopes of this Journey were now grown cold and desperate.

The Queen seeing her self deluded, and this opportunity stoln from her, by those whom she before so mortally hated, sets her own brains a working, to invent a speedy remedy. She was therein so fortunate, as to pretend a Journey of Devotion and Pilgrimage to Saint *Thomas* of *Canterbury*, which by her Overseers was wholly unsuspected. Things thus prepared, by a faithful Messenger she gives *Mortimer* the knowledge of her Design, who prepares himself with a more dangerous Stratagem to meet it. Her eldest Son, her dearest comfort, and the chief spring that must set all these wheels a going, she leaves not behind, but makes him the Companion of her Travels.

The King's Joy was great, that saw by this occasion, he should gain a free liberty to enjoy his stoln Pleasures, which were before so narrowly attended by the jealous eyes of his Queen, that in this kind had been so often wronged.

The aspiring *Spencers* were well pleased, that to be assured would have given a free consent to her perpetual absence. A short time brings her to the end of so short a journey, where she makes her stay of the same measure. *Winchelsey* had the honour to have the last farewel of this pair of

precious

precious Jewels. Thither comes *Mortimer*, having made a fortunate Escape, and with the Earl of *ane* resolves to venture his Life in the Attendance and Service of so brave a Mistress. An Exploit so weighty and dangerous gave no time of stay or ceremony. They immediately Embark, and make a tryal where they may find another Climate more propitious and fortunate. The watry Billows and the peaceful Winds, as if they were consenting to their Enterprise, entertain them with an aspect clear and quiet, sending them with a fresh and pleasing Gale safe to their desired Port of *Bulloign.*

The King and *Spencers* being truly enformed, are startled with the matter and manner of their Escape. They knew the Birds were too far flown to be catcht or reclaimed; and did imagin the Plot was too surely laid that had so prosperous a beginning. Now all the former Resolutions are useless; new Deliberations are required how this Breach may be handsomly sodered, or the threatning danger prevented. All other ways are deemed short, that one of taking off the King of *France* was believed most sure and easie. They knew the *French* strain to be giddy, light, and covetous, and applied themselves in the right Key to fit these several humours.

The King, whose presaging soul misgave his welfare, grows sad and melancholly, calling to mind the Injustice of his own Actions, and the fair Cause his Wife had to seek her right and refuge. The neglect and breach of Wedlock was so great an Error, but so to contemn so sweet and great a Queen, was a fault, in his own thoughts, deserv'd

D 4   a

a heavy censure. She had not only felt a particular share of her own grief, but suffered deeply in the general sorrow of the whole Kingdom. Those which had erected their petty Tyrannies over the Subject, were in like sort authoris'd by him that ought to have had an equal share of her affliction, more and more to abuse her.

The sad Impressions of these Disorders, and the reeking Blood of so many noble and brave Subjects, so basely spilt, do seem to cry for Vengeance. This, for a while, wrought deeply in his distressed thoughts, but a small intermission brings him back to his former temper. A customary habit of a depraved Nature, dulleth the sense of the Soul and Conscience; so that when our better Angels summon us to restitution and repentance, the want of a lively true apprehension, leads us blindfold into a dangerous despairing hazard.

The *French* King having notice of his Sister's arrival, with a wondrous plausible and seeming Joy, doth entertain it with an honourable Attendance, fitting more her Estate, Birth, and Dignity, than her present miserable condition: she is waited on to *Paris*, where she is soon Visited by the Royal King, her Brother. When she beheld the refuge of her hopes, she falls upon her Knee, and with a sweetly coming modesty, she thus begins her Story.

The King, unwilling to suffer such an Idolatry from her that had a Father, Brother, and Husband so great and Royal, takes her up in his Arms, and then attends her Motives.

Great

Great Sir, (quoth she) *behold in me, your most unfortunate Sister, the true Picture of a dejected Greatness, and the essential substance of an unhappy Wedlock. I have with a suffering, beyond the belief of my Sex, overcome a world of bitter Tryals. Time lessens not, but adds to my Afflictions; my Burthen is grown too heavy for my long abused Patience: Yet 'tis not I alone, but a whole Kingdom, heretofore truly glorious, that are thus unjustly wronged. My blushing Cheek may give you knowledge, I too much Honour the Cause of mine Affliction, to let my Tongue discover it. Yet this in Duty and Modesty I may ingenuously confess, My Royal Husband is too far seduced, his Ear is too open, his Will too violent, and his Heart too free, to those bewitching Syrens, that make his Errors their Profit and Glory. All hope of his return is lost, so long as they shall live, and remain his Leaders. How many of his noblest and bravest Subjects have attempted his freedom, and by an unjust and inglorious Death miscarried? Alass! all expectations are vain and desperate; if I had not known the impossibility to disinchant him, I had not in so mean and miserable a case stoln to you for Succour. You have a fair way to make known to the World, the truth of your own Glory and Goodness. Fortune leads you by the hand to an Action not more Just than Honourable, if you would dispute it. Can there be a more precious Motive to invite you, than the view of these unhappy Ruins? See here two Royal Branches of the* Flower-de-luce *withering, sullied, and depressed. Would you truly consider, how great and noble a Work it is, to support those that are unworthily oppressed, Heaven and Earth must witness*
the

the true value of your Worth and my Petition.
Let it not breed a Jealousie or Discouragement, that I
appear before you, and seek your help with so poor
a Train and mean Attendance. Besides the Justice of
my Cause, I bring with me the Griefs and Hearts of
a Kingdom, that have both Sworn and Vow'd to defend
it. Nor may you with reason doubt their Integrity,
while you have my wretched self, and the Heir ap-
parent to be your Pawn and Warrant. For God's
sake, Sir, by your own Virtue and Goodness I desire
it, and in the challenge of that Royal Blood whereof.
by the Laws of God, Men, and Nature, I have.
so large a Share and Interest. Let not after Ages
taint your Memory with such an Aspersion, That
you are the first of all the Kings of France *, that*
denied to relieve a Sister so deeply wronged and di-
stressed.

She would have spoken more, but here the big
swoln Fountains of her watry Eyes discharge their
heavy burthen. Her Tears, like Orient Pearls,
bedew her lovely Checks, while she with a silent
Rhetoric invites a noble pity. Her sad Complaint
won a general remorse, and her liquid Tears, a
deep and strong compassion. Her Brother vows
Revenge, and promiseth to make *England* and the
World know she was his Sister.

The Lords and Peers of *France* tender their
ready help and assistance; the Service is so hotly
pursu'd, that the poor Queen, with an abused confidence, believes she shall be speedily and strongly
righted. 'Twas not alone her Error, it is a general Disease. We easily credit that News we most
desire and hope for.

The

The *Spencers*, whofe watchful eyes were foon informed of thefe Paffages, too late condemn their own Improvidence and Folly, that gave the wronged Queen fo fit and fair an advantage. They fear not all the Power of *France*, but fufpect Inteftine danger, where they knew the Hearts of all were alien'd and eftranged. They well enough underftood the vanity of Female Paffion, but fufpect, that the rifing Son would be follow'd and admir'd, whilft their declining Mafter would be left forfaken and dejected. Thefe Conceits work fo deeply, that they conclude they muft fall, if they could not ftop the Foreign Danger. The *Englifh* were Cow'd, there was in them no fear, unlefs the ftrangers ftrength gave them new Life and Spirit. In fo weighty a Caufe there was no time left for delay or dalliance. They difpatch prefently away their Agents to the *French* Court, laden with the Treafure of the Kingdom, and many glorious Promifes. They inftruct them how to apply themfelves to the Time and prefent Neceffity; and teach them the way to work and undermine the Queen's Proceedings.

Thefe Meffengers arriving at *Paris*, find the *French* heat well qualified and cooled. This gave them more time and hope, to bring their Mafter's Will and their own Imployment to a fpeedy perfection. They fet upon the Pillars of State, fuch as in their Mafter's Ear or in his Council had moft fway and preheminence: they give freely and promife more, till they have won a firm and fair affurance. No one had an Intereft, and was known to be a favourer of the adverfe Party, but his Tongue is tied with a golden Chain to a perpetual filence.

When

When thus this Practice was ripe, the King is perfuaded of the danger and peril of fo great and weighty an Action. His Sifter's Reputation and intemperate Carriage, though tenderly, is often touched. A Woman's Paffion is believed too weak a Reafon to engage two fo Warlike Nations in a War, wherein themfelves had formerly fo often fuffered.

The King, for all his firft great and high Expreffion, had much rather have to do with the *Englifh* in their own Kingdom than in *France*, yet was well enough content not to try their Arms in either. Yet ftill he feeds his forrowing Sifter with good words, pretending many vain Excufes, which made her fufpect and doubt his meaning. She arms her felf with a noble patience, hopeful at leaft, that fhe and her fon might there remain in peace and fafety.

By the intercourfe of Meffages that had fo often pafs'd and repafs'd, the *Spencers* are affured, that their Affairs in *France* went fairly on, by which they were well onward in their Journey.

There could be yet no certain or affured confidence, until they had again gotten the Queen and her Son into Poffeffion. No Promife or Perfuafion is left to win her to return, but her Ears were ftopt, fhe too well knew the fweet Enticements of fuch alluring Serpents. This Project falling fhort, a folemn Letter is fram'd from King *Edward* to the Pope, and a Meffenger after their own hearts appointed to carry it. The Contents were full of Humility and Bitternefs, complaining to his Holinefs, That his Wife had, without juft Caufe, forfaken both Him and his Kingdom, carrying

carrying away his Son, the ftay of his Age, without his leave or licenfe ; a Traytor to Him and his
Crown, that had publickly acted a Rebellion, and
was taken and Imprifon'd for it, had made an efcape,
and was now her fole Companion ; and though
he was not hafty to report or credit, ye he had
juft caufe to fear he was the abufer of his Wedlock. The King of *France*, with whom he had
fworn fo folemn and firm a League, being Summon'd, had denied to reftore her.

 Thefe goodly Gloffes and Pretexts find a ready
paffage, and an eafie belief where there was none
to contradict, or juftifie. If thefe Afperfions had
been as they were pretended, juft and true, the Fact
had been odious, and juftly deferved a fair and
fpeedy reformation. The greater *Cardinals*, that
were at that time moft great and eminent, had
tafted deeply of the King's bounty, which gave
the Pope a daily inftigation to pity and reform
fo great and grofs an Error. On which an Admonition is prefently fent out to the *French* King,
that he caufe immediately the Queen of *England*
to depart forth of his Dominions.

 Whilft this device was in action, the *Englifh*
difcontented Barons fend privily to the Queen,
informing her, that they were almoft crufh'd to
pieces with their fuffering. They folicit her to
haften her return, and promife really to engage
themfelves and their Eftates in her Quarrel. With
a joyful heart (as it deferves) fhe entertains this
loving proffer. And the more to advance her declining Affairs, fhe inftantly acquaints her Brother
with the tender. He had then newly received
his Summons from the Pope, which taking out of his
Pocket,

Pocket, he delivers her back, wishing her to peruse and read it. The amazed Queen, when she beheld so sad a Sentence, falls humbly on her Knees, and desires, That his Majesty would grant her but so much favour, that she might more truly inform his Holiness, and justifie her self by a fairer and noble trial. With Tears she instanceth the malice of her Adversaries, that had taken so strange a course both to abuse and wrong her. Her Brother, glad of such a Protection to shadow his dishonourable and unnatural falshood, lets her know the necessity of his Obedience, and that he must not for her sake adventure the Censure and Interdiction of himself and a whole Kingdom. He wisheth her to arm her self with patience, and to return and make a peace with her Husband, in which Act himself would use both the persuasion and strength of his best Power and Interest, letting her withal know, that she had but a short time to deliberate, for she must instantly leave his Kingdom. Scarcely had he ended these his last unwelcom words, when away he flings, with a seeming discontented shew of sorrow, rejoyceing inwardly, that he had freed himself of the Expence of her Entertainment, and found so fair a colour to avoid the Justice of her daily Importunity.

The drooping Queen, thus abandoned, with an amazed grief, relates this unkind sad passage to her faithful Servants, *Cane* and *Mortimer*. Their valiant hearts make good the loss of their hopes; they accuse the injustice of time, and exclaim against the *French* unnatural baseness. *Mortimer*, whose inflamed Passion flew a higher pitch, breaks out, and with a bold freedom, would have fallen

to

to a bitter Expoftulation. The Queen, that knew the danger, and was loth to hazard that little miferable freedom fhe had left, with fweet and mild perfuafions reclaims him to a milder temper. She had a fecond doubt, left in fuch a conteftation fhe might be fent back againft her will to her Hufband. This makes her temporize, and cunningly feem to provide for a voluntary return, which might prevent that danger. She failing in the Mafter, yet tafts a-new his Servants, and leaves no means unattempted to bring about and alter fo hard and ftrickt a Cenfure. They that were the firft betrayers of her hopes, do now with a more confidence and conftancy exprefs it, and with one voice fing the fame Tune with their Mafter; declining Mifery, the touchftone of Friendfhip, finds it felf fhunn'd, like fome infectious Feaver. The funfhine of Fortune hath as many Profeffors as Beams, but if her Glory be once eclipfed, they all, with a coward bafenefs, feek fome other fuccour. This Leffon, that is fo frequent and familiar, fhould guide our election more by judgment than affection. They are not to be chofen or valued, that in the pretence of Love, though it be for our proper good or fervice, will act any thing that is bafe and unworthy; the fame in the leaft change will not be fqueamifh, for a poor advantage to confirm their former practice, though it be to our lofs or deftruction. Where Virtue guides our choice, it begins with truth and honour, ending with a like refplendent glory. No worldly crofs, nor height of affliction, leffens the worth and value of fuch a Friend, who, like a goodly Rock, in fury of the greateft Storms, makes good his

proper

proper ſtation. Mutual correſpondency in affe-ctions ought to be pure and innocent; if private reſpects taint the ſincerity of the intentions, it makes this traſſick rather a commerce than friend-ſhip. Opinion of faith is a powerful Motive, yet not weighty enough, unleſs it become as well with real ability, as appearance, the ſubject of our Election.

But to proceed, The Queen being in this di-ſtreſſed Agony, finds an unexpected refuge. The gracious God of Heaven, who never forſakes thoſe which are his, ſends her a comfort when her dying hopes were almoſt ſunk and deſperate.

Robert of *Artois;* a Man as truly Valiant, as Noble, was one of the firſt that in the *French* Court had tendered the Queen his Service. He was a wiſe, grave, and ſteddy, well reſolved Gentle-man; his firſt Devotion was not led by matter of Form or Complement, but was truly grounded on a true Compaſſion and Honour. This brave Friend beholding with a noble eye, the Vanity of his fel-low Friends and Courtiers, and looking into the Miſery of the Queens forſaken Condition, ſets up his reſt to appear like himſelf, a Friend in all her Fortune, firm and conſtant. In this reſolution he waits a fitting opportunity to let her ſee and know it. The time was favourable, he finds her in her melancholy Chamber, confuſed in her reſt-leſs thoughts, with many ſad diſtractions. She fancying the occaſion of the coming of ſo great a perſon was great and weighty, with a ſilent and attentive Ear expects his Meſſage.

Madam,

Madam, (quoth he) *It is the most excellent part of Wisdom, with an equal Virtue, to entertain the different kinds of Fortune. This World is but a meer composition of Troubles, which seems greater or less, as is the quality of the Heart that entertains them. I confess the Justice of your Grief, and truly share it, but Tears and Sorrow are not meant to relieve or right you. The just Heavens assist those that with an active and lively hope invoke their Succour. The tenderness of your Sex, and former free Condition is yet a stranger to these Trials; Time will let you know they are the familiar attendants of our frail structure of flesh and blood, when you will confess it too great a weakness to sink under the burthen of our Afflictions. For your own goodness (Noble Queen) erect and elevate your thus dejected Spirits: behold in me the Character of an unworthy, but true Friend, that am resolv'd my Life and State shall attend and run with you the self-same Fortune. You may no longer make this unthankful Climate, the place of your Birth, the stage of your abiding; the way is pav'd with Gold to your destruction. Wherefore, if my Advice may sway, let speed prevent your danger. The confines of the sacred Empire are near adjoining, where are many brave Princes, who may happily afford you Succour; at the worst, you may there enjoy a more assured peace and safety. Neither do I presume to direct this course, but lay it humbly before you, offering my faithful Service to attend you, to what part soever of the Universal World your resolution shall fix on, desiring you to be assured my Life, before my Faith shall perish; for I have vow'd my self, and will continue your everlasting Servant.*

E

Infinitely was the Queen rejoyced in this so
grave and sincere an Expression, she doubles a
world of Promises and Thanks for this so free an
offer, and with a secret and wary Carriage she
speedily provides to begin her thus resolved Journey. Though here she saw a far less appearance
of hope, when her dearest Brother, and her Native Kingdom had forsaken her, yet she resolves
the trial rather than to return, without a more
assurance. She knew she had too far waded, and
incens'd her malicious Adversaries, to expect a
reconciliation, and feared to be mewed up from all
hope of future advantage. These Considerations
made her with a sad heart and weeping Eyes forsake the fruitful limits of ingrateful *France*, and
betake her self to her last, but most uncertain
Refuge. The Condition that is truly miserable,
finds few real Friends, but never wants Infidelity
to increase its sorrow.

Stapleton, Bishop of *Exeter*, who had fled to the
Queen, and made himself a sharer in this weighty
Action, forsakes her Party. He seeing the *French*
hopes vanished, and these remaining so poorly
grounded, thought to work his Peace by losing
his Faith, and in this conceit, in haft, returns for
England. His Intelligence reconciles and wins
him favour, but it was purchas'd at too dear a rate,
that stain'd the Honour of so high a Calling, and
made him most unworthy of so divine and grave a
Profession.

By this Treachery, the King and *Spencers* understand both the Queen's Resolution and Weakness. They fear not the *German* Motions, that
were

were a dull sad Nation, that seldom use to fight
for nothing. Time hath at last brought our Royal
English Pilgrims to the shrine of their devotion.
The Earl of *Heynault*, a Man truly noble and virtuous, understanding her arrival within the Pre-
cincts of his Jurisdiction, gives her a free and loving welcom. This bountiful honest Earl, esteems
it his glory to entertain so Princely Guests like
themselves, and to become the Patron of their so
weak condition. He had a Brother that made
his Arms the honour of his Profession, who thinks
the Estate of this forsaken Queen in justice deserv'd a true relief and pity. He renders her his
Service, and believes the occasion happily offer'd,
that might leave to ensuing Times the Memory of
his Virtue, Worth, and Valor.

So fair a Morning puts the Queen in hope the
Evening would prove as fortunate : By all those
winning graces of a distressed Beauty, she strives
to confirm and more engage this first and fair affection.

The Earl having knowledge of his Brother's
resolution, thought the Attempt too full of hazard, and with a grave and mild temper, com-
mending the nobility and greatness of his Spirit,
adviseth him to quit the Action; he lays before
him the weakness of the Foundation, the Queen
was in want of Men and Money, and had not such
a Correspondency in *England*, as might warrant
her against her incensed Husband, who was waited
on by so warlike and valiant a Nation. He in like
sort acquaints him, how impossible a thing it was
for him to raise such an Army as might credit the

E 2   Cause,

Cause, and countenance the beginning. True Valor confisting not in daring Impoffibilities, but expofing it felf where Reafon, Judgment, and Difcretion were the leaders.

Sir John with a quiet patience hears his Brother's Admonitions, which he knew fprung from the freedom of an honeft and a loving heart, but he imagined Age had robb'd his Breaft and Head of all their Noble Vigor.

Sir, (quoth he) *If You and all the World forfake this Noble Lady, my fingle Arm fhall maintain her Quarrel, fince I had rather lofe my Life than my Faith, fo full and freely engaged. After Ages fhall not blot the Glory of our Houfe, fo great and noble, with fo inglorious a ftain of bafenefs and infidelity: fuch Precedents are feldom feen, and ought to be more tenderly regarded. A Queen and the Heir apparent of fo great a Crown pleading fo juft a pity, nor may, nor fhall be forfaken. If in the Reafon of State you lift not to be an Actor, referve your felf, and make not the King of* England *your Enemy. Know I have both Arms and Friends, I will pawn them all, rather than in the leaft degree falfifie my Word and Promife.*

These words fpoken with fuch a refolution and fearlefs bravery, ftopt all reply and contradiction. The Queen, that had already both a *French* and an *Italian* Trick, had no lefs reafon here to doubt it. She knew no means would be left unattempted from her Domeftic Spies, to make her once more forfaken. This enforceth her with a more Importunity

tunity to haften and advance her Enterprife. All
the good Offices, that might fpur on the enflamed
heart of her brave Protector, fhe makes the Handmaids of her Female Wifdom. But alas they needed not her careful Agent, they had quickly gotten
together a voluntary Troop of Three Hundred well
refolved Gallants, that vow themfelves to follow
him even into the mouth of the Canon. He ftays
not to encreafe his number with a multitude, but
believes if there were an anfwering Correfpondency
in the *Englifh*, with thefe, to overrun the Kingdom. Arms, Shipping, and all Provifions neceffary
attend their coming. They, with the glory of
their hopes, lead the revived Queen a Shipboard.
Now do they expofe themfelves to the firft tryal
of their Fortune, aiming at *Donge Port* to take
their hop'd poffeffion. The Heavens, that favour-
ed their Defign, out of their prefent fear preferves
them beyond belief or expectation. Her Adverfaries had a forerunning knowledge of their intended place of landing, and had there provided
to give them a hot and bitter welcom. The raging Billows and the bluftring Winds, or rather
the Divine Providence, after the fecond day's extremity, brings them aland fafe at *Orwel*, near *Harwich*. They were ignorant, being driven to and
fro by the violence of the Weather, what part
of the Kingdom they had light on; and were
as much diftreffed with the Unfhipping of their
Men and Baggage, as with the want of Harbour
and Victual. Three whole days in diforder and
confufion they make the bleak and yielding Sands
their habitation, perceiving the vanity of their rafh

and

and defperate Attempt, which in the leaft oppofition or encounter muft have wrought their confufion. It was in vain to attend longer here, where
they faw fo fmall fign of better Entertainment;
this makes them march on with this little weather-
beaten Troop, to win and Conquer a Kingdom.
St. *Hammonds*, an Abby of black Monks, was honoured with the welcom of their long loft Miftrefs;
here fhe and her Princely Son had their firft Reception and Entertainment.

The bruit of this Novelty, like a *Welch* Hubbub, had quickly overtaken the willing Ears of
the difpleafed Commons. Who, ever defirous of
Innovation, like Bees, in fwarms, do run to her
affiftance. The Barons fo deprefs'd and unjuftly
grieved, with itching Ears attend the News of this
advantage. When the tydings of their arrival
came to their knowledge, with fo liberal a relation, which made her Army ten times greater than
it was, they lofe no time for fear of fome prevention.

Henry of *Lancafter* was the firft, who was feconded by many others of the braver Peers of the
Kingdom. By this means the Queen and her
adherent ftrangers lofe the depth of that Agitation, that till now had kept them doubtful.

The King, that till this time had flumber'd out
the Prologue of this enfuing Danger, fecure in
the belief of the *Spencers* Strength and Providence,
in fo general a Revolt, awakens from his licentious
Pleafure, and beholds nothing but a grim and fearful face of Sorrow. The Council of his Cabinet,
accompanied with their own guilt, are affrighted
.in

in the fad apparitions of their approaching ruin. The time of prevention is loft, their abufed confidence had only labour'd to fhut the Gate, but not affur'd the Family. The prefent neceffity admits no long deliberation, this flame was too violent to be quenched, and fuch a courfe is to be taken as may rather affure them time to temporize, than with a ftrong hand to ftrive to repel it.

The City's Guard is recommended to *Stapleton*, that had fo unhappily; and with fo little credit changed his Mafter. The King and the *Spencers* forfaken, but yet ftrongly attended with the guilt of fo many and fo foul Errors, fly to *Briftol*, a Town ftrong enough, and well provided. *Arundel*, and the elder *Spencer*, undertake the defence of the City, while the King and the others make the Caftle their hope and refuge.

The Queen being informed, that the King had forfaken his Royal Chamber, and had ftoll'n a flight to *Briftol*, fhe foon apprehends, and lays hold of the advantage, addreffing a fair but mandatory Letter to the Mayor, to keep the City to the ufe of her and her Son, that was fo like to be his Soveraign. The inconftant Citizens, that ever cleave to the ftronger Party, are eafily perfuaded and entreated. *Stapleton*, that forefaw and fear'd the danger, fummons the Mayor to furrender him the Keys of the Gates for his affurance. *Chickwell*, that was then Lord Mayor, incenf'd with the Imperioufnefs and Injuftice of this Demand, apprehends this inconfiderate Bifhop, and without all refpect to his Place or Dignity, makes his Head the Sacrifice to appeafe the angry Commons. This

act

.act had too far engag'd him to recoil, he must now wholly adhere to the Queen's Faction. Four of the gravest and most substantial Burghers are sent, to let her truly understand their Devotion. They are graciously and lovingly received, the Mayor hath thanks for his late bloody Act, which was stiled an excellent piece of Justice.

This Gap thus stopp'd, with her Army she marcheth to the Cage that kept those Birds, whose Wings she would be clipping. She knew if she struck not while the Iron was hot, the heat of a popular Faction would quickly sink and lessen. All the way of her Journey, she finds according to heart's desire, a free and noble welcom. Her Troops, like Snow-balls, in her motion more and more increasing. When she came before this great and goodly City, she saw it was a strength by Art and Nature, and did believe it furnish'd to outwear a Siege of long continuance, which made both her and her adherents more jealous, and suspect the issue. Where the Person of an anointed King was at stake, there could be no assurance. But smiling Fortune, that had turn'd her wheel, resolves this doubt, and makes the Action easie. The Citizens, that knew not the Laws of War or Honour, will not expose their Lives and Goods to the mercy of the Strangers, and the hazard of an unruly Conquest. They had too much tasted the afflictions of the Kingdom, to think the Quarrel just, or to adventure their Protection at so dear a hazard, for those that had been the cause and instrument of so much Blood and Trouble.

From

From this Confideration they fend an humble Meffage to the Queen, and defire as well to capitulate for their Commanders, as their own Intereft. All other Conditions are defpifed and difdained; if they will have Grace, they muft purchafe it with the refignation and delivering up their Captains. This doom was efteemed heavy, they would have been glad that fhe had had her will, but were themfelves unwilling to be the Actors. But the time no more Imparleance admitted, neither could they have a delay or remedy. The Queen, that had won fo far upon their yielding hearts, knew their Condition well enough, and would not give them refpit, but calls upon their prefent Anfwer.

This round and fmart Summons brings with one and the fame art, *Arundel*, *Spencer*, and the City, into her poffeffion. This part of the Prey thus gotten, no time is loft to call them to a reckoning. Sir *Thomas Wadge*, the Marfhal of the Army, recites a fhort Calendar of their large Offences, when by a general confent they are approved guilty, and without Judge, or other Jury, they are fentenc'd to be drawn and hanged, and their Bodies to remain upon the Gibbet. The rigour of this doom, *Spencer*, the Father, feels, that was Ninety years old, and could not long have liv'd by the courfe of Nature.

The Caftle-walls, and the eyes of the King, and his unhappy Son, were witneffes of this fad Spectacle and his difafter. This *praludium* gives them the fenfe of their enfuing ftory, which with a world of melancholy thoughts, they ftudy to prevent

vent or alter. A defpairing refolution at length
wins them to a defperate hazard. While the Queen
was labouring to furprife their Fortrefs, which
was like too long to hold good, if fome ftratagem
were not found to get it, there were no Citizens to
betray them, it needed not, themfelves were foon
the Actors. They fteal into a fmall Bark that rode
within the Harbour, hoping by this means to
make an efcape undifcover'd ; they find the merci-
lefs waves and winds a like cruel. Twice had they
gain'd *St. Vincent's* Rock, but from that Reach were
hurried back with fuddain Gufts and Tempefts.
The often going off and return of this unguided
Pinnace, begets a fhrewd fufpicion. At length
fhe is furpriz'd, and in her Bulk is found that
Treafure that ends the War, and gave the work
perfection.

The King is comforted with the fmooth Language of thofe which had the honour to take him,
and believes the Title of a King, Father, and
Husband, would preferve his Life, if not his Soveraignty.

The Queen having now made the Victory perfect,
no Enemy or other work remaining, refolves with
her felf to ufe it to her beft advantage. Yet fhe gives
her incenfed paffion preheminence, revenge muft
precede her defire and ftrong ambition. No fooner
had Sir *Henry Beamond* brought the imprifon'd
King and his dejected Favorite to the Army, but
fhe difpatcheth away her Husband to *Barkley-*
Caftle, and *Spencer* is deliver'd over to the Martial,
and immediately hath the like entertainment only,
he hath fomewhat a longer time, and a far more
cruel

cruel Sentence than his Father. All things thus order-
ed, the Queen removes to *Hereford*, and in all the
places of her paſſage is welcomed with joyful Acclamations. With a kind of inſultant triumphing
tyranny, far unworthy the Nobility of her Sex and
Virtue, ſhe makes her poor condemned adverſary
in a ſtrange diſguiſe attend her Progreſs. He
was ſet upon a poor, lean, deformed Jade, and
cloathed in a *Tabarce*, the Robe in thoſe days due
to the baſeſt Thieves and Raſcals, and ſo was led
through all the Market-Towns and Villages, with
Trumpets ſounding before him, and all the ſpight-
ful diſgraces and affronts that they could deviſe to
caſt upon him.

Certainly this Man was infinitely tyrannical
and vicious, deſerving more than could be laid upon
him, yet it had been much more to the Queen's
Reputation and Honour, if ſhe had given him a
fair and legal Tryal by his Peers, according to
that ancient and laudable Cuſtom of *England*,
wherein by his death he might have given both
the Law and his Adverſaries a full ſatisfaction.
It is certainly, give it what other title you will,
an argument of a wondrous baſe condition, to in-
ſult or to tyrannize over thoſe poor Ruins which
Fortune hath thrown into our power. A noble
pity is the argument of an honourable and ſweet
diſpoſition, and the life of Man is great enough to
expiate all offences. To ſatisfie our paſſions with
the bittereſt extremity of our power, may juſtly
be ſtiled rather a ſalvage and barbarous Cruelty,
than true and perfect Juſtice. No queſtion it was
a pleaſing ſight to all the wronged Subjects, to ſee
ſuch

such a leprous Monster so monstroufly used. But when the heat of blood was past, and men had recollected their sences, it then appeared to be too great a blemish to a Queen, a Woman, and a Victor. But whether she were now weary with impofing, or he with suffering, *Hereford*, on a lofty Gibbet, of an extraordinary height, erected on purpofe, gives him the end of all his Torments. Which being performed, Order is left behind for the Execution of *Arundel* four days after, which is accordingly performed.

I could never yet read a fair and juft caufe, why this Earl loft his Life, unlefs it may be counted Treafon not to forfake his Lord and Mafter, to whom he had fo folemnly fwore his Faith and Obedience. It certainly was no fuch capital fault, to accompany and feek to defend his Soveraign, when he was by all others forfaken, that by their Vows and Oaths ought to have been as deeply engaged. If being taken with thofe that were fo corrupt and wicked occafion'd it, I fee yet no reafon, why he alone was Executed, and thofe, that in their knowledge, were his only Instruments and Creatures, were fuffered to live, and be promoted. But we may not properly expect Reafon in Womens Actions, whofe Paffions are their principal guide and mover.

Now she is come to *London*, and received with all the Honour due to fo great a Queen and Conqueft, the People croud to fee her, and with applauding shouts extol her, that in the leaft change of Fortune would be the firft should cut her Throat, or do her any other mifchief.

A

A Parliament is immediately call'd and affembled, in which the Pack was before-hand eafily laid, for *Edward* had loft the Hearts and Love of all his People; the Errors and Abufes of the Kingdom are there with too great a liberty againft a Sacred King yet living, laid open and difcourfed. All men were of one mind, a prefent Reformation muft be had, which, in a true conftruction, was but a meer politic Treafon. The three Eftates prefently affent to the depofition of the Elder, and raifing the Younger *Edward*, to the fole Regiment and guidance of the Kingdom; not a Peer, Bifhop, Knight, or Burgefs, fpeaks a word in defence of him that was their Mafter but; divers are fent from both Houfes to the yet King, to let him know their Declaration. When they were come into his prefence, *Truffel*, Speaker in the lower Houfe, in the Name of the whole Kingdom, refign'd up all the Homage due to him, and then pronounceth the Sentence of his Deprivation.

Edward, that long before had notice of thefe Proceedings, arms himfelf to receive it with patience. He gives them back no Anfwer, knowing a conteftation or denial might haften on his death, and a confent had made him guilty by his own confeffion.

Thus did this unfortunate King, after he had with perpetual agitation and trouble, governed this Kingdom Eighteen Years, odd Months and Days, lofe it by his own Diforder and Improvidence, accompanied with the treachery and falfhood of his own Subjects. And that which is moft miraculous, an Army of three or four hundred men,

entred

entred his Dominions, and took from him the Rule, and Governance, without so much as a blow given, or the loss of one Man more than such as perished by the hand of Justice. In a declining Fortune all things conspire a ruin, yet never was it seen, that so great a King fell with so little Honour, and so great an Infidelity. But what could be expected, when to satisfie his own unjust Passions, he had consented to the Oppressions of his Subjects, tyranniz'd over the Nobility, abus'd his Wedlock, and lost all fatherly care of the Kingdom, and that Issue that was to succeed him. Certainly it is no less honourable than proper, for the Majesty and Greatness of a King, to have that same free and full use of his Affection and Favour, that each particular Man hath in his œconomic Government; yet as his Calling is the greatest, such should be his Care, to square them always out by those Sacred Rules of Equity and Justice; for if they once transcend or exceed, falling into an extremity, they are the Predictions of a fatal and inevitable Ruin. Let the Favorite taft the King's Bounty and enjoy his Ear, but let him not engross it wholly, or take upon him the sway and governauce of all the Affairs of his Master; this begets not more Envy than multiplicity of Error, whose effects do for the most part occasion a desperate Convulsion, if not the destruction of that State where it hath his allowance and practice. As Kings ought to limit their Favours, so ought they to be curious in the Election, for persons of baser or meaner quality exalted, are followed at the heels with a perpetual murmer and hatred.

Neither

Neither is it fafe or proper, that all the principal Dignities or Strengths of a Kingdom fhould be committed to the Fidelity of any one particular Subject, though never fo gracious or able. There muft be then a kind of Impulfive neceffity ftill to continue his Power, and approve his Actions, elfe, having the Keys in his hand, he may at all times open the Gates to a Foreign Trouble, or a Domeftic Mifchief.

The Number of Servants, as it is the Mafter's Honour, fo is the knowledge of their Ability his Glory. Where by a difcreet diftribution, they find variety of Imployment, and are indifferently heard, both in Advice and Action, they more fecure their Mafters fafety and greatnefs. Kings, in their Deliberations, fhould be fwayed by the whole body of a Council, and, in my opinion, fhould take it ill, to have any Servant efteemed much wifer than his Mafter. Their Royal Glory fhould be pure and tranfparent, fuffering not the leaft eclipfe, or fhadow: Be the advice of a fingle Wit never fo grave and weighty, let the Act and Honour be folely the Kings, which adds more and more to the belief of his ability and greatnefs.

If once the Royal Heart be fo given over to Senfuality, that the befitting and neceffary Cares of a Kingdom feem a burthen, and by Letter of Attorney affigned over to the Fidelity of another, he is then by his own Indifcretion no more an abfolute King, but at fecond hand and by direction. It is the Practic and not the Theoric Act of State that aws and affures the heart of the Subject, this being once doubtful or fufpect, eftrangeth the will of
our

our Obedience ; and gives a belief of liberty to the Actions of Diforder and Injuftice.

Neither is the Error and Imbecillity of a Crown more prejudicial to it felf, than dangerous in the Example. Majeftic Vanities and Vices find a ready imitation and practice, fo that it may be concluded, an ill King may endanger the Virtue and Goodnefs of a whole Kingdom. Our Nature is prone to the worfer part, which we more readily are inclined to practice, with the condition of time, and fo powerful and eminent a Precedent.

Kings that are fubject to a natural weaknefs, or grown to the practice of any other particular Error, by corruption, fhould act their deeds of darknefs with fuch a referved fecrecy and caution, that there be not a fufpicion to taint him ; for if it once win an open knowledge, befides the particular afperfion, it brings with it an enfuing fuppofed liberty of Practice, both in Court and State, by his Example.

As thefe are moft proper to the Affections, fo are there fome as neceffary Inftructions for Kingly Paffions, which, of the two, are more violent and dangerous.

Though it a while delay the concluding part of this Hiftory, yet my Pen muft not leave them untouched. I muft confefs, if Man could mafter and govern thefe rebellious Monfters, he might juftly merit rather the name of an Angel than a mortal Creature. But this, in a true perfection, is moft impoffible. It is yet in Divinity and all Moral Conftruction, the moft abfolute Mafter-piece of this our Pilgrimage, to difpofe them fo, that

they

they wait on the operations of the Soul rather as
obedient Servants than loofe and uncontrouled Vagabonds. A King that is in thefe deficient, having
fo unlimited a .Power , and making his Will his
Law, in fhort time lofeth the Honour of his Calling, and makes himfelf a Tyrant. Intemperate
and heady Actions beget but diforder and confufion, and if they end in blood without a warranty
of apparent Juftice, or inevitable Neceffity, they
cry to Heaven for a deferved vengeance. The
Law hath Advantages and Punifhments enough for
thofe that lie. at his mercy. Let not incenfed ,haft
betray the Royality of a Crown, to make it felf
both Judge and Executioner. Kings are Gods on
Earth, and ought in all their Actions to direct the
imitation after a Divine Nature, which inclines to
Mercy more than Juftice. Mens Lives once loft cannot be redeemed; there ought therefore to be a tender confideration before they be taken, left the injuftice of the actor in time be brought to fuffer In tha
fame meafure. As is the quality of the Fact, fo is the
condition of his Agent to be maturely deliberated,
wherein there may be fuch dependencies, that it is
for the Crown more profitable, fafe, and honourable,
to fave, or delay the Execution of the Law, than
to advance or haften it. Howfoever, it is the more
innocent and excellent way to offend in the better
part, and rather to let the Law, than once own
Virtue and Goodnefs to be vifibly deficient, and
difefteemed. The Actions of Repentance are
numbred with the Regifter of our Mifdemeanours,
where none appear more fearful than thofe, which
an inconfiderate Fury, or the violence of Paffion,

F   hath

hath acted with too much haft and cruelty. Let then the height of fo great and excellent a Calling be fuited with as fweet a temper, neither too precipitate or flow, but with a fteddy and well-advifed Motion.

As thefe Confiderations are in the one part neceffary, fo ought there to be a correfpondent Worth and Care in him that hath the happinefs to enjoy in fo great a meafure his Royal Mafter's Ear and Favour. If the Actions of the King be never fo clear and innocent, yet he muft favour or protect the Error of fo great a Servant, which makes him an Acceffary, if not an Actor, in the unjuft Oppreffion of his Kingdom. It is not difcretion, neither hath it any Society, with the well grounded Rules of Wifdom, for the Subject to exalt or amplifie the height of his own Glory, it is in the Eye of all, too great a prefuming Infolence, and Kings themfelves will rather alter their Affections, than to be outfhined or dazled in their own Sphere and Element.

He that hath made his Mafter's Love, and hath afcended the Stairs of his Preferment, fhould make the fame Vertue the ftay of his Advantage, framing his carriage to his Equals and Inferiors, with a like fweet and winning Temper. If he fwerve from this facred Rule, and arrive to win Fear, or a vain Adoration, let him know, the firft is the Companion of Truft and Safety, the other of a jealous Diffidence, that muft betray his Life and Honour.

But to return to our Hiftory, which now removes *Edward* the Father to *Killingworth*, where
he

he remains under the keeping of the Earl of *Lan-caster*, while his unripe Son is crowned King, and the Queen, with *Mortimer*, take into their hands the whole Sway, and Adminiſtration of the Kingdom. Their firſt Act ſends *Baldock* the Lord Chancellour to *Newgate*, a fit Cage for ſuch a Haggard, though far unworthy the Eminency of his height and dignity.

Now do the recollected Spirits of the Kingdom begin to ſurvey and examin the injuſtice of that Act, that had diſrobed and put down a King, their unqueſtionable Soveraign, that had been ſo ſolemnly Anointed, and ſo long enjoyed the Regiment of the Kingdom: They find the condition of their Eſtate but little altered, and according to the vanity of their Hearts, are as ready to attempt a new Innovation. Many Suits are made to the King, and the Protectors, to releaſe him out of his Impriſonment, but all prove vain and fruitleſs. The Black Fryers were in this requeſt more earneſt, who in their denial, ſought to bring it to paſs by force or ſurpriſal. They make *Donhead*, one of their number, their Captain, but he knew better the uſe of Church-Ornaments, than how to handle his Weapons, or manage an Army; he is intercepted and ſent to Priſon, where he dies, before he had ſo much as muſter'd his Congregation.

This Cloud diſperſed, the Queen believes it a fit time to take her leave of her aſſiſtant Strangers, who mainly haſten their departure. She was unwilling they ſhould be witneſſes to the unnatural ſucceeding Tragedy, which was too much for her

own

own Kingdom, and unfit for the Strangers Climate, which was filled with the belief of her Vertue and Honour. She liberally and freely requites to each particular the minute of his Pains and Travel, but Sir *John* of *Henalt*, and the better fort, are honoured with many rich Jewels and Gifts, befides continuing Annuities, and annual Revenues. They hold themfelves nobly contented, and taking a folemn leave, are honourably attended to *Dover*, leaving the Kingdom with a merrier Eye, than when they firft beheld it.

Now is the Earl of *Lancafter*, who, though he had leaft caufe, was nobly difpofed towards his old Mafter removed, and delivers over his Charge by Indenture, to Sir *Morice Barkeley*, and Sir *John Mattrevers*, who lead him back to his firft place of Imprifonment, where, in the prefence of his Keepers, he one day in a melancholy Paffion, doth thus difcourfe his Sorrows :

Alas ! Is my Offence fo great, that it deferves nor pity nor affiftance ? Is human Piety and Goodnefs fo wholly loft, that neither in Child, Wife, Servant, or Subject, appears the leaft expreffion of Love or Duty ? Admit my Errors unexcufable, wherein I will not juftifie my felf, nor accufe others : though it hath taken from me the Glory of my former Being, I am yet a Father and a Husband, thefe titles are without the jurifdiction of Fortune. If I be fo, where is the Affection and Duty that becomes the Child, and Wedloc? Sure my Mifery hath not made me fuch a Bafilisk or Monfter, that my fight fhould beget or Fear or Hatred; can they believe a danger in the vifitation of a poor
diftreffed

diftreffed Captive? I know their hardned Hearts are not fo noble and apt for Compaffion, that they need fufpect themfelves or me in fo poor a courtefie. What then occafions this neglect or eftrangement? Are they not content to enjoy all that was mine, as yet by the Laws of God, Man, and Nature, but they muft defpife and forfake my withered Ruines?

-. Alas! I know my poor Children are Innocent, both they, and my injurious Queen, are betrayed by cunning wicked Mortimer, whom if I had paid with his juft defert, when Heaven, and his own Guilt, had laid him at my Mercy, I had not lived to endure this Affliction, nor he to be the infulting Inftrument of my Difhonour. But Time, and this fad Trial, hath taught me Patience, and learned me how to know the height of my Misfortunes, which (if my divining Spirit err not) will not be long unfeen and unrevenged. Am I unworthy to be feen? I am then unfit to live, and will receive it as a well-becoming pity, if my Death may fend me hence from this fo great a Sorrow.

When he had thus ended, and with a few manly Tears fmother'd in the depth of that heart-breaking figh that enforc'd his filence, he was by one of his Attendance made this ruff uncivil Anfwer:

" My Lord, your Wife and Children are jea-
" lous, and fearful of your cruel furious Nature,
" whereof both they and the Kingdom have too
" true a knowledge to truft you: Befides, they
" are informed your refolution is fixed to do them
" mifchief, if they approach your danger. This

" keeps

" keeps your Queen from you, she once so truly
" loved.

My Queen, (quoth he) *hath she that remaining Title, while I that made her so am less than nothing.   Alas poor wretched Woman!. Hath she, nor could she find no other more tolerable excuse than this, so faint a pretended fear and danger? Is there a possibility in her suspicion? Or have I the means (if I were so resolved) to do it, that am here a poor forsaken Man, as far from Power as Comfort?. And, fellow, thou that takest so audacious and saucy a Liberty, to character thy Soveraign's Disposition, which thou art bound to Honour, and not to question: Know Edward's Heart is as free from thy base Aspersion, as thine from Truth or Honesty.*

When he had ended these words, he retires himself to his Chamber sad and melancholy, believing his case was hard and desperate, when so base a Groom durst face to face affront him.   The Queen and *Mortimer* revelling now in the height of their Ambition and Felicity, had yet a wary Eye to the main, which they knew did principally rest on the safeguard and sure keeping of the deposed King.   Though they had all the marks and essential parts of an absolute Soveraignty, the Name alone excepted, yet they had unquiet and troubled thoughts in the fear and imagination of losing it. They saw their plausible Incomes was dully continued, and there was a beginning murmur against the manner of their Proceedings.   They knew there was no constancy in the People, that would
be

be as ready to take them off, as they were to bring
them on, in any new ftirring or Innovation. The
Lords that were their principal Supporters were
content, but not fatisfied, all things concurring to
make them fufpect their own condition.

Edward the Father's faults were extenuated,
his Vices afcribed to thofe that had betrayed him,
and his Eftate infinitely pitied, that had fo difhonourable a ufage, far fhort of what in juftice ap-
pertained to the honour of his firft Calling. Thefe
Reports made their Ears tingle, and incites them
in time to think upon fome befitting Remedy.
Many ways and devices are thought upon, but
they all are fubject to fome manifeft imperfection.
On this *Mortimer* falls to the matter roundly, and
tells the Queen plainly, That there is no way left
to make all fure, but abfolutely to take away the
Caufe, and to leave the Party by *Edward*'s death
hopelefs, that by his life fought to make a new
Combuftion.

The Queen, whofe Heart was yet innocent of
fo deep a Tranfgreffion, was deeply and inwardly
troubled with this unhappy Propofition. She believed his fufferings were already greater than his
faults, and was unwilling to ftain the opinion of
her worth and vertue, with fo foul an Act of injuftice. She was affured it could not be fo done,
but it would be difcovered; if the Eyes of Men
could be blinded, yet that all-knowing power of
Heaven would reveal and punifh it. Such deep
Actions of crying Sins are feldom long unrevenged, which made her moft unwilling that her
confent fhould pafs, or be affiftant. To kill a

F 4 King,

King, her Husband, that had once so dearly loved her, was more than an Act of Blood, nor could she expect, but that the Son grown up would revenge the death of the Father. *Therefore* (quoth she) *sweet* Mortimer, *let us resolve rather any other hazard, than this which is waited on with so great Infamy and certain Ruin.*

Mortimer replies, " Madam, who hath the
" benefit of time, and neglects the advantage,
" if he fall is justly unworthy pity or compassion.
" Have you exposed your self to all the bitter
" Tryals of Fortune, suffering so meanly, so
" many Miseries, and having overcome them ac-
" cording to your desire, are you willing to return
" to your own condition, and former sorrow ? If
" it be so, *Mortimer* is wretched in sacrificing his
" Devotion and Heart to such a Female weak-
" ness. In cases of extremity, a tenderness of
" Conscience begets a certain danger, nor is it
" disproportionable so to continue a Crown, that
" by blood was gotten and surprised ; had *Edward*
" known I should have liv'd to see his Ruin, my
" Head had paid my ransom. The impressions of
" Fear make his subject less in sence than appari-
" tion ; think not me of so poor a Brain, but I
" as well know how to work as move it, such Acti-
" ons are not to be done, but such a way as may
" prevent proof, if not suspicion. But why do
" I seek thus to charm your Ears, if you be wil-
" ling he shall live, let him, let the inclining People
" set him free to call you to an account for his op-
" pression, let him parallel his *Spencer's* death in
" your Affliction, perhaps he'l spare you for your
" Bro-

" Brother's fake, who he knows fo dearly loves
" you, and did fo bravely witnefs it in your Affli-
" ction, perhaps he'l fuffer you ftill to guide the
" Crown, and your fair Son to wear it. If you
" be pleas'd you may abide the Trial. *Mortimer's*
" refolv'd, fince you neglect his Judgment, you
" will as foon forget his Service, which he will in
" time prevent, before it be debarred.

With this he flings away, as if he meant, to
give his words a real Execution. The amazed
Queen purfues and overtakes him. *Stay, gentle*
Mortimer, (quoth fhe) *forgive my Error, I am*
a Woman fitter to take advice than give it. Think not
I prize thy Love fo little as to lofe thee. If Edward
muft dye, I will not feek to divert it, only I thus much
beg, I may not be partaker, or privy to the time,
means, or manner.

" Madam, leave that to me, who will alone
" both undertake the Act and Danger; all I re-
" quire from you, is but to feal a Warrant to
" change his former Keepers.

Sir *Morris Barkley* had been tamper'd withal,
and was fo far from confent, that he plainly declared he did abhor the Action. This Anfwer fuddenly difchargeth him, and commits his Mafters
Guard to Sir *Thomas Gourney,* and his former Partner *Mattrevers.* They having received both their
Warrant and Prifoner, convey him to *Cork-Caftle,*
the place in all the World he moft hated. Some
fay he was foretold by certain Magic Spels, that
this place was to him both fatal and ominous. But
whatfoe're the caufe was, he was at his firft arrival deeply fad and paffionate. His Keepers, to
repel

repel this humour, and make him less suspicious, feed him with pleasant Discourse, and better Entertainment, while his misgiving Spirit was heavy, sad, and melancholy.

The Night before his Death he supp'd heartily, and went to Bed betimes; scarcely were his heavy Eyes lock'd up in silent slumber, when his forsworn traiterous Murderers enter his Chamber, and finding him asleep, inhumanly and barbarously stifled him, before he could avoid or resist it. The writers differ mainly in the manner of his Death; but all conclude him murder'd, yet so, that the way, on search and view, could not be known or discover'd. A small passage of time gave the most part of all these Actors of his Death, an end fit for their deserts, and this so bloody an Action. Their several Relations and Confessions occasion so many various Reports, and different kinds of Writing; the truth whereof is not much material, since all agree, he came to an unnatural and untimely Death.

Thus fell that unhappy King *Edward* the Second, who was Son and Father to two of the most glorious Kings that ever held the Monarchy of the *English* Nation. Main Reasons are given probable enough to instance the necessity of his fall, which questionless were the secondary means to work it. But his Doom was regiftred by that inscrutable Providence of Heaven, who with the self-same Sentence punish'd both him, and *Richard* the Second his great Grandchild, who were guilty of the same Offences. The Example of these two so unfortunate Kings may be justly a leading precedent to all Posterity.   Cer-

Certainly we have had other Kings as faulty and vicious, that have o're-liv'd their Errors; and died not by a violent hand, but by the ordinary and eafie courfe of Nature. The condition and quality of thefe, was not in themfelves more perilous and exorbitant, than hurtful and dangerous to the Eftate, Peace, and Tranquillity of the whole Kingdom. If by height of Youth, height of Fortune, or a corrupt natural Inclination, the Royal Afflictions loofely fly at random; yet if it extend no farther than the fatisfaction of the proper Appetite, it may obfcure the Glory, but not fupplant the ftrength and welfare of a Monarchy. But when it is in it felf not only vicious and ill affected, but doth patrocine and maintain it in others, not blufhing in fuch a juftification, it is a forerunning and prefaging evidence, that betokens a fatal and unpitied Ruin.

It is too much in a King, that hath fo great a Charge delivered to his care and cuftody, to be diffolute, or wantonly given, but when it falls into a fecond Error, which makes more Kings than one in the felf-fame Kingdom, he opens the way to his own deftruction. The Subjects hearts, as they are obliged, fo are they continued by the Majefty and Goodnefs of a King; if either of thefe prove proftitute, it unties the Links of Duty and Allegiance, and hunts after Change and Innovation.

It is of fo fingular and great a confequence, that Kings ought to be well advifed, and fparingly to accumulate their Honours and Favours, wherein both the Time, Perfon, and Occafion, ought to be

both

both worthy and weighty; for the Eye of the Subject waits curiously on his Actions, which finding them degenerating from his own Greatness, and inclinable to their Oppression, vary their Integrity to a murmuring discontent, which is the Harbinger to a revolt and mischief. Nor is it proper (if the Soveraign's Affections must dote) that the Object of their weakness should sway the Government of the Kingdom. Such an Intermixtion begets confusion and Error, and is attended by a perpetual envy and hatred.

Is it possible but there must be perpetual Error and Injustice, where all things are carried more by Favour and Affection, than Law and Reason? Or can the lesser Fountains be clear, when that main Spring that feeds them is tainted and polluted? Alas, common and familiar Experience tells, that the Actions and principal Use of a Favourite, is to make good by his strength and favour, those Designs that are in themselves unjust, perverse, and insupportable.

A good Cause in the Integrity of Time, needs no protection but its own Innocence; but where the sacred Rules of Justice are inverted, the sincerity of the Law abused, the conscience of the Judge corrupted or enforced, and all things made Mercenary, or carried by indirect Favour, what expectation can there be, but that Kingdom, which is the Theater of so infamous a practice, should fall speedily into a fearful and desperate Convulsion. Though the Histories of these times are plentifully stor'd, and few Common-wealths are free from the Examples of this nature, yet I shall
not

not need any other inftance than the ftory of this unfortunate Prince, whofe time prefents a perfect Mirror, wherein enfuing Kings may fee how full of danger and hazard it is, for one Man's love to fell the Affections and Peace of the whole Kingdom.

Had *Edward* in j c j own particular been far worfe than he was, he might have ftill fubfifted, but when for his inglorious Minions *Gavefton* and *Spencer*, who fucceffively engrofs him, he fell to thofe injurious and diffolute Actions, that made all Men, and the Kingdom, pray to their infolent and imperious Humours, he quickly found both Heaven and Earth refolved to work his Ruin. Not only his own, but theirs, and thofe of their ignoble Agents, were made his proper Errors, which took fo wholly from him the Love and Hearts of his Subjects, that he found neither Arms nor Tongue to defend him. A more remarkable Mifery I think no time of ours produceth, that brings this King to deftruction, without fo much as any one Kinfman, Friend, or Subject, that declared himfelf in his Quarrel.

But he found the Climacteric year of his Reign before he did expect it: And made that unhappy Caftle, which he ever hated, the witnefs of his cruel Murder; where I muft leave him,'till he find a more honourable place of Burial, and my weary Pen a fortunate Subject, that may invite it to fome other new Relation.

F I N I S.

Books fold by John Playford, *at his Shop near the* Temple-Church.

MUsic's *Recreation* on the *Viol Lyra-way*, containing a Collection of New Leſſons, with Inſtructions for Beginners. Price 2 *s.*

Apollo's Banquet for the *Treble-Violin*, containing new Theater-Tunes, Ayres, Corants, Sarabands, Jigs, and Horn-pipes; to which is added, the Tunes of the new *French* Dances: Alſo Rules and Directions for Practitioners on the *Treble-Violin.* Price 1 *s.* 6 *d.*

The Treaſury of Muſick containing three Books of *Select Ayres* and *Dialogues* to ſing to the *Theorbo-Lute*, or *Baſs-Viol*; Compoſed by Mr. *Henry Laws*, and others. All bound in one Volum in Folio. Price 10 *s.*

Choice *Ayres*, *Songs*, and *Dialogues*, being moſt of the neweſt Songs ſung at Court, and at public Theaters. Compoſed by ſeveral Gentlemen of His Majeſties Muſic, in Folio, newly reprinted with large Additions. Price 3 *s.*

The Muſical Companion, containing Catches, Ayres, and Songs, for two, three, or four Voices, bound up in Quarto. Price 3 *s.* 6 *d.*

The Introduction to the Skill of Muſic, both Vocal and Inſtrumental, by *J. Playford*, in Octavo. Price bound 2 *s.*

www.ingramcontent.com/pod-product-compliance
Ingram Content Group UK Ltd.
Pitfield, Milton Keynes, MK11 3LW, UK
UKHW020400010325
455677UK00021B/561